TITANIC

WHY SHE COLLIDED, WHY SHE SANK,

WHY SHE SHOULD NEVER HAVE SAILED

TITANIC

WHY SHE COLLIDED, WHY SHE SANK, WHY SHE SHOULD NEVER HAVE SAILED

Senan Molony

LYONS
PRESS

Guilford, Connecticut

An imprint of Globe Pequot, the trade division of The Rowman & Littlefield Publishing Group, Inc.
4501 Forbes Blvd., Ste. 200
Lanham, MD 20706
www.rowman.com

Distributed by NATIONAL BOOK NETWORK

First Lyons Press edition published in 2021

Originally published in 2019 by Mercier Press, Cork, Ireland. *Titanic* is published by arrangement with Mercier Press.

British Library Cataloguing in Publication Information available

Library of Congress Cataloging-in-Publication Data available

ISBN 978-1-4930-5549-4 (paper)

In memory of G

CONTENTS

The officer was a young man, Joseph Boxhall, Fourth Officer of the *Titanic*. I took him up to the bridge, to report to our Captain.

Without preliminaries, Rostron burst out, excitedly: 'Where is the *Titanic?*'

'Gone!' said Boxhall. 'She sank at 2.20 a.m.'

In the moment of stunned silence that followed, every man on the bridge of the *Carpathia* could envisage the appalling reality, but not yet to its fullest extent. It was now 4.20 a.m.

Boxhall added in a voice of desperation: 'She was hoodoo'd from the beginning ...'

Carpathia Second Officer James Bisset,
Tramps and Ladies, p. 286

PROLOGUE

On the day the *Titanic* left Southampton, first-class passenger Mrs Henry B. Harris encountered a man in a corridor as the ship was negotiating the Solent, the body of water between the English mainland and the Isle of Wight.

The stranger addressed her, asking: 'Do you love life?'

Mrs Harris nodded, stupefied.

'Well then, get off this ship at Cherbourg,' he advised, 'if we get that far! That's what I'm going to do.' With that, the unknown approacher hurried down the passageway, away from the startled woman.

Irene Harris, who would suffer the loss of her Broadway producer husband on the voyage, recounted this story the moment she made landfall – on another ship – and told it frequently in the years thereafter.[1] But why would any individual urge someone to get off at the earliest possible moment with the voyage barely begun?

Who was this peremptory person – could it have been a fellow passenger? Mrs Harris mysteriously never made this clear. And why was the man so agitated and importuning?

There had been, admittedly, a little excitement at the start of the maiden departure, when the American Line's *New York* snapped her ropes by dint of her nascent rival's suction, nearly colliding with the slowly outgoing *Titanic*. But despite this little bit of drama, no passenger booked through to America disembarked in Cherbourg, only those who had booked the short cross-channel trip. In Ireland, again, only the expected offload went down the gangplank to the tender, including trainee priest Francis Browne (with his subsequently famous shipboard snaps). No short-hop travellers might have been expected to fret, as they were getting off so soon – they might rather suppress their discomfort, no matter how eerie they found the ship. It would thus appear that the prophet of doom failed to follow his own advice.

So was Mrs Harris making it all up about the frazzled man fixated on escaping the *Titanic* at the first opportunity? Or did an actual incident lodge in her mind, one that ended up being frequently described because it took on sepulchral significance in light of later events?

And yet, if it were not a fellow passenger who urged her to 'Get off this ship at Cherbourg' if she loved life, but instead a member of the crew, the perplexing incident becomes more plausible and more meaningful. What if he were an insider, anxious about a continuing and out-of-control situation below decks that had not been quelled since Belfast, wherefrom the ship had sailed over a week ago? He might then indeed have reason to hurry, rather than saunter, down a passageway. Perhaps the whole snatched conversation was born out of a nagging sense of a threat to the success of the maiden voyage.

Irene Harris always used the word 'man' in her story, never specifying passenger or crew. Perhaps the individual actually straddled the two. The *Titanic*, like her sister ship *Olympic* the year before, carried a team of technical experts from the builders, Harland & Wolff, to sort out operational snags on the maiden voyage. Members of this nine-strong 'guarantee group' were listed as passengers, not crew, on the ship's papers. One of their original ten, a manager of interior decoration named Joseph Thompson, had disembarked at Southampton on arrival from Belfast. The remaining shipyard men wore civilian clothes. Six were accommodated in second class, with three in first.[2] One of the first-class trio just might have had words, however gloomy, with wealthy Mrs Harris. The pledge that the man himself would get off in Cherbourg could have been added for emphasis and to help convince his listener, even if the speaker were in fact wedded through work to sailing all the way.

These shipyard men already possessed much inner knowledge. They were intimates of the debutante steamer's deepest secrets.

1

OUTWARD BOUND IN APRIL

A CAUTIONARY TALE

A stately ship stood dockside on an April day in England. Wisps of funnel-smoke were panting steadily in the crisp morning air and the transatlantic passenger vessel seemed as if she were already straining to start.

On the quayside all was busy with last-minute sailing preparations, not least among the arriving swarm of passengers. Many emigrants were set to board, buoyant themselves, optimistically bent on a fresh start in the New World. They included a significant component of Russians and Armenians, the majority of them Jews fleeing pogroms for the promised peace of the United States. Also embarking was a party of returning American cattlemen. The ship's four masts stretched impressively above them, and she was a striking 461 feet long – quite a sight to eyes unaccustomed to the exceptional Cunarders *Mauretania* and *Lusitania*, to which there was as yet no equal. She was the steamship *Cairnrona* and the year was 1910.

On this trip the liner would carry 879 passengers, yet she only had 800 lifebelts. Thus, if any disaster should occur, some would have to go without (including all the crew). As well as this, the vessel carried just ten lifeboats, capable of accommodating 500 persons, and two smaller craft, sufficient to hold but a further thirty-two.[1]

On 6 April the *Cairnrona* slipped her moorings at the Surrey Commercial Dock in Rotherhithe, London, bound for Portland, Maine, after being inspected and cleared by the Board of Trade. The Cairn Line steamer was under the experienced captaincy of Charles Thomas Stooke, commanding a crew of no fewer than 116 hands. That made the entire complement on board just five short of 1,000 souls.

The *Cairnrona* proceeded to sea. Within a short time the ship began to be enveloped by the slow descending shades of night and was presently out of communication with the coast. Yet at 7,682 tons, she was of sufficient size and importance to warrant carrying a wireless set, one of a tiny minority of shipping to do so at the time. She negotiated the narrow straits of Dover in the early hours, sighting the lights of other steamers off her port side, towards the French coast. Soon she was fully into the heavily trafficked English Channel and the lookouts strained their eyes for potential hazards.

The ship's chronometer limped into Thursday 7 April. At length, the lights of Folkestone were sighted on the starboard side, and next the small seaside settlement of Dungeness swam into view, leading on to the twinkle of battle-famed Hastings, until all eventually fell away into the ship's wake. It was now that the rosy glow of a welcome dawn appeared on the port side of the ship, the deck fixtures growing in definition as darkness cleared, but still too early for the passengers to bestir themselves.

The officers noted with satisfaction the Eastbourne lighthouse to starboard, at the base of Beachy Head, its rhythmic two flashes every twenty seconds so familiar to them. Only eight years in existence, this edifice of Cornish granite was already proving its worth. By now some emigrants were up and active, enjoying the early seascape. Breakfast had begun at 5 a.m., and early risers were keen to escape the claustrophobia below decks.

Then, at precisely 6.15 a.m., a powerful explosion tore through the silence of the morning, blowing off a forward hatch and killing assistant steward Frederick Longhurst. It grievously maimed a strolling pair of third-class passengers and severely injured three further members of crew. A swathe of more minor injuries were inflicted, as the blast reverberated to the far-off chalk cliffs. Two further concussive blasts followed, the force of which smashed into the women's quarters and blew over bunks, while sections of hatch timber struck several passengers.

Then, after a numbed pause, a tremendous wail arose. From the deck came a shout that a baby had been blown out of its mother's arms and overboard. The shout was ignored, however, because panic had broken out throughout the ship. Emigrants 'ran about the decks wringing their hands and hindering the officers of the ship in the efforts they were making for the safety of all'. One man was seen 'rushing madly with his head ablaze'.[2] A woman, whose clothes were on fire, begged to be thrown into the sea.

A stunned Captain Stooke burst from his quarters and took over from the officer of the watch as crew rushed to the aid of the wounded. Stooke soon received reports of structural damage, with smoke issuing in quantities from the hold. He heard one alarming dispatch that four passengers, afraid for their lives, had already jumped overboard.

Herschel Schenef, a Russian, recalled how he fled onto deck from his steerage berth. He could see thick black smoke billowing from the vicinity of the engine room and heard a crackling sound. Next came 'a terrible rush for the gangway'. Soon he saw sailors brandishing boathooks 'in order to keep back the crowds of excited passengers [from the lifeboats]'.[3]

By this time the wireless operator was transmitting the CQD ('Come quickly, danger') signal, requesting urgent help and giving the ship's position. The message was picked up at Dover and two tugs were promptly dispatched. The Liverpool steamer *Kanawha* was already in view, and within a few minutes was turning to the stricken ship's assistance, while a wireless response came flashing in from the unseen Swedish steamer *Upland*.

Captain Stooke ordered life rings thrown and a lifeboat lowered for those already in the sea, directing further that all boats be uncovered and prepared for launch. As the boats were cleared and swung out, the master ordered they be loaded and, in the age-old tradition of the sea, intoned: 'Women and children first.'

Despite this injunction in favour of those considered weak and helpless, 'several men endeavoured to thrust them aside, but were prevented by the crew,' said *The Times*. The British sailor noble once more. Emigrant Schenef saw one of his fellow Russians attack a crewman, with others joining in. 'There was a general fight. Women also engaged in the struggle.'[4]

English passenger William Forster, emigrating with his wife and three children, saw things sternly. 'There was no justification for the way they acted,' he said of foreigners in the fray. 'They would not listen to reason and to see them fighting with the women and children to try and get into the boats was enough to make one's blood boil. I gave the crew what little help I could in beating back these men, and we succeeded in getting the women and children away first. The crew acted splendidly; but for their pluck there might have been much loss of life.'[5]

The panic gradually subsided. With order somewhat restored, the lifeboats were launched and those who had earlier gone overboard were hauled in from the sea, all still alive, if exhausted. They now steered for the *Kanawha*, ever closer at hand, whose men were opening gangway doors in the ship's hull and deploying ropes and ladders.

Back on the wounded vessel, a crewman's hand had been mutilated by the explosion and it was already lying in a bucket, severed by the swift chop of Dr Heron, the *Cairnrona*'s surgeon. Nearby, a Polish woman lay paralysed on a stretcher, victim of a suspected spinal fracture. Outside in the doctor's corridor was a piteous line of groaning burn victims, two screaming children already treated and bandaged, and several crew also needing assistance.

Hoses had been playing on the angry blaze in the bunker, and now the steamer *Upland* and a trawler named *King Fisher* were on the scene. The transshipment of passengers got underway in a more or less organised manner over a matter of hours with the sea mercifully calm. Luckily the *Cairnrona* stayed afloat. Eventually these passengers were all brought ashore, the most severely injured being landed first and rushed to hospital. The crippled ship staggered back to Dover, arriving late that same night. Over 100 of her passengers would refuse ever to go to sea again.

An official inquiry was convened. It determined that the explosions, three in total, were 'probably' caused by hot embers in a coal bunker, having drifted there when fires were drawn from furnaces after completion of the last voyage. This finding seems highly unlikely, however, as somehow those embers would have had to sustain themselves until tons of fresh bunker coal came hurtling down on top of them in preparation for the next trip. It was also found there had been no inspection of the starboard bunker prior to departure, and its condition was not known to the master or chief engineer, the latter thus not having taken 'proper and sufficient measures' to guard against danger.[6]

As the ship sailed, the report continued, there was a slow combustion and generation of gas in the bunker. The subsequent working out of coal for the furnaces allowed air to be admitted. Combining with the gas, it became an explosive mixture. When the coal got low enough to admit air to the seat of the hidden fire, 'a flame or spark broke out which ignited the gas', the report found. It would have all happened in a fraction of a second.

The chief engineer was severely censured. But he staunchly maintained he had indeed inspected the bunker prior to coaling and found it in a proper state – as had a foreman from the supplying colliers. This would appear to implicate the embarked coal itself. Yet no proper consideration was given at the inquiry to the very real possibility of spontaneous combustion, even though it was heard that an undesirable mixture of fractious American and Scottish coals had been loaded. This auto-ignition idea was briskly dismissed, the conclusion already forming in the court's mind that hot ashes entering the starboard bunker had been the author of the calamity. This was based on a ridiculous allegation that a Portuguese crewman had failed to dampen raked-out coals after the previous arrival. But that man insisted he had wetted the ashes as ordered, and the task had in any case been on the *port* side. No information was provided as to how embers could enter a far-off bunker and last for days to await an influx of fuel.

Nonetheless, the catastrophe had occurred, and it was down to a bunker fire, whatever the cause. In August the formal investigation issued findings. For all masters and shipping companies there was a dire and forbidding stipulation in paragraph 5:

The vessel ought not to have taken to sea with the bunker coal in such a condition.

The judgement was widely circulated, by way of precaution. Yet two years (and three days) after the *Cairnrona* diced with disaster, the mighty newcomer RMS *Titanic* – with staggeringly vast bunkers – cast off her moorings for a similar crossing of the Atlantic. And her coal was arguably in even *worse* condition.

2

THE PRICE OF UNREST

A NATIONAL COAL STRIKE

No fewer than twenty-nine boilers, each weighing over ninety tons, were laboriously installed by crane into the new Harland & Wolff hull at Belfast, yard number 401. That overwhelming mass of metalwork, over 2,600 tons in total, delivered 159 furnace mouths. It would need a small army of firemen to feed them all – together, of course, with thousands of tons of coal.

John Kelly & Company, coal merchants, made several deliveries prior to the *Titanic*'s departure in 1912 for her sea trials in Belfast Lough and transfer to Southampton. The final supply was made on 25 March, a week before the off, when 200 tons of Scottish steam coal was chuted into the ship's innards. This fuel cost £350, an exorbitant thirty-five shillings per ton. This fee is worth careful consideration, because the price of a ton of liner coal had been less than £1 (twenty shillings) in February 1912. It had thus jumped by 75 per cent in the space of one month. And at the beginning of the year it had been just sixteen shillings a ton for Best Welsh, which had fetched fourteen shillings the previous September.

The reason for the increase was the first national coal strike ever called across Britain. Miners had long been feeling the strain of their dirty and dangerous calling, with its low wages, claustrophobia and long-term health implications. Even then it was recognised that 'miner's lung' cut lives short. A number of the surviving firemen from the *Titanic*, for example, had lifespans only into their prime. (Leading hand Fred Barrett, who gave evidence to both subsequent inquiries, died at forty-eight from tuberculosis, while fireman John Priest succumbed to pneumonia aged forty-nine. Fred Sheath died of asthma at forty-two, and George Combes from TB aged thirty-eight.) Pit barons had increasingly been attempting to shave money from their operating costs, often by playing off one colliery or mine against another, and it was estimated that

steadily rising shop prices had eroded workers' pu⁊
in recent years. Minor disputes had broken ov
briefly laid up the *Titanic*'s newly operational
failed; in the latter case due to blackleg (oppor
northeast and sent to Southampton under pₒ⩃.

Finally, however, the men everywhere had had enoᵤ₆
miners commenced on New Year's Day 1912, and a proposal tₒ⩃
action was resoundingly endorsed by a margin of four-to-one when votes ⸳⸳
counted on 12 January. If there had been an expectation of the employers coming
to the table, however, it was misplaced. Instead, backed by a virulently anti-union
national press, the malcontents were warned that their 'sabotage' of homes and
industry could not succeed and would not be tolerated. The *Pall Mall Gazette*
accused them of 'blackmailing the nation'. Nevertheless, the strike went ahead.

Beginning in Derbyshire from mid-February, and spreading immediately to
Wales and Scotland, hundreds of thousands of miners stayed away. Pit after pit,
working after working fell idle. Soon over 800,000 men were withholding their
labour. With the necessary breaking, chiselling and quarrying not performed,
and vital 'black diamonds' not reaching the surface, the national implications
soon became obvious as hardship deepened across the land. After all, coal was
the vital ingredient for cooking and heating in nearly every home at the time,
with electricity or gas still bit players, usually reserved for the upper classes and
not even dominant there. As a result, many families suffered during this period,
devoid of their source of fuel.

'No longer do men with few ideas talk on the subject of the weather and
crops,' wrote *The Sketch*. 'The typical clubman no longer asks his friends whether
their gout or rheumatism is better, and how this damp weather affects their
bronchial tubes. "How much coal does your cellar hold?" is the question now
of first importance; and "How much did you pay a ton?" comes next.'[1] This
was because, understandably, the price of coal soared in the wake of the strike.
Poverty pushed the scarce commodity out of reach for ordinary workers, with
many workplaces soon left with no option but to close for the duration. Ireland
– geologically short of mineral wealth in any case – was as paralysed by the
dispute as the rest of the United Kingdom.

The worsening situation alarmed the government. On 20 February Prime
Minister Herbert Asquith summoned both the pit owners and the Miners'

of Great Britain to a crisis meeting. However, the hostile press ensure the conference failed. Some newspapers called for troops to in.

ebruary passed into March, and the suffering grew worse. Rail services were verely curtailed, hampering commuters attempting to get to those workplaces that were still open. Occupancy restrictions were lifted on trams and trains, and top-hatted gentlemen were depicted in the popular prints as packed into the guard's van.[2] Food shortages became a reality, with wagons of goods unable to roll. As a consequence, producers scaled back their output, and so one problem compounded another.

The Times decided that the strike was 'the greatest catastrophe that has threatened the country since the Spanish Armada', although this time English ships were unable to put to sea.[3] A Conservative MP called for food rationing and the imposition of martial law to defeat 'socialist' agitation. There were thefts and tragic fatalities, with children diving into canals to look for lost lumps from barges, and a deep gloom pervaded parliament as a result of the 'overwhelming tragedy of the coal strike'.

One cartoon showed Asquith as the embodiment of capital, grappling with a representation of labour. They were portrayed as roped-together mountaineers on the edge of ruin. John Bull, connected in turn, was shown clinging to the cliff face, saying: 'If you two fellows keep quarrelling you'll both go to destruction, and what's more you'll pull me down with you.'[4] Another caricature featured John Bull tugging the sleeve of a policeman as a runaway horse and lorry (marked 'coal strike') careered towards the grocery barrow of British Trade & Industry. 'I don't care how you stop it, but stop it you must,' Britain's everyman demanded of Constable Asquith. 'I can't have my whole bloomin' apple cart upset.'[5]

Eventually the cabinet met (by candlelight, it was claimed) and caved in. A government proposal setting out somewhat improved minimum wage terms for miners, named the Coal Mines Bill, was introduced on 19 March. However, it was as economical as possible in its surrender to organised labour, meaning many miners were unsure whether it represented any kind of victory at all. Nonetheless, the union leadership accepted the parsimonious deal on offer, leading to the renewed balloting of members. There were still rejectionist pits, but the national picture soon clarified into one of grudging acceptance. The strike came to an official end on 6 April, after thirty-seven days, although large parts of the country would end up having no coal for fully six weeks.

As a result of the strike, much shipping had been laid up and many schedules abandoned because there had been no fresh stock for empty bunkers. In Belfast, coal from other ships had been laboriously dug out and transferred to the *Titanic*'s cavernous repositories to enable her to make the trip to Southampton.[6] Much of this cannibalised coal was Welsh, of various grades; Scottish coal was also used. The Scottish stuff was inferior, with a value of 14,200 British Thermal Units to the Welsh coal's power of 16,000. It meant that exactly the same weight of the former would produce less output than the latter – and consequently would result in considerably fewer miles sailed. But, as *The Irish Times* reported from Belfast on 2 April, 'the stock of best English coal is rapidly approaching vanishing point. The price is listed at 42 shillings, while Scotch is being bought at 35 shillings.' White Star, galled by the giddy prices of the former, opted for the latter.

A photograph of the *Titanic* taken the day before her departure from Belfast shows a column of thick black smoke coming from her forward funnel, the pillar of smoke folded over by the wind. The sheer darkness of that pillar indicates either poor quality coal was being burned, or that low-fire furnaces were being overwhelmed with new fodder. The former, of course, is by far the more likely.

In Belfast the *Titanic* took on 2,600 tons of coal, more than three times enough to get her to Southampton, although she still had enormous spare capacity. Given the final price of 35 shillings, it was clear that there was virtually no coal to be had in Northern Ireland, and the White Star Line must have hoped to do better in southern England.

Despite the severe problems posed by the coal strike, there remained every chance the vessel would be able to meet her scheduled maiden departure on Wednesday 10 April. In fact, the Line would make sure of it, regardless of any inconvenience or disruption.[7]

A crew of just 280 was aboard when the cold streaks of early morning Tuesday 2 April saw the *Titanic* glide out of Belfast Lough for her deep-water baptism. After speed trials and various tests, all apparently satisfactory, she made a brief return to her Lagan cradle. Finally, at 8 p.m., the *Titanic* hoisted anchor and aimed for the Saxon shore.

3

CROSSING THE LINE

BELFAST TO SOUTHAMPTON

As a substance, coal's properties are many and various, chief among them instability and unpredictability. The modern mind might revolt at such a notion, but the relative stability of oil and diesel has robbed the collective memory of a time when the mainstay fuel was distinctly dangerous.[1]

In making comment on the 1912 coal strike, an article in the *Fort Wayne Sentinel* referenced 'the problem of storage of coal on a large scale'. It explained that 'the ages produce coal by crushing decayed vegetable matter under great weight and pressure in the depths of the earth, far from atmosphere. Through some chemical or physical action of the air upon coal that has been taken from the mine, the product generates heat of its own and spontaneous combustion results. This is one of the mysterious forces of nature that has baffled many scientists and engineers. Without the application of any internal heat or inflammatory matter, a pile of coal sometimes will ignite itself and burn with dangerous intensity.' The article then added: 'The phenomenon is encountered most frequently at sea. Steamers must store large supplies of coal in their bunkers. The frequent result is bunker fire, caused almost always by spontaneous combustion.'[2]

Contact between air and the coal is enough to trigger combustion, which initially need not be 'fire' as we ordinarily understand it. Dr Guillermo Rein, an expert in thermal energy at Imperial College in London, says there may be no outward sign at all – no fumes, no odour, nothing resembling smoke – yet burning is nonetheless underway. His counterpart in the *Titanic*'s time, Ozni Porter Hood, chief mechanical engineer at the US Bureau of Mines from 1911 to 1926, pointed out that the area exposed to air by a ton of coal was tremendous: 'Each lump presents a surface and so does each powdered grain. The normal coal pile is not so tightly packed as to prevent the passage of the oxygen-bearing air through interstices to practically every particle of the coal.' Hood concluded that there was approximately one acre of surface to every ton of coal, a finding the press labelled 'astounding'.[3]

According to Dr Rein: 'The scary thing about smouldering coal is it doesn't need an ignition event. It's spontaneous. It's self-heating. It doesn't need an arsonist. It doesn't need an accident. Just the bed of coal … The kernel of the bed will start to slowly heat up and will continue spreading, until actually over the course of weeks it reaches a very high temperature. So when someone detects a smouldering fire in a big bed of coal, the fire has been going on for days for sure. Weeks, probably. The difficulty is that by the time you get a smell or signs that there is a fire in your bunker, it's already too late. And it's really difficult to suppress a smouldering fire.'[4]

That such a spontaneous coal fire had broken out in one of the towering starboard bunkers of the *Titanic* – and had done so in Belfast, weeks before the maiden voyage – has been confirmed and corroborated by 1912 evidence, including, for example, the testimony of Charles Oskar Hendrickson, a twenty-eight-year-old fireman, who joined the *Titanic* at Southampton. 'The first watch we did from Southampton we started to get it out,' he said, referring to attempts to suppress what was by then an outright blaze in the bunker.[5] It was plain the outbreak stemmed from before he came aboard. Hendrickson declared: 'I heard it commenced at Belfast.'[6] Someone aboard evidently told him as much.

Hendrickson was also asked at the British inquiry into the sinking: 'Is it a common occurrence for fires to take place on boats?' He replied, 'No.' The question repeated, he again denied it, pointing out that he had been five years in the White Star Line and he 'never saw one before'.[7]

A fire that began in Belfast, and in a coal bunker three storeys high – immeasurably higher and deeper than repositories of old – was obviously a dread development, and the crew's subsequent inability to extinguish it before the ship departed on her maiden voyage was proof, *ipso facto*, of a serious blaze. It is not surprising, therefore, that after the sinking of the *Titanic*, White Star was anxious not to encourage any other view but that the fire was discovered only after leaving Southampton, and was not previously known about, no matter what Hendrickson said. The implications of prior knowledge, plus a failure to disclose it to officialdom in Southampton ahead of the Atlantic crossing, did not bear thinking about.

Nonetheless, the company was ultimately forced to acknowledge that the fire had indeed begun in Belfast. The admission would eventually come from the patrician Harold Arthur Sanderson, deputy chairman of the Oceanic Steam Navigation Company, operators of the Line and its fleet. Sanderson succeeded the ill-starred J. Bruce Ismay as chairman when the latter resigned, having controversially survived the foundering of the *Titanic*.

Aged fifty-one and distinguished by his height, silver hair and a cavalry officer's moustache, Sanderson came from a long-established shipping family, of 'traceable Norman roots'.[8] Just before attending the third day of the British post-disaster proceedings (an inquiry that was set up as a major public tribunal in response to an *ad hoc* inquiry by American senators), he was handed a Marconigram, or wireless message, from Ismay, who was then halfway across the Atlantic on the *Adriatic*. He responded: 'I am up to my neck in this wretched B of T Inquiry – It looks like going on for weeks', then added '[White Star solicitor John] Furniss is coming to Queenstown to interview *Titanic* officers, etc., coming up [St George's] Channel [to Liverpool]. Good luck to us all, and a stout heart for yourself.' Sanderson himself would not give evidence for another month, but his communication of 7 May with Ismay shows White Star was legally protecting itself from the earliest.[9]

The *Adriatic* arrived in Queenstown on Friday 10 May. Furniss was on board as she proceeded from Ireland to England, almost certainly advising Ismay and the surviving *Titanic* officers on overall strategy and how to conduct themselves when giving evidence.

When Sanderson finally testified, he was shown appropriate deference and was soon flourishing a report from just before the ship sailed, written from Southampton by Captain Smith of the *Titanic* and dated 10 April. He read from it: 'I herewith report this ship loaded and ready for sea. The engines and boilers are in good order for the voyage, and all charts and sailing directions up-to-date. Your obedient servant, Edward J. Smith.'[10] Sanderson answered nearly 300 questions on his first day in the witness box, all inoffensively asked by Sir John Simon, Solicitor General of the United Kingdom.

On the next day he was tackled in cross-examination by William Harbinson, counsel for some third-class passengers. During this cross-examination it emerged that Sanderson had personally made the delivery trip from Belfast to Southampton. He had been aboard with the skeleton crew.

Clement Edwards, counsel for the Dockers' Union, who questioned Sanderson next, managed to draw out some key disclosures. He first referred Sanderson to the White Star Line's own Rule 248 from its operational handbook.[11] Under the title 'Examination of Coal Bunkers', the rule declared: 'The respective senior engineers of each watch, before going off duty, must go through the coal bunkers, and note their condition on the log-slate, and should there be any signs of spontaneous combustion taking place, they are at once to report same to the Chief Engineer, who is immediately to notify the Commander. All [affected] coal should, as often as possible, be worked out of the bunkers.' This was White Star's own standard procedure. If a bunker fire was underway and detected – and reference to 'each watch' meant several inspections of every bunker every day – then it should have been reported at once to Chief Engineer Joseph Bell. He, in turn, would immediately notify Captain Smith.

An appalling vista may have opened in the mind of Harold Sanderson as Clement Edwards then asked: 'We have had it in evidence there was a fire in one of the bunkers when the *Titanic* was coming over from Belfast to Southampton?'

Sanderson's reply was terse: 'Yes.'

Edwards next asked: 'Would a copy of the log of the *Titanic* be taken for the use of the company before she left Southampton?'[12] The implication was that the Line would therefore have a record extant of what occurred on the delivery trip, despite the subsequent loss of the ship herself.

'The Engineers Log from Belfast to Southampton?' queried Sanderson in what can only be interpreted as playing for time. 'I presume there would be one, but I do not remember it. It is a very short trip, and perhaps the ordinary regulations might not have been carried out on it.'[13] With this, he did not quite answer the original question – whether a copy had been taken off the ship and retained by the company to that very moment.

It is tempting to imagine a pause at this point as it sank in that this emollient bigwig, faced by two unpleasant possibilities, chose to suggest his great enterprise could very well not have complied with 'ordinary regulations' and, more to the point, its own internal procedures. Might this have been the lesser of two evils in Sanderson's eyes?

One thing is clear. The White Star standing rule meant the ship's high command had to have known about the fire. The implication, then, was of wilful deception at the very highest level, meaning that a government fitness-to-sail inspector was not told of a long-term unextinguished fire.

Mr Edwards persisted with his line of questioning: 'You cannot tell me whether there was any entry in the log as to the fire?'

'I could not tell you,' replied Sanderson, 'but I know that there was a fire.'[14]

There it was, then, an important admission. It went beyond strange heat in a storage bunker, or a suspicion of incipient combustion, to an actual fire having been reported on board.

At the inquiry, Sanderson portrayed himself as a disinterested and disengaged passenger on the voyage (despite his shipping company, of which he was a director, taking formal legal possession of this new vessel at the time). This was the same inert posture J. Bruce Ismay would adopt in testimony about the maiden voyage itself.

Sanderson was then asked about when he first learned of the fire he had just described. 'I heard it at this inquiry first of all,' the White Star principal maintained, referring to Hendrickson's evidence. 'I then sent down to Southampton, and they said, "Yes, there was a small fire."'[15] With this answer, Sanderson confirmed that the Line had known about the blaze on the voyage from Belfast to Southampton (unlike a mere deputy chairman aboard), even as he actively sought to trivialise it.

Commissioner Lord Mersey summed up 'that there was a fire in this bunker between Belfast and Southampton', but he did so in the course of long judicial interruptions that threw Edwards off his interrogation, and as the trade union counsel and the bench fenced with each other, Sanderson stayed silent in the box. Eventually Edwards returned to the issue, asking whether the fire in the bunker had been reported to Sanderson 'independently of anything which might possibly appear in the log?' The witness, who had indicated no direct knowledge despite his seniority, now said: 'I have no doubt it was reported to the Superintendent at Southampton.' He added: 'It would not have come to my knowledge unless it was important.'[16]

It may have suited Sanderson to characterise the on-board blaze as small and unimportant, but a report to the White Star Line marine superintendent at Southampton meant it had also been previously reported to the ship's command in accordance with Rule 248. Thus Chief Engineer Joseph Bell and Captain Edward John Smith must both have known about the existence of a bunker fire on the positioning voyage from Belfast to Southampton and that it was not extinguished before they departed Southampton. The wider duty of such honourable gentlemen, one would think, would have been to make sure the authorities on land were made aware of the outbreak, since those powers were tasked with safeguarding the travelling public. Yet no word on the fire was disclosed.

Towards the end of his evidence Sanderson was again asked if engine-room logs were retained. 'Certainly they are kept,' he replied, finally appearing to answer the question of whether the delivery log papers could be produced.[17] Their supply would be attended to, the court was given to understand. But no such documents were ever entered into evidence at the inquiry and nothing of the kind is known to exist today.

4

AN OLD MAN'S MEMORY

TROUBLE IN THE STOKEHOLD

Joe Mulholland nearly didn't make the *Titanic*'s debut onto the shipping lanes of the world. He was the second-last man to sign on for the delivery trip, joining at Belfast on sailing day, 2 April 1912. The seemingly endless new leviathan – she was one-sixth of a mile in length, or 882.5 feet – had actually been due to depart the morning before, April Fool's Day, but had been delayed by high winds.

Mulholland got his job in the stokehold only because someone else had failed to turn up – John Rowan, a dock labourer from Little York Street, did not appear at the appointed hour. Another no-show was John Gillen, a forty-four-year-old marine fireman from Smithfield in the city. Captain Smith wrote up the paperwork stating that this pair had 'failed to join' and Mulholland and Thomas Holland, a stoker from Lancashire, were engaged in their stead.

Joe had hooked the big one. The last ship he had worked on, *Troutpool*, was 3,281 tons. *Titanic* was fully fourteen times larger. His story was told on the fiftieth anniversary of the *Titanic*'s sinking by the *Sunday Independent*:

Old-time seamen are notoriously superstitious and 79-year-old Joseph Mulholland, of Upton Street, Belfast, who sailed from Belfast in the Titanic *on the first leg of her ill-fated maiden voyage, can still recall his feelings as he stoked down in the engine room of the ship which Belfast boasted was 'unsinkable'.*

Silver-haired and vigorous despite his great age and a lifetime at sea, from square-rigged grain ships on the Australian run to White Star liners on the Atlantic, 'Big Joe' Mulholland says:

'There was something about that ship I did not like and I was glad to lift my old bag and bid goodbye to my shipmates, like Hughie Fitzpatrick and Pancake Baker, when she arrived at Southampton. Hughie offered me a job as storekeeper on the trip across the Atlantic, but I

did not accept. Hughie was lost when she hit the iceberg, but Pancake was picked up and I met him years later at La Plata.'

Big Joe is still fond of cats and perhaps he has reason. He recalls that on his way down to the Titanic before she set sail from Belfast with bands playing and crowds cheering, he took pity on a stray cat which was about to have kittens. He brought the cat aboard and put her in a wooden box down in the stokehold.

At Southampton, when ruminating whether to take on the job of storekeeper on the trip or sign off, another seaman called him over and said: 'Look Big Joe. There's your cat taking its kittens down the gangplank.'

Joe said, 'That settled it. I went and got my bag and that's the last I saw of the Titanic.'

But there was plenty of drama on the journey down the Irish Sea as the great ship – the pride of the Belfast shipyard – headed for Southampton to take on board its complement of passengers, a cross-section of the social registers of England and America.

In Belfast in those days it was hard to get an experienced stokehold staff. Joe Mulholland said they scoured the Salvation Army hostel, the dockside and eventually got together a scratch team ranging from milkmen to dockers.

'I had to mind six stokeholds, and the Chief Engineer [Joseph Bell] *told me to get the men to break up the big clinkers* [lumps of impure residue]. *I told them, but they must have lifted up the covers and kicked the clinkers down and affected the hydraulic pumps because the seas came back* [in] *and we were soon standing up to our thighs in water.*

'A young whipper-snapper of an engineer came galloping up and gave off something shocking. We got the water away, but I did not fancy that young fellow.'

Joe recalls a meeting in the engine room with Thomas Andrews, the designer of the ship, director of Harland and Wolff, and a member of the noted Comber [Co. Down] *family.*

'I knew Mr Andrews because I often stoked ships on their trials after they were launched at Belfast. He came down to me and pointed to some insulting slogans about the Pope chalked up on the smoke-box. Some of them were filthy and I had already heard about similar slogans which had been painted on the hull before the Titanic was launched.

'Mr Andrews said, "Do you know anything about these slogans?" I did not, so he said, "They are disgusting," went off and returned with some sailors and had them removed. Mr Andrews was a very decent man. He went down with the ship.'

Joe has his own theory about the disaster. 'I was never in deep water in a White Star liner that we were not trying to win the blue riband for speed. That was the cause of the disaster. They were on a northerly course to break the record for the Atlantic crossing.

'Any seaman can smell the ice from miles away, but instead of changing course south they

kept on and hit that berg. The blue riband was the cause of the disaster and all those folk losing their lives.'[1]

Old Joe was taken to see the premiere of the film A Night to Remember *because he helped James [sic] MacQuitty and his advisers with details for the production. He sat in the front row with the Belfast Lord Mayor.*

What did he think of the film? 'Not much,' he said. 'It would make all the old sailors turn in their graves. The tiny crew they showed in the engine room would remind you of a coal boat.'[2]

Mulholland neglects to mention a bunker fire. It would later be shown that this had broken out in boiler room 6, the most forward stokehold space in the vessel. It may be that he was concerned only with his own compartment, which could have been located much further aft. But whether or not Mulholland knew of its existence (or had simply forgotten it in the half-century since), the bunker fire did exist, as confirmed not only at the inquiries, but also in press interviews with the surviving *Titanic* firemen in New York, even if news of it had been withheld from two Board of Trade inspectors and from passengers on the maiden voyage.

We must be grateful for what Mulholland did recall. He is the only fireman to describe in vivid detail this leg of navigation through the Irish Sea. His overall tenor punctures inflated and enduring notions of the *Titanic* as some perfect prow knifing through the waves, puffed up by White Star publicity as that image may have been.

'There was something about that ship I did not like,' says Mulholland mysteriously, while making revealing remarks elsewhere in his story. Others on board would soon make similar remarks, hinting at underlying doubts.

Of the two shipmates, Hughie Fitzpatrick and Pancake Baker, that Big Joe bade goodbye to at Southampton, Fitzpatrick would be lost within a fortnight in the chill, still North Atlantic. An exact contemporary of Mulholland, from a neighbouring street, he left a young wife pregnant with their first child. Also doomed to shipwreck and death from hypothermia was the full complement of twelve men who served aboard the *Titanic* for New York as junior storekeepers – the job Fitzpatrick had offered Mulholland.

The 'Pancake' mentioned by Mulholland in the news article was John Baker, a fireman six months his junior. He did not have to be saved because he, too, disembarked at Southampton, even if that fact was unknown to Big Joe at the time. Baker was thus not on the maiden voyage to be 'picked up' during the rescue, as Mulholland suggested in the interview. Baker usually served in the Ulster Steamship Company, also known as the 'Head Line' – his previous ship to the *Titanic* was the *Bray Head*. He returned to his old employer following his time on the *Titanic* and visited the port of La Plata (thirty-four miles southeast of Buenos Aires) on both the *Dunaff Head* and *Kenbane Head* in the early 1920s, and it was on one of these visits that he once again encountered Mulholland.[3]

The stray feline about to have kittens that Mulholland took pity on and brought aboard (he was photographed cradling a cat in the 1962 article) was mentioned by *Titanic* stewardess survivor Violet Jessop in her memoirs.[4] She claimed the cat's name was Jenny – Mulholland's later seaman's card shows that he sported a tattoo declaring 'Jennie', whereas his wife's name was Sarah. It would be nice to think that he perhaps had it inked to commemorate the life-saving mouser.

The blocked pumps and the seawater coming into the boiler room is an uncorroborated story from Mulholland, but does lead on to important elements, while causing a worry over the ability to expel water during the flooding that was to come. His row with the 'whipper-snapper' engineer finds another echo in the record, albeit again from Mulholland himself. Four years earlier, in 1958, he had mentioned the quarrel to Belfast-born film producer William MacQuitty during the making of *A Night to Remember*. A snippet quoting Mulholland appears in an outsize publicity book compiled for the press.[5] Joe says: 'I had a dispute with an engineer officer and I took my bag out of her at Southampton.' Twice Mulholland refers to the engineer being 'young', although only a few were younger than he, the youngest being twenty-two-year-old junior sixth William McReynolds. The engineers, notably, were drowned to a man.

The story about Thomas Andrews, whose humanity was legendary, and the offensive slogans has the ring of truth. However, if the Harland & Wolff chief was indeed down in the boiler rooms during the leg to Southampton, then it seems likely that he would have known about the condition of the bunker in boiler room 6 (if Smith and Bell knew about it, so must he as chief designer). Indeed he could have been passing through Mulholland's boiler room towards it when he noticed the graffiti (a shipyard photograph shows the milder 'No Home Rule' chalked on the *Titanic*'s hull before her launch). After all, there must have been a reason for Andrews' sudden manifestation at the bottom of the vessel.

Now to the 'clinkers' that Mulholland references – of which poor quality coal produces many. Clinkers are brittle shards that do not burn because they are the product of impurities. These glazed formations, which are basically lumps of vitrified ash, have to be removed from the furnaces. The literature says that poor quality coal produces lots of clinkers, just as there are fewer impurities and better burning in the best. The *Titanic*'s coal generated big clinkers that were hard to break and dispose of, and according to Mulholland, these clinkers eventually affected the pumps.

We thus have primary eyewitness evidence that the *Titanic* was burning poor quality coal on this run, likely as a result of taking on the stock of other vessels in her native city. Poor quality equals less propulsion and therefore less distance travelled per ton of coal.

It's all consistent with the Line's readiness to accept an inferior crew, also alluded to by Mulholland, as if on a 'needs must' basis. With or without the bunker fire, his unvarnished and candid account of the trip to the English south coast makes being aboard the *Titanic* sound distinctly unpleasant, with a worse-than-usual gulf between those in command and the sweat-salted singlets who found themselves literally working at the bottom of the heap.

* * *

The *Titanic* cancelled a stop at her home port of Liverpool en route to Southampton (whereas her sister ship *Olympic* had been open for public inspection on Merseyside during her own debut), the decision supposedly the result of a weather delay at Belfast, or so it was said at the time.[6] There are indications that she kept close to the coast of Ireland in her transit of the Irish Sea, well away from England and Wales, before making a late diagonal run to the southeast.

The Belfast News-Letter, the oldest daily paper in the world, was keeping a close eye on her progress. It reported she 'made a good run', passing Land's End at 12.30 p.m. on 3 April. That same afternoon the *Cornishman* reported: 'Considerable interest was aroused in Penzance on Wednesday in a remarkably fine steamer observed crossing the Bay. She proved to be the White Star liner *Titanic*, on her way from Belfast to Southampton.' The next paragraph might have merited some pause for thought: 'The *Titanic* shaped a course considerably nearer the land than that usually taken by liners, and, as the day was fine, a good view of her was observed.'

Why was Captain Smith hugging the coast in what was plainly stated to be an unusual course of action? What could have prompted him to want the land so close to hand?

The new vessel arrived in Southampton in darkness, having covered over 530 nautical miles in twenty-eight hours, at an average speed of smarter than 19 knots. She was 'safely moored in one of the Southampton docks' at midnight, as a handwritten note on the crew agreement declared. It also mandated: 'Firemen to clean down after arrival, as may be required.'[7]

5

THE LAST WORD

UNFINISHED

The *Titanic* was 'the last word in shipbuilding'. The newspapers all said so after her launch in Belfast, heavily prompted by White Star publicity agents, and they dutifully continued to use the phrase as her service debut neared. American press correspondent Ernest Townley sampled her salons at Southampton on sailing day itself – and, for readers on the other side of the Atlantic, pronounced the *Titanic* 'assuredly the last word in comfort and luxury'.[1] Second-class passenger Lawrence Beesley, whose book about the voyage was published in 1912, wrote: 'The machinery and equipment of the *Titanic* was the finest obtainable and represented the last word in marine construction.'[2] A surgeon from her sister ship *Olympic*, Dr J. C. H. Beaumont, called her in his memoirs 'the last word in engineering'.[3] And the *Cork Constitution*, on the day before the disaster, applied this phrase to the food on offer: 'the kitchens represent the last word'. Even Francis Browne SJ – who took wonderful photographs on the maiden voyage, but who had the good sense to get off in Queenstown (after being ordered to do so by his religious order) – called her 'the last word in marine architecture'.[4]

But being the 'last word' did not mean she was a completed creation. In fact, she was far from finished. If the plain truth is told, it had been a rush to get her even approximately ready. Proof lies in a photograph taken at Easter 1912 in Southampton, as the ship awaited her maiden voyage: in it, a party of men, lowered on rope platforms, are tending to her aft port quarter, apparently touching up the ship's paint. A similar photograph, also taken over the holiday – when overtime might have commanded a premium price – shows workers harnessed by guy wires applying fresh coats to the giant funnels.

The temporary chief officer of the *Titanic*, William McMaster Murdoch (he would step down to first officer on sailing day), admitted unreadiness in a letter to his sister, penned on the ship's stationery on 8 April 1912. Murdoch wrote: 'The holidays are on down here, and it takes me all my time to get men to work, even at overtime rates, but we are nearly ready for the road.'[5]

The previous day Henry Tingle Wilde, the man who would replace Murdoch as chief officer, boarded the vessel and he wrote to his family on Resurrection Sunday: 'I am on the *Titanic* but not sure I am sailing on her yet ... I have been kept very busy on board all day on Good Friday and again today Sunday with the crew getting the ship ready. She is very far behind to sail on Wednesday. Working on her night and day.'[6]

Because the ship was unfinished – workmen arriving on board at Southampton noticed paint on the lockers was still wet – the White Star Line decided it could not open her to public viewing, as had been popularly expected. Even before her arrival, the *Southampton Times* of 30 March sulked that 'sightseers need not apply'. Even so, spectators came. The town's *Pictorial* reported: 'Though the *Titanic*, the world's last word in shipbuilding construction has not been open to inspection by the general public since her arrival from Belfast, hundreds of sightseers have visited the docks to catch a glimpse of the leviathan as she lies moored.'[7]

One civilian who managed to be shown around was the sister of Second Officer David Blair, who was about to transfer to another vessel. Blair's daughter, Nancy, recalled: 'Aunt told me years later my father took her on a tour of the ship the day before she sailed. This took several hours and the ship was still a hive of activity, with carpets still being laid and decorators busy until the last moment.'[8]

Storekeeper survivor Frank Prentice bluntly declared in 1978: 'She was rushed through, not ready for [the] sea.'[9]

George Beedem, a steward, was feeling defeat at the pressure of work as the date for departing Southampton neared. He wrote to his loved ones: 'This is the last night and thank goodness we are off tomorrow. I shall never do another week as long like I have this one ... I have no news to tell you, only the last three days I've felt rotten and what with no dusters, or anything to work with, I wish the bally ship at the bottom of the sea.'[10]

Similar scenes had been observed in her last few days at Belfast. On 6 April a photo was published of the *Titanic*'s stern.[11] In front, on the dock, was a dray cart loaded with 'numerous carpenters' chests' and a higgledy-piggledy heap of furniture. 'A scene of great activity was witnessed at the Deep Water Wharf, Belfast, on Monday morning, when quite an army of workmen, who for some considerable time past had been busily employed in fitting out the new White Star leviathan *Titanic*, came ashore with their tools,' it was reported. 'Several lorries were requisitioned to carry these outfits back to the yard, and several others were laden with trestles and other impedimenta [tools and other items] which had been used in completing the ship.' Clearly, it had been an almighty scramble getting her even approximately ready.

Will Jeffery, twenty-eight-year-old bookkeeper in the à la carte restaurant, wrote to his mother from Belfast of the 'worry around trying to get various necessary jobs done. Until the workmen are out of the way we can't touch anything.' Jeffery died in the sinking, but his letter serves as another indication that the *Titanic* was in a race against time to be ready before she left her birthplace.[12]

Senior surviving officer Charles Lightoller testified that the *Titanic* had not steamed straight to Southampton after sea trials in Belfast Lough, but had returned to the Lagan. Fifth Officer Harold Lowe told the US inquiry the vessel was there anchored for half or three-quarters of an hour and that 'We sent all workmen ashore by tender to Belfast.'[13] She then put out to sea again, Lightoller said, 'after taking on board a few things that had been left behind, which were required for the completion of the ship'. He gave a couple of examples to the American inquiry: 'requisites down in the galley, cooking apparatus, a few chairs, and such things as that'.[14]

Lightoller observed in his memoirs: 'Putting a new ship in commission is, at the best of times, a pretty strenuous job. With the *Titanic*, it was night and day work, organising here, receiving stores there, arranging duties, trying and testing out different contrivances, (and) makers of the hundred and one instruments with chits to be signed certifying that this, that, and the other was in perfect working order.'[15]

A striking account was given by fireman John Thompson in the wake of the disaster. He referred specifically to a 'rush job' readying the ship.[16] 'Thompson said many workmen – electrical fitters, plumbers, carpenters and machinists – who had been taken on board at Belfast were let off at Queenstown, where the *Titanic* last touched,' said the New York *Sun*, referring to the ship's final port of call in Ireland. 'The fireman didn't know how many of these there were, but he said there must have been close to 100. "We heard that there hadn't been time to complete the ship before taking her out and that the line made a rush job of it between Belfast and Southampton. I don't know whether anything vital, like the working of the watertight compartments, was left to the last minute.'"

This last remark insinuates something alarming. Although there has been a blanket assumption in modern times that the electrically operated watertight doors worked perfectly on the *Titanic* when the accident occurred – Lightoller said so, after all – as we have already seen in the previous chapter the hydraulic pumps did not cope with clinkers on the delivery trip to Southampton.[17] Might there have been an issue with the watertight doors, too?

How the watertight doors and compartments operated was explained in a puff piece about the new liner in the *Cork Constitution* on Saturday 13 April – the eve of their being put on trial in a real emergency. A long description of the vessel occupied page four and, under a crosshead that read 'Practically Unsinkable', the reading public was assured: 'The *Titanic* is as complete in her safety devices as in her luxurious outfit. She is divided into upwards of 30 steel compartments separated by heavy bulkheads. An automatic device on the bridge controls all these heavy steel doors, making it possible for a single hand to close them all in case of danger. The priceless time conserved in closing them in case of accident may thus be saved. Each of these doors in turn is electrically connected with a chart on the bridge, where each floor is represented by a small electric light. When one of these doors closes the light will burn red; while it remains open it will remain dark. The officer on the bridge will thus be able to see at a glance if all the compartments are closed.'

The point of the puff piece was to assert, despite all evidence to the contrary, that the *Titanic* was indeed the finished article and 'as complete in her safety devices as in her luxurious outfit'. When one part of this equation – the outfit – was obviously lacking, what confidence can be reposed in the other? Was everything really in perfect order, as Second Officer Lightoller claimed?

Fireman Thompson had his doubts, and he was not the only one, specifically in regard to the watertight doors. A letter surfaced at auction in 2008, written home in the wake of the tragedy by *Titanic* lookout Archie Jewell. He confessed: 'If the watertight doors had worked she would not have went [*sic*] down.'[18] First-class passenger Elmer Zebley Taylor, a chemical engineer, wrote in his 1949 memoirs: 'There were steel doors in these bulkheads that could be opened or closed at will from the navigator's quarters on the bridge. I recall explaining to Williams [his companion, first-class passenger Fletcher Williams] how the gears, levers and gadgets of these doors operated from the bridge. A sailor who heard the conversation stepped up and said, "Sir, you are right for the most part, but this door has not been connected. They did not have time to complete all the work before we sailed."'[19]

There is a yawning gap of thirty-seven years between the accounts of crewmen Thompson and Jewell, and passenger Taylor. Yet no gap separated Thompson's *Sun* interview and the recording of a startling remark made by Taylor's fellow passenger Fletcher Williams, as reported in the *New York Herald*. It came second-hand. Williams was named by the Countess of Rothes as hastening to her after the collision to exclaim frantically: 'The watertight compartments must surely hold!'[20]

Perhaps what Williams had heard about the incomplete work and the unconnected door had been preying on his mind. He was forty-three (Taylor was forty-eight) – hardly an impressionable *ingénue* likely to be taken in by a sailor's tall tale. Unfortunately he could never corroborate Taylor's disturbing account.[21] Fletcher Williams died in the sinking.

Many other passengers on the maiden voyage decidedly did not think that *Titanic* was the acme of perfection, and were ready to complain about it afterwards. One, Imanita Shelley, went aboard at Southampton with her mother, Lutie, thinking they had bought 'the best second-class accommodation sold by said company'. Instead, they were taken to 'a cell'. It took eleven trips to the purser (the officer in charge of passenger needs) to secure transfer to another room, she said in her affidavit to the American inquiry.[22] This new cabin 'looked in a half-finished condition … just as cold as the cell from which we had been removed … as the heating system for the second class cabins refused to work'. Her mother 'was obliged to go to bed to keep warm' as the rooms were 'like ice houses' (an unfortunate phrase).

Afterwards, when on board the *Carpathia*, Mrs Shelley 'took pains to inquire of steerage passengers as to whether or not they had heat in the steerage of the *Titanic* and received the answer that there was the same trouble with their heating plant too,' wrote public notary Simon Wilson of Montana on Mrs Shelley's behalf a month after the calamity. He documented another two pages of her grievances. She had been sick, for example, but the stewardesses could not even procure a tray to bring her meals, and she was brought 'plates and dishes one at a time'. She deposed 'that in the ladies' toilet room only part of the fixtures had been installed, some of the said fixtures being still in crates'. Even when finally in her lifeboat 'the tackle refused to work' to lower it, and only after considerable time did it reach the water – when 'the casting-off apparatus would not work and the ropes had to be cut'.[23]

The last word from 1912 about malfunctions and mishaps must go to first-class passenger Daisy Minahan from Wisconsin. At the end of her US deposition she made an arresting statement that chimes with the misgivings of Thompson, Jewell, Taylor, Williams and the unnamed sailor informant about the watertight door. Daisy declared: 'A stewardess who had been saved told me that after the *Titanic* left Southampton there were a number of carpenters working to put the doors of the air-tight compartments in working order. They had great difficulty in making them respond, and one of them remarked that they would be of little use in case of accident, because it took so long to make them work.'[24]

James Witter, a second-class smoke-room steward, took part in a 1956 BBC television recording of some *Titanic* survivors, captured for posterity in ghostly black and white. More than forty-four years had elapsed by this point, yet the catastrophe remained a source of popular fascination, boosted by the new book *A Night to Remember* (later adapted into a movie). Witter was nonetheless laconic about his experience: 'I didn't think she'd hit anything. I thought she'd dropped a blade. From the propeller, you know,' he began, matter-of-factly.[25] 'I went down to the working alleyway where my cabin is, No. 7 glory hole, and I was standing there talking to two or three fellows, and the carpenter [John Maxwell, who had been asked to sound the ship (search for flooding) by Captain Smith] came along, and I heard him say: "The bloody mail room's full of water!"'

'I said, "What's that, Chip, mail room full of water?" and he said, "Yes." I said, "Well, what about those bulkhead doors forward?" and he replied, "They're not holding, Jim."'

'Of course, then I walked into my cabin ... I called everybody, I said "Come along, fellas, get up, she's going down!" I took out some matches, some cigarettes, and I said, "Come on, fellas, get up" – "Ah, what the hell are you talking about," they said, "get out of here." And someone threw a boot at me.

'I said, "Goodnight, gentlemen." Just as easy as that.'

And Witter walked back out to fend for himself.

6

OFFICIALDOM

DESPONDENCY AND CONFIDENCE

The *Titanic* had arrived to a climate of despondency and some desperation in Southampton. A large department store on Bridge Street had just been burned to a gutted shell, with damage estimated at £25,000. Hart & Co. advertised a 'gigantic salvage sale' of household furniture, carpets, linos, ironmongery, bedsteads and bedding, all at 'astoundingly low prices owing to the late disastrous fire'.[1] Most of the despondency, however, was due to the effects of the coal strike on the port. A relief fund had recently been inaugurated by the city's mayor, Henry Bowyer, following a town hall meeting. According to *The Belfast News-Letter*, it was clear that 'distress is growing more acute' in the city.

A press announcement by the American Line during this period held particular meaning. All its sailings from Southampton to New York were 'temporarily suspended during coal strike'.[2] Both this company and White Star were owned by the J. P. Morgan conglomerate known as International Mercantile Marine (IMM). They featured together in publicity about services operated by the 'White Star and American Lines'. But, on this occasion – with coal still in desperately short supply – IMM was willing to cut the American Line loose. It intended to pillage coal stocks from other vessels, specifically the *St Paul, St Louis, New York* and *Philadelphia*, in order to fill the *Titanic*'s yawning dearth.[3]

White Star's *Olympic* also sailed from Southampton for Cherbourg and New York just hours before her former captain, Edward Smith, arrived in his new command on 3 April. But the elder sister could only go because, said *The Times*, she 'took on board sufficient coal at New York to ensure her sailing on the return voyage'.

Left behind by the *Olympic* was a stowaway who had crossed from America, an actor named Edward James Rich.[4] He appeared in court charged with failing to pay his fare, with the out-of-work thespian claiming he was also a 'mechanic, electrician and fireman'. He received one month of jail time in default of paying his passage. Penniless, the misnamed Rich mounted the steps of a Black Maria taking him to prison. The felon was lucky; he might have been ordered to work his way home as a fireman on the next available liner – if they could have been persuaded to take him. British crews were doughty, uncompromising and fiercely distrustful of outsiders. And they were often solely out for themselves, as demonstrated by a court decision involving a sailor and fireman, delivered the day before *Titanic* tied up at the Ocean Dock.

Able seaman William Weller was already aboard the new ship, having joined in Belfast, and had yet to learn the result of a legal action brought by him against White Star. He and a stokehold pal had launched an audacious claim arising from the cancellation of the *Olympic*'s crossing the previous September after a collision with Royal Navy cruiser HMS *Hawke* in the Solent. A huge gash had been torn in the liner's starboard quarter. Weller wanted compensation, as his engagement had been for the whole voyage, to New York and back again. But *Olympic* had promptly returned to Southampton, the trip cancelled, and he was paid only three days' wages. He and fireman Thomas Fraser sought a month's money, £6 and £5 respectively, and their case was taken up by the British Seafarers' Union.

The defendants in the case were relying on Section 158 of the Merchant Shipping Act, 1894: 'When the service of a seaman terminates before the date contemplated in the agreement, by reason of the wreck or loss of the ship ... he shall be entitled to wages up to the time of such termination, but not longer.' The decision, therefore, turned on whether the *Olympic* was a 'wreck' under the circumstances. With a lower court deadlocked, papers were sent to Admiralty Judge Bargrave Deane, who heard it was very difficult to define a wreck. Stroud's *Judicial Dictionary* saw it as where 'a ship is perished on the sea, and no man escapeth alive out of the same'.

The plaintiffs maintained that what befell the *Olympic* did not make her a wreck, even if it rendered her unfit to proceed, and based their claim on Section 162, seeking damages for wrongful dismissal. However, Frederick Laing, barrister for White Star, pointed out that the ship's passenger certificate, which was effectively her licence to sail, had been taken away, which did render her a wreck. She did not get this licence back until after repairs (made at Belfast), and only resumed transatlantic service two months later on 29 November. So what wrong had the owners of the *Olympic* committed, he argued.

William Weller arrived with the *Titanic* to find he had lost his case. And so it was in early April 1912 that the *Olympic*, not the *Titanic*, was legally and officially a wreck.[5] Too bad, Weller might have consoled himself in a quayside tavern. It had definitely been worth a try.

Yet this test case was to have major implications within weeks. The High Court had limited the obligations of a shipping line to crew members in the case of an aborted voyage. So when the *Titanic* sank, the Line initially ended workers' wages at the moment she left the surface, thereby causing huge public opprobrium on both sides of the Atlantic. As a result, the men who were cast up as flotsam and jetsam in America were shown huge public generosity, which shamed the company. Charities piled in with fresh clothes and even cash, as did the mayor's office and newspapers, on foot of reader appeals. Guillotined pay by the company was interpreted as a cruelty, not a legally sound protection against a grasping crew.

A far more damaging idea about the Line could also take hold as a result – if the White Star Line had such a policy, might it not suggest that calamities were never too far from the firm's door? Who, then, would sail with such an outfit?

Incidentally, William Weller was one of the first in the queue for a lifeboat place after the *Titanic* struck. His fellow able seaman Archie Jewell was asked in evidence: 'Did you count as one of the two seamen for this boat (Lifeboat 7)?'

'Yes.'

'Who was the other?'

'Weller.'[6]

The disappointed litigant's fortunes soon improved. He was paid £8, twelve shillings and sixpence in expenses by the British inquiry ($44 in 1912), though never called.

* * *

By mid-April the Lord Mayor of Southampton's second appeal for relief had been launched – this time for the survivors of the *Titanic* tragedy. Bowyer told the *Daily Telegraph*:

I have said the distress is very great. Why, it will be asked. The answer is easy and convincing.

Nearly one-half of the rank and file of the dead crew are victims of the coal strike. A large proportion of the men on Titanic's *glorious roll would have been sailing in other ships if their vessels had not been laid up through shortage of coal.*

To these men and their families the disaster is a coal strike tragedy; but it is small comfort to the bereaved to be told that if their loved ones had not been lost, others would.

The men of some of the liners laid up in Southampton Docks for want of bunker coal were out of work for four or five weeks before the Titanic's *crew signed on. Some of them had made many voyages in the ships from which they were discharged, and the* Titanic *was able to have the pick of the seamen and firemen in the port.*

She had as fine and efficient a crew as ever sailed in a British merchant ship, but as the majority had been idle for some time they left very little behind them. This is why destitution has so swiftly overtaken those who know only too well that their fears of widowhood are correct.[7]

In another interview, Bowyer said: 'The distress is very bad … they [sailors and firemen] left their people in very low water, and the wives have been selling furniture and clothing to buy food.'[8]

* * *

The first thing to be done with the *Titanic* after her arrival at Southampton was to make sure she was coaled. One might have expected the master to stay aboard for this minimum four-day process since there was a burning bunker fire that he certainly knew about – stemming from 'poison pills' among lumps of coal the vessel had ingested at Belfast (so much for the perennial Ulster boast that she was 'all right when she left here')[9] – yet Captain Smith nonetheless left the ship for several days. But in his haste to get home to his family, Smith broke the rules. This time it was not a matter of defying regulations in any failure to note the spontaneous coal fire on the engine room log, nor to duly inform the shore authorities, but a genuine bureaucratic oversight.

James Percival Dodd was the thirty-six-year-old deputy superintendent at the Board of Trade's mercantile marine office in Southampton. He received the *Titanic's* crew agreement for the trip from Belfast, dropped off by messenger. The punctilious Dodd, son of a solicitor, was piqued to see Board requirements had not been complied with. The master, Captain Smith, had not signed the document to 'hereby declare to the truth of the entries in this agreement and account of crew, &c.' The line for Smith's autograph was conspicuously blank. Dodd's handwritten note, in scolding scarlet, fills the place allowed for the master's signature and can be seen today in the Public Records Office of Northern Ireland. He scrawled: 'Capt. Smith was informed he had not signed agreement. He sent a message [from his home] that if he could not call before he sailed he would do so on the return of the ship.' Dodd appended his initials, his unhappiness emphasised by an understroke.[10]

Captain Smith promised to return the *Titanic* to Southampton. The world knows that he did not do so. Therefore this particular crime against proper procedure stands for all time, although he appears to have regarded it as being of trifling importance. He was never going to come from his home to the docks simply to satisfy some jobsworth's desire for correct paperwork.[11] Smith was too eager to spend time at home before departing in his new command. The *Faringdon Advertiser* reported: 'Captain Smith is essentially a home man. His beautiful sylvan retreat near the New Forest is, with his wife and thirteen-year-old daughter, the Captain's chief interest ashore.'[12]

The sixty-two-year-old commodore of the White Star Line, nearly one-third of a century with the same employer, was undoubtedly adept at adjusting to company machinations, so mere bureaucrats could be brushed aside. After all, Smith had hobnobbed ashore with no less a figure than J. P. Morgan, America's leading financier. Once, while sharing Morgan's big touring car on a trip along the US eastern seaboard, Smith, then of the *Adriatic*, found himself treated to speed mania on land. Having missed a rendezvous with a railroad service known as the Millionaires' Express for New York, Morgan ordered it be caught by pursuit. There followed a race between limousine and locomotive over twelve miles from Pittsfield to Lee. Morgan's driver averaged fifty miles an hour, often exceeding sixty – with the captain and the plutocrat hurled back in their seats. But they made the vital interception. 'When Mr Morgan boarded the train he gave the chauffeur five dollars,' reported the *Hartford City Telegram*.[13] The effect on Smith is unrecorded, but evidently Morgan, owner of the White Star Line, believed in the utmost celerity in pursuit of all objectives. The tycoon had made sure to attend the launch in Belfast of RMS *Titanic*, then the largest moving object wrought by the hand of man.

Charles Lightoller, soon the senior surviving *Titanic* officer, had always admired Captain Smith, writing: 'He was a great favourite, and a man any officer would give his ears to sail under. I had been with him many years, off and on, in the mail boats, *Majestic* mainly, and it was an education to see him con [navigate] his own ship up through the intricate channels, entering New York at full speed.

'One particularly bad corner, known as the South-West Spit, used to make us fairly flush with pride as he swung her round, judging his distances to a nicety; she heeling over to the helm with only a matter of feet to spare between each end of the ship and the banks.'[14]

Smith confirmed this impulsive impression in an interview to mark the New York arrival of the *Adriatic* on her 1907 maiden voyage. 'The love of the ocean that took me to sea as a boy has never left me,' the *Washington Post* heard. 'A certain amount of wonder never leaves me, especially as I observe from the bridge a vessel plunging up and down in the trough of the seas, fighting her way through and over great waves, tumbling, and yet keeping on her keel, and going on and on – I wonder how she does it; how she can keep afloat in such seas, and how she can go on and on to port. There is a wild grandeur, too, that appeals to me in the sea. A man never outgrows that.'[15]

Elsewhere in the interview, Smith showed even greater confidence in the safety of modern steamers: 'Shipbuilding is such a perfect art nowadays that absolute disaster, involving the passengers, is inconceivable. Whatever happens, there will be time enough before the vessel sinks to save the life of every person on board.

'I will go a bit further. I will say that I cannot imagine any condition that would cause the vessel to founder. Modern shipbuilding has gone beyond that.'

An *Adriatic* officer who heard the remarks, put in: 'Don't forget, when you write of the Captain's uneventful life, to put in that it's the great Captain who doesn't let things happen.'[16]

7

EXODUS

SIGNING OFF AND ON

Ship papers signed by Harold Sanderson as 'managing owner' in late March gave the terms on which seafarers had gone to Northern Ireland in order to 'bring her round' (i.e. transfer the *Titanic* to Southampton). These stipulated: 'members of the crew signing herein shall proceed from Southampton to Belfast, mustering at West Station at 2.30pm on Tuesday 26th March 1912'.[1]

One of these crew members was George Herbert Hinckley, a thirty-nine-year-old steward of six years' experience with the White Star Line. He was from Derby, and it was a pleasure for him to pass through his home town in the train heading to Liverpool for the Irish Sea crossing. After taking the *Donegal* to Belfast and getting settled into the new ship, George sat down to write to his sister Ida, who still lived in Derby, helping to run the Lonsdale dairy on Uttoxeter Road. He told of seeing familiar gables and gardens from the carriage window as he 'and about a hundred others went to fetch the *Titanic* down from Belfast Lough'.[2] The letter demonstrates that plenty of Englishmen were involved in the transfer of the vessel from one port to another.

Ironically, Hinckley had been glad to get switched from the *Olympic* because a significant body of men regarded her as 'an unlucky ship', a phrase used in his letter.[3] The *Olympic* had, of course, collided with HMS *Hawke* the previous year, and had also thrown a propeller blade and bumped a tug boat or two (supposedly nearly sinking one) on her maiden arrival in New York, but some of the dread at least seemed to stem from her official number, which started with two thirteens. The *Titanic*, on the other hand, had only one thirteen in hers. Hinckley referred to the incident with the *Hawke* and how she had knocked a large triangular hole in the *Olympic*'s starboard side, saying those aboard 'hardly felt the shock'. This would soon become a familiar refrain, but to Hinckley the *Titanic* seemed steadier and a great deal better.

Hinckley also wrote to his sister from Southampton: 'We had a fine run down from Belfast, hardly knowing we were on board.' The optimist, 'a single man of very kindly disposition, very popular with nephews and nieces', stayed aboard for the maiden voyage and predictably perished.[4]

It was the firemen who were the pessimistic members of the crew. Of those who stoked the *Titanic* from Belfast to Southampton, no fewer than 95.6 per cent departed the ship at her first landfall.[5] The figure is stark. While it is true that those from the birthplace of the behemoth had been promised a paid-for return to their point of origin, they could have stayed aboard thereafter. The crew agreement stated: 'Food and bedding will be provided on the way round to Southampton, also tickets for the return journey to Belfast.' Very likely this return ticket to Belfast was open-ended, so could have been used on the men's return to Southampton from New York. Hinckley's letter also shows many non-Ulstermen were aboard, so they did not require to be returned en masse to Belfast. It was not a case of the entire stokehold being Ulstermen anxious to get home from a heathen land. Clearly something unsettling must have caused this stupefying number of tough taskmen to simply walk off the job.

Inducements for these men to stay were clearly offered to some at least. We have already seen how Big Joe Mulholland was offered promotion to storekeeper but chose to leave the ship regardless. Another example is suggested in a story from *The Belfast News-Letter* on 26 April.[6] It began, 'The story of a fireman's fortunate escape from sailing in the ill-fated White Star liner *Titanic* was told yesterday in the Belfast Custody Court,' and continued:

Patrick Morgan, of 32 Shore Street, was charged with having assaulted his wife in their home. Mr Osborne, who appeared for the accused, said his client was the son of a distinguished old soldier, and might consider himself a lucky prisoner. He was a ship's fireman, and had accompanied the ill-fated Titanic *as far as Southampton, when, for some mysterious reason unknown to himself, he absolutely refused to sign on for the voyage and returned to Belfast.*

He now found himself in the dock on a charge of assaulting his wife, when instead he might have been at the bottom of the Atlantic.

Sir Andrew Newton-Brady RM, having heard the evidence, adjourned the case generally, remarking the man should be thankful for his escape, and resolve never to return to the dock in the Police Court again.

Patrick Morgan 'absolutely refused' to sign on for the maiden voyage – this implies repeated attempts at persuasion. There must have been a reason he didn't accept whatever offer was made, but it was not stated in court. Yet Morgan, like other shipmates, was very likely spooked by the spontaneous coal fire in the bunker and tales of malfunctioning hydraulic pumps. Most probably, he had no desire to stay for a voyage in which something could go wrong in mid-Atlantic, stranding him well below the waterline. And fear spreads like wildfire, even among men accustomed to constant combustion.

Perhaps the row with his wife came about because Maggie didn't expect to see him home so soon. He'd been out of work for weeks thanks to the coal strike, and had promised to provide. How were little Patrick and Joseph, aged three and one, supposed to eat? His wife worked as a flax spinner, toiling for hours in their little home, and they needed every penny they could get. But a nagging worry, deep in the stokehold over long hours on the Irish Sea, could have drowned out the fear of what his wife would say at his unexpected reappearance.

Back in Belfast, the court heard a maddened Morgan had resorted to his fists in a domestic argument. He had come home drunk, of course. However, by the time the case was called, Maggie's wrath had cooled. Asked to give evidence, she stated that she did not wish to press the case. She was simply relieved Patrick had not gone down on *Titanic* and that she had him home safe and well. The defendant was discharged, popping his flat cap back on his head as he left an unfamiliar kind of dock. Following this Morgan's marriage appears to have endured, although its level of plain sailing can only be guessed at.

Mulholland, Morgan … who else was made an offer? Following broadcast of a television documentary about the bunker fire aboard the *Titanic* on New Year's Day 2017, a man in Scotland addressed a letter to the editor of *The Times* of London. Published on 3 January, it read: 'Sir, my grandfather was a young steward/barber and his elder brother a stoker on RMS *Olympic* when they were transferred to RMS *Titanic* for work before departure from Belfast. On the passage to Southampton my great-uncle said to my grandfather, "Tom, we have to get off. There's a fire in the bunkers and we've not been able to sort it [out]." They were offered extra money but they got off.'

Overall, 174 members of the stokehold – leading hands, firemen, greasers and trimmers (those who brought coal in barrows from the bunkers) – wantonly walked down the gangway at Southampton, abandoning ship. Another fireman, John Coffey, deserted at Queenstown (his story will be dealt with in more detail later). By meagre comparison, only eight of the original stokehold men opted to stay. The only leading hand to do so, Joseph Beattie, drowned or froze to death. Also fated to die among the few who remained were four firemen – William McQuillan, Richard Turley, Thomas Connor and Hugh Calderwood. Three of the original firemen survived: William Murdock, John Haggan and Thomas Graham. The last-named was called to the British inquiry, but was never asked to give evidence. Haggan never talked about the disaster. Murdock, in contrast, did consent to be interviewed by the press and 'recounted his thrilling experiences in a simple, straightforward manner'.[7] He was so cool that, on being ordered to crew lifeboat 16, 'before entering it, went below to obtain additional clothing, wading waist-deep in water to secure it. On his return to the deck he assisted in placing women and children in the boat.'

Clearly Murdock was not one to be put off by scare stories of a blazing bunker. Naturally he was not asked by the newspaper about his *Titanic* experiences prior to her final night, nor anything that occurred pre-collision. It is the collision that has defined this story, first overshadowing, then seemingly eradicating, all that went before.

* * *

So why did 174 of the stokehold leave and only eight stay to re-engage for the maiden voyage? Arguably at least half of the original stokehold crew – around ninety men – would have been expected to have stayed in what was an exceedingly good berth, particularly given the painful economic pinch being felt at the time on foot of the prolonged coal strike.

On 6 April, in the middle of a *Titanic* layover lasting just short of a week, the *Southampton Times* made this very point. It proudly quoted the *Shipping Gazette* in its report that 'the conditions of service on liners sailing from the Hampshire port are quite satisfactory from the sailors' point of view, [as] is frequently evidenced at the signing-on of crews. Only four days ago, when the crew of the *Oruba* was signing on, there were practically no changes. The men who had made the previous voyage were re-employed for another trip.'

While seafarers were famously mercurial – they failed to join, deserted, and generally shipped as the mood took them – on this occasion there was a powerful added incentive to stay at work in the aftermath of the coal strike, which had denied all earning opportunities for weeks past, 'and there was no unemployment benefit', as Alfred Fanstone, himself a greaser, pointedly put it.[8]

On the morning after arrival in Southampton, *Titanic* Second Officer David Blair wrote home that he was leaving 'to make room for [the] Chief Officer of the *Olympic*, who was going in command [of another ship], but with so many ships laid up, he will have to wait [for his own captaincy]'. Henry Wilde had been due to become master of the *Cymric*, but she was one of the many ships that were idle in early April. Paying berths for crewmen were as rare as hen's teeth in such straitened times.

Delivery and maiden voyage documents for the *Olympic* a year earlier are not obviously extant – either they are not catalogued or are no longer in existence. Thus a direct comparison cannot be made between the two sisters as to crew propensity to stay for the longer voyage. It seems impossible to believe, however, that there could have been an attrition rate of 95.6 per cent of firemen in the case of the *Olympic*'s entry into service in 1911, despite other jobs being easy to come by at the time, and with coal both plentiful and cheap.[9]

The unease evidenced by messmates about the fire in the coal bunker would probably have been enough to encourage those told about it to leave the ship, even if they hadn't direct knowledge of it themselves. Anyone who doubts that word-of-mouth would be sufficient to drive so many stokers off the ship should look at the parallel in the case of the *Olympic* mutiny, weeks after the loss of the *Titanic* in 1912. In that case firemen did not trust the collapsible crafts that were stacked aboard her in the wake of the *Titanic* sinking, considering them unseaworthy. They refused to sail as a result. All were of a like mind. Consequently, the entire voyage was abruptly cancelled.

A lack of confidence among the 'Black Squad' is, therefore, demonstrably sufficient cause to result in virtually the whole stokehold complement refusing to remain in service.[10] In the case of the *Titanic*, this loss of faith resulted in the exodus of 95.6 per cent of these men, suggesting this 'small' fire, as it was labelled by Harold Sanderson at the inquiry, must have been much more significant than the Line was willing to admit.

8

MEN OF AFFAIRS

SOME CONSULTATIONS

Not all crew took part in the exodus, of course. Those taken on at Belfast who were placed higher than the stokehold – i.e. the stewards and pantrymen, scullions and cooks – almost uniformly remained aboard for the maiden voyage. Their continued presence on both the Irish Sea trip and the maiden voyage highlights a glaring disparity when compared with the 'Black Squad's' walking off. Sailors, quartermasters and deckhands also stayed en masse, bar the usual minor comings and goings, including officers David Blair and Henry Wilde. Remaining, too, were the engineers who had been below as the ship was stoked to Southampton.

These engineers were made of stern stuff. Their devotion to duty was widely hailed when they were later lost to a man. The young whipper-snapper who 'gave off something shocking' (see p. 31) is to be both pitied and admired for what soon transpired, despite the tantrum Mulholland claims he threw. Their higher calling meant they had to stand by the ship.

As well as the crew who remained with the ship, the first passenger had also been aboard since Belfast, despite the ship's unfinished state. The intriguing presence of Wyckoff Van Derhoef on the positioning trip has led to an argument that the trip to New York should in fact be classed as the *Titanic*'s second voyage, and that the maiden voyage (with its single paying passenger) had been from her fitting-out wharf to where a dockland peninsula separates the Trent and Itchen rivers in Southampton.

Van Derhoef looked almost exactly like Captain Smith, which must have alarmed the crew, as if the skipper were wandering incognito in civilian clothes among them. Although a year younger, he, too, sported snowy hair and a full white beard – albeit his only extant photograph, from some years before, shows him solely with a moustache. He had been visiting his Brooklyn-born sister,

Mary Long, who lived with her merchant husband in leafy College Park East in Belfast, close to both the Botanic Gardens and Ulster Museum.

Wealthy Van Derhoef, who had not been out of the United States in years, was gratified to find a vessel locally to hand that would 'bring him all the way back to his native soil. He paid £33 and ten shillings for the first-class privilege, which entitled him to full board from the moment he ascended the gangway on the Queen's Island. It must have been profoundly strange and lonely being the sole customer in an echoing dining saloon capable of holding 600. Nonetheless, full menus were printed for his benefit. On 3 April, the day after leaving the Lagan, he chose between hors d'oeuvres, various soups and supreme of chicken, filet mignon, roast duckling, halibut or saddle of mutton for the main course.

It so happened that this sole person aboard the *Titanic* who was not an employee of the White Star Line was instead a specialist in fire insurance. Van Derhoef was the secretary and largest shareholder in the Williamsburg Fire Insurance Company, having worked his way to the top after beginning as a clerk three decades before. Naturally, he was exceptionally well insured for personal risk during his trip, and his estate would soon be probated with a sum in excess of $100,000. His will, drawn up in 1898, left $250 to the Green Wood Trust Co. for the perpetual care of his grave – and $500 for a monument to be selected by his widow. It was as well, then, that his body was recovered from the cruel sea. His physical description, including beard, was noted by corpse-retrievers from a chartered cable ship – along with his gold ring, gold watch and fob, gold medallion, gold cufflinks and $62 in cash.[1] He now lies in Green Wood, Brooklyn, his stone a last terse accident report. It gives the cause of demise as S.S. *Titanic*.

But what were the factors that contributed to his and the whole *Titanic*'s loss? Interestingly, Van Derhoef's cousin, George Chauncey, who was the president of the Mechanics Bank, told the *Brooklyn Daily Eagle* of 16 April 1912 that he did not blame Captain Smith for the sinking: 'I was a passenger on board the *Olympic* on her first eastward voyage when Captain Smith was in command of her. I found him a fine gentleman and first-class mariner. He inspired everybody on board with confidence. I cannot believe he was to blame for this disaster.' He added: 'Icebergs are treacherous and barely discernible in the night. The *Titanic* must have been going at a terrific rate of speed. She must have struck head on and been almost completely telescoped. Many with accommodations forward must have been crushed to death.'

His impressions, framed early on, proved wide of the mark in one way – his cousin's corpse was not crushed – but Chauncey did accurately gauge that the *Titanic* had been travelling at high speed, as would subsequently be revealed at the inquiries. This ought to have been all the more perplexing for the bereaved because White Star had explicitly stated the ship would not do so. After the vessel's arrival in Southampton, the company issued a press statement, printed on 6 April, four days before the maiden departure: 'Arrangements to ensure the regular sailing of the mammoth liners *Olympic* and *Titanic* have been made by the White Star Line. To economise coal, the liners will be run at a speed of 20 knots instead of 23.'[2] Yet the truth is the *Titanic* was doing a rampant 23 knots before she struck the iceberg. The contradiction made no sense at all to those who noticed it.

Neither did the exodus of firemen, if all was well with the ship. In fact, the haemorrhage of stokehold staff in Southampton must have seriously alarmed White Star, because bosses resorted to a very unusual tactic – throwing themselves on the mercy of a militant trade union. There was an approach on the afternoon of 4 April (the day the stokers were paid and strayed) to the British Seafarers' Union (BSU), formed in October 1911 by the firebrand labour organiser Tommy Lewis. It must have been distasteful to local managers to beg a man whom they considered to be a base agitator for assistance, yet Lewis was asked to kindly make his members aware that the *Titanic* desperately wanted crew and would pay good rates. The BSU was asked to supply firemen, trimmers and greasers to replace those who had left, as well as stewards, if they had any, since few had been needed hitherto in the absence of passengers.

Nothing could be done the next day, Good Friday. Instead White Star set up a hiring hall on the docks bright and early on Saturday morning and it was thronged all that day. A total of 228 signed up from the BSU's ranks, with another hundred from the National Sailors' and Firemen's Union. More followed in another engagement fair on Monday, making it clear that the appointed date for the maiden voyage would be handsomely met, despite recent troubles.[3] Tommy Lewis was able to tell Lord Mersey on the second day of the British inquiry that his union had a membership of 4,000. 'Practically the whole of the seafarers of the *Titanic* are members of our union.'

It seemed there was no need for any bothersome Belfast men, after all. Yet some of the eager local firemen may have heard rumours of the fire from the previous stokehold staff, as a number decided against going aboard at the last moment, which later translated into a general unease about the ship. Elizabeth Burrows of Clarence Street told the *Southampton Times* of her son, Harry, a trimmer, who expected to engage on the *Titanic*: 'He went down to the docks to sign on, but at the last moment changed his mind and came away, for which we are very thankful. I can't explain why he changed his mind; some sort of a feeling came over him, he told me.'

On 20 April the same paper reported the tale of three lucky Slade brothers, firemen all. They had signed on, yet, on sailing day, were cut off from joining the *Titanic* by a long train that passed – painstakingly and providentially – in front of them while the ship's gangways, obscured in the distance, were taken away. Their grateful mother, widow Sophia Slade, was overheard in conversation with another mother of crew members (likely also firemen). The unidentified matriarch declared: 'You may not believe in dreams, but Mrs Slade, I'm telling you the truth when I say one of my boys had a dream about the boat the night before sailing and he afterwards said he had a dread of her. I knew they were not very keen on going, but nevertheless, they went.'

Possibly there was word on the wind, however – mention of an uncontrollable blaze that served to deter. Wait for another ship, said the old-timers. When this one succumbed to ice, not fire, the prior misgivings lost their factual roots and became instead psychic forebodings.[4]

Helen Podesta, wife of *Titanic* fireman Jack, told Canadian radio in 1972 that she and others at Toogood Seeds were allowed to go down to the docks to watch the new liner depart.[5] 'When she was sailing out, the rumours went about that she was going to sink,' she declares on tape. 'We didn't take no notice.' But next she observes: 'My brother and brother-in-law and a friend of mine was going on that boat [*Titanic*], and they actually done [*sic*] what they call a dockhead jump – they didn't go on the boat, they went on the *Olympic*.'

Most of the new stokers who signed on at Southampton were sent straight back home on leave as the majority of the ship's furnaces were cold. *Titanic Voices*, the Southampton oral history, declares: 'Some stokers, however, had to remain on the *Titanic* in Southampton as a fire was smouldering in Number 10 coal bunker [in boiler room 6] – they were working the coal, hosing water on it, and shovelling it away to try to get to the base of the pile, to keep the situation under control.'[6] It seems the blaze was in fact a serious cause for concern, but there remained optimism in the senior ranks that it would ultimately come to heel and be no impediment to getting away on Wednesday. In light of the *Cairnrona* ruling, however, that 'the vessel ought not to have taken to sea with the bunker coal in such a condition', they realised that there would have to be a veil drawn over the matter.

The period immediately prior to embarkation of passengers and departure is intriguing. But a crucial admission was made two years after the disaster in 1914, by J. Bruce Ismay, managing director of the White Star Line, that throws a faint light on preparations. It was unremarked upon then, with a world war imminent, and has not been spotted by scholars since. Ismay revealed in a deposition seeking limitation of liability for his company (against US victims' relatives seeking compensation) that he had made 'an arrangement' with Chief Engineer Joseph Bell 'at Southampton, two or three days before the ship sailed' about the conduct of the Atlantic passage.[7] It seems inescapable that this conversation with Bell must have included mention of the fire in the coal bunker. Just as it was written in the White Star rules that the chief engineer had to inform the captain of any such outbreak (a measure of its potential seriousness), Bell had a similar duty to acquaint Ismay with the fact of the fire in the course of their arrangement.

There is oblique corroboration that this consultation occurred – if not that the bunker fire was discussed – in the fact that a statement was issued by White Star in the same time frame that the *Titanic* would be run at a restrained speed of 20 knots in order to economise on coal. The reason for such a public announcement will be examined later, but sections of the press printed it on 6 April, which in Ismay's later recollection became 'two or three days' before the ship sailed on the tenth. Yet without doubt, *any* internal company discussion on the *Titanic*'s coal and intended speed must have involved disclosure of the bunker fire, because that was the chief engineer's duty. There can thus be no doubt that Captain Smith and Managing Director Ismay both directly knew of this troubling combustion 'two or three days before the ship sailed', and knew at Southampton.

According to his biographer, Ismay was in London and did not travel to Southampton until the very eve of the maiden departure, raising questions about the circumstances of the 'arrangement' he later disclosed. His discussion with Bell could thus not have been made in port 'two or three days' prior to sailing, because Ismay was not physically there.

The *Titanic* had an internal telephone system, but it had no connection in turn to the wider network administered by the Post Office. How, then, did the personal 'arrangement' between Managing Director Ismay and Chief Engineer Bell come about? Either Ismay (or his biographer) is wrong about dates, or else the possibility arises of a personal trip by Bell to see Ismay in London 'two or three days before the ship sailed'. An impetus to report might have originated with Bell himself, possibly in conjunction with the captain. This would then invest the discussion and 'arrangement' with arguably even greater significance, reflecting a concern that had originated on board.

It turns out that Bell had exactly the kind of close relationship with Ismay that would allow him to take it upon himself to broach difficult subjects with his company superior. Ismay himself confirmed this encounter, and in truth Bell was a close confidant and deeply trusted lieutenant on whom Ismay relied extensively. Indeed the latter spoke warmly about Bell in the immediate wake of the tragedy, in which the chief engineer died: 'He had had a very long experience, and he was an extremely good man,' said Ismay. 'He was sent over to Belfast when the *Olympic* was being built, and he remained in Belfast during the whole of the time she was being built, superintending her construction, making any suggestions which he thought would lead to improvements [i.e. making those suggestions to Ismay, whose approval was required].

'He brought the ship out to New York on her first voyage as Chief Engineer. We then brought Mr Bell again ashore, and he was present during the whole time of construction of the *Titanic* and brought her out as Chief Engineer.'[8]

In short, Bell may even have outstripped Captain Smith in Ismay's estimation. He was more familiar with the *Titanic* than anyone else aboard (with the possible exception of chief designer Thomas Andrews), having spent months at a time in Belfast during the building, and was also undoubtedly a close personal friend of the managing director. Ismay's admitted consultation with him provided Bell will the perfect opportunity to raise anything that was on his mind, prior to the ship being put to sea.

It accordingly seems certain that he would have told Ismay about the fire, and done so days before departure from Southampton. But it is probable that the White Star chief already knew, because an even closer associate of his was his deputy, Harold Sanderson.

This foreknowledge of the fire amongst the senior staff and managing director meant the maiden voyage not only defied safety warnings but ran a flagrant risk when set against an undersupply of lifeboats.

The New York *Sun* special correspondent reported from the British inquiry on 5 June:

[Ismay] *stood at the witness table ... his hands clasped behind his back, and swayed to and fro almost ceaselessly as he stood shifting from one foot to the other ...*

Lord Mersey sharply reprimanded Mr Ismay when he hesitated in answering questions ... Ismay admitted he had never considered the possibility of the Titanic *having to use her lifeboats to save the lives of her passengers ... he regarded the boats more as a means of taking people off other vessels that were in trouble.*

When Lord Mersey asked: 'Supposing there was a fire on board, might not you want lifeboats then?'[9] the *Sun* witheringly reported: 'Mr Ismay this time had no answer.' It portrays him stuck for words, as if uneasy that Mersey might privately have learned the seriousness of the outbreak.

No pause is shown in the official transcript. It carries Ismay's response, eventual as it may have been, amounting to meek capitulation: 'Yes, if the passengers had to leave the ship on account of fire, you would need lifeboats.'

9

PASSING MUSTER

ARRIVALS AND ABSENCES

Ismay's biographer, Wilton Oldham, wrote that 'Mr and Mrs J. Bruce Ismay motored down from Hill Street [their imposing Mayfair residence, just off Berkeley Square, London] with their three children in the big Daimler Laundalette ... they all stayed the night [before sailing] at the South Western Hotel, Southampton. At 9.30 a.m. on April 10, the family went aboard the *Titanic* as she lay in the Ocean Dock; at noon the liner sailed. Mrs Bruce Ismay and the children watched her depart, and then set off on their motor tour of Devonshire and Wales.'[1]

The managing director might have independently arrived in Southampton, but most passengers took a train to begin their transatlantic journey, albeit rail travel was still restricted in the wake of the coal strike. Some, like nineteen-year-old Joseph Nichols from St Ives, came early just in case. On checking into a boarding house he dashed off a postcard to relatives: 'Got up all right. Now had supper. Sailing tomorrow 12 o'clock. Cheer up.'[2]

At Waterloo Station in London, '*Titanic* Special' departures were laid on early on sailing day. The lower orders went first, allowing their 'betters' extra time in bed. Second- and third-class passengers, as well as servants and attendants to first class, left at 7.30 a.m. on the London and South Western service to Southampton. They arrived dockside some two hours later, the maids and valets summoning help to carry aboard the clutter of first-class baggage sent down in their charge.

Nellie Becker, who was returning to the United States with her family, expressed doubts about the untried monstrosity looming above them. A purser's clerk, overhearing, said she did not have to be the least bit afraid. 'If anything should happen to this ship, the watertight compartments could keep it afloat.'[3]

At the altogether more civilised hour of 9.45 a.m., a total of 202 first-class passengers, suitably unencumbered by anything other than a parasol or newspaper, boarded in London. For these the train journey was made express, taking just one hour and forty minutes, and arriving at 11.25 a.m., comfortably more than half an hour before the ship was due to sail.

Francis Browne, a student for the priesthood taking the vessel as far as Queenstown, Ireland, wrote: 'My first glimpses of the ship had been from the train as it slowly steamed through the streets and the docks of Southampton.'[4] The carriages inched parallel to the waiting vessel (an arrivals shed separated the two), with brake squeals preceding the flying-open of doors and expressions of admiration at her profile as the well-to-do disgorged themselves onto the quayside.

At this stage, even though passengers were heading aboard, many crew members were still in town, eagerly consuming their last drop of alcohol before a sternly abstentionist trip. Able seaman Fred Clench later told the somewhat puritanical American inquiry: 'As for any intemperance, you seldom saw anything on a boat like that. I mean to say you can not get anything to drink there, so you are bound to be a teetotaler.'[5]

For the crew already on board, there had been a boat muster on deck at 8 a.m., followed by a boat drill, as two lifeboats were lowered to the water from the starboard side and then re-hoisted. Interestingly, the firemen didn't attend. This boat drill at Southampton engendered a lot of discussion at both the American and British inquiries – particularly over the lack of participation by the 'Black Squad'. The sense conveyed by witnesses was that it was ultimately down to the recalcitrance and stubbornness of the stokers.

Harold Sanderson grappled with the no-shows in his evidence to the British inquiry, not the first time he had to address his company's seeming indifference to official regulations (in this case, the regulation was that all crew should attend the drill). 'I should like to say in regard to this boat muster or boat drill, that we have experienced very great difficulty in carrying it out,' he confessed. 'In the first place we have a difficulty, which is a natural one, from the fact that we carry large numbers of passengers, and that many of the crew cannot be spared from their duties. But over and above that, we have experienced a very serious difficulty arising from the unwillingness of certain portions of the crew to comply with the company's regulations. To such an extent that they at times refuse duty on the voyage.'

He then made clear: 'I am particularly speaking of the firemen.'[6]

Only within the past two years had they rebelled, he added, lest the court think the company had encouraged such slackness. 'Up to that time we had no difficulty of the kind.'

In this specific case, however, their absence may have at least in part stemmed from the firemen being needed below to address that outbreak of spontaneous combustion in a three-storey coal bunker. Even getting them to attend to that problem probably took extensive cajoling and the promise of generous and sympathetic consideration. As far back as 1906 it was observed in a magazine article that 'the work of this department is so arduous while at sea that men receive liberty for the entire time the ship remains in port, their places being taken by a special shore force which remains aboard until sailing day'.[7]

Maurice Harvey Clarke, the Board of Trade surveyor at Southampton who gave the *Titanic* her vital certificate of clearance to sail on the maiden voyage, also addressed the firemen's absence from the drill in his testimony. Clarke first told of witnessing the mustering of the crew, with members of different departments summoned to separate decks because of the ship's size. It was his job to see that the numbers were correct and the names tallied off as each passed by. He spoke of watching a total of two lifeboats swung out and lowered. He claimed that it was 'entirely' to his satisfaction, with eight sailors and an officer in each boat (although the *Titanic* had barely enough deckhands, and when disaster struck would not be able to spare even two to a boat). There were no firemen or stewards at this important drill, Clarke confirmed, despite his own belief that all classes of crew should be exercised in handling the boats.

A question from trade union counsel Thomas Scanlan MP was beguilingly placid: 'Up to the time of the *Titanic* disaster that had not been the practice?'[8]

'Not in the White Star Line,' Clarke conceded, next admitting that all other shipping lines nonetheless managed to muster their different grades, firemen included, at boat stations.

Lord Mersey, president of the court, then got involved in the probing, and Clarke allowed that he had personally heard White Star firemen object to the boat drill in Southampton. As to why White Star allowed their slacking off, and not the other lines, he lamely offered: 'I don't know; I couldn't tell you.' He could only confirm that he had never seen firemen at a White Star boat drill. He agreed, however, that he himself could have demanded their presence. He did not do so because it was 'the custom'. The system was 'not very satisfactory', he granted. Asked if he always followed custom, though bad in practice, Clarke weakly managed: 'You will remember I am a civil servant. Custom guides us a good bit.'[9]

Surveyor Clarke further indicated he had not got down to the stokehold because certain doors were locked. 'The reason for having those doors locked is to keep the firemen and stewards and other people from passing through into the different places on sailing day,' he said, in apparent contradiction of the need for firemen to attend drills.[10] 'The ship is very congested from a lot of visitors – something like a thousand visitors.'

Yet he had also inspected on two occasions before sailing day, when the ship lay quiet, with no visitors: on the day of arrival for 'a very short time' he said and then on the day before sailing. The locked doors – which had been locked then, too – had only in those instances discouraged the surveyor from venturing into the bowels of the vessel. It was all a bit limp, and Clarke further relied on the fact there were not enough surveyors at Southampton, as if to ward off anyone looking askance at his own performance. He stated that there ought to be getting on for double the number of ship-checkers.

'Have you ever represented [that deficiency] to the Board of Trade?' he was asked.

'That would not be in my province.'

To the suggestion that, if such was his view, it was his duty to say so, Clarke showed his essential cowardice: 'I should get a very severe snub if I did.'[11] Yet this was the man on whom a mass of emigrants vicariously relied for safe passage and new lives.

One thing Clarke could do it seemed, was shut a stable door. He made sure to testify that he saw three watertight doors closed in his presence. Those ones worked, at least, although whether he selected which ones were to be closed himself or not is unclear. He also did not say whether they were of the electrical type or designed to be manually cranked shut from the deck above.

Clarke also provided a classic example of acting after the horse has bolted. Firemen were now taking part in boat drills, he was pleased to report. 'We are doing it now. We fill boats with stewards and with firemen; in fact, the men like it, now I have instituted it. Since the *Titanic* disaster, they like it.'[12]

Clarke's resurgent and certified self-satisfaction must have nauseated some in his audience, or reading newspaper coverage – particularly those who had lost loved ones. What is clear from his testimony, however, is that he had not seen the stokehold with its incriminating bunker. He instead relied on the reassurance of the White Star Line, a company that had shown itself practically impudent in its apathy towards official regulation.

Asked whether any report had been made to him about a fire, Clarke replied in the negative. It was put to him that, if there was a serious fire before the ship sailed, it ought to have been brought to his attention. Clarke replied: 'Yes, if it was a serious fire it ought to have been reported to me.'[13]

He then followed up, to cover his own dereliction: 'It is not an uncommon thing to have these small fires in the bunkers.' He used the same adjective as Sanderson, whether he knew it or not, when neither had actually seen the fire. But Clarke could not have known whether it was a small fire or a serious blaze for the simple reason that he had not bothered to look in the place where he might find it. The *Titanic* was indeed vast – and some of her bunkers were massive in proportion.

It must be plainly observed here that the heads of the White Star Line – if it indeed had been a 'small' fire – could easily have ingratiated themselves with the surveyor through cloying 'full disclosure', along with demonstration of all the steps they were taking to ensure its early extinguishment. But the fact that it was not reported tends to the other pole – that the fire was indeed serious, not small, and would have resulted in a cancelled crossing had the surveyor known of its existence.

Dockers' Union lawyer Clement Edwards, who had skewered Sanderson on this burning issue, commented now to Clarke that the fire damage was later 'regarded as so serious by the Officer [Chief Engineer Joseph Bell] that it ought to be reported to the makers [Harland & Wolff's guarantee group]'.[14] But that was when the ship was halfway across the Atlantic.

Surveyor Clarke, however, appeared to be a man accustomed to the slapdash. Even the non-reporting of a roaring inferno might not have mattered to him.

10

DRILLING DOWN

ATTEMPTS AT DECEPTION

It was unfortunate for Second Officer Charles Lightoller that he spoke of Maurice Clarke at the official inquiry in America as the very paragon of oversight and zeal. Lightoller's overriding concern was to preserve the fiction of the *Titanic* as the 'last word in shipbuilding' and all that went with it, having become convinced that the future of the company, and its entire employment, was at stake in the post-tragedy environment. That meant a need to convey that the official examination had certified the ship as utterly without blemish prior to sailing, while the accident itself was a once-in-a-century freak occurrence. He memoired: 'The disaster was due to a combination of circumstances that never occurred before and can never occur again. That may sound like a sweeping statement, yet it is a fact.'[1]

To the American inquiry in 1912, he said: 'Speaking of Capt. Clarke, we call him a nuisance because he is so strict.' His innocent listeners must have been impressed, long before the object of Lightoller's praise would cut a lonely figure in London, stripped of credibility. 'He carried out the tests required by the Board of Trade,' the senior surviving officer maintained. He had been with him about four hours on the ship, he said, adding that the marine superintendent of the White Star Line at Southampton, Captain Benjamin Steel, accompanied Clarke 'the whole time'.[2]

Riding shotgun with the government inspector, therefore, was the very man whom Harold Sanderson testified had been informed about the fire on the ship's arrival – but who, in Clarke's company, appeared to firmly keep his mouth shut.[3]

Steel was later put into evidence for twenty minutes on 11 June 1912 in the course of the British inquiry. He was principally examined by Raymond Asquith (son of sitting Prime Minister Herbert), junior counsel for the Board of Trade. Three other lawyers then asked a few questions each. Maddeningly, absolutely none asked Steel about his knowledge of the fire. But he was asked about the absence of firemen at the lifeboat drill, which he confirmed, only to then contradict Clarke on their eagerness to take part since the disaster. He stated that they had been offered half a day's pay to come down the day before sailing to take part in boat drills. 'Not one appeared,' he said. 'That was equal to a refusal.' Even if given a half day's pay for what he estimated to be two hours' work, 'I do not think they would, not from our past experience.'[4]

He doubted some of them would come even if offered the sum of five pounds, a month's salary. But he added an exculpatory remark: 'Well, of course, I have not much to do with the firemen. That is the Superintending Engineer's business.'[5]

Now, let us return for a moment to Lightoller's defence of Clarke. 'He makes us fork out every detail,' the officer marvelled in his United States evidence. The surveyor would insist upon equipment being brought out on deck every time, he claimed. His attendance meant all boats being uncovered and cranked out, all tanks and water containers examined, oars counted, rudders tried, all the davits tested. 'There was innumerable detail work. The boats lowered, put in the water, and pulled out, and brought back again, and if he was not satisfied, sent back again,' said Lightoller. This was a wild exaggeration – certainly in the case of the *Titanic*, anyway. Clarke had asked for only two boats to be lowered. Numbers 13 and 15 were sent off from starboard for twenty minutes, under Fifth and Sixth Officers Harold Lowe and James Moody respectively.[6]

Clarke had no doubt sensed impending danger for his career when tragedy struck, drawing up private notes for himself in advance of the inquiry. The very first paragraph of his first page of notes (a page later auctioned for £5,200 from those consigned by his descendants) stated: 'Started boat drill about 8.30 am on the 10th Ap. No instruction compelling E. officer [emigration officer; i.e. himself] to have boat or fire drill before granting clearance.'[7]

Clarke had mentioned the 'fire' word. In his notes he also wrote that he had to pass men as ordinary seamen 'who have never been to sea' and spoke about 'crew going ashore' contrary to regulations during the boat drill. He wrote of the *Titanic*:

All hands were mustered on deck. Officers and ABs [able seamen] *under the forecastle, engineers and firemen in the working alleyway known as Scotland Road on E deck, the stewards, stewardesses and restaurant staff on A deck.*

A clerk from the company's office then read out the names, each man passing doffing his cap and answering. Absentees were noted and vacancies filled up before sailing, and the physically unfit rejected by the doctors, of which there were four.

I only tested and lowered the usual number of boats. I would respectfully add that it is not an uncommon occurrence to find at our emigration clearances ABs wholly incompetent to row in even a moderate weather and sea, but to reject such men on the score that they cannot handle an oar would, I most respectfully suggest, have annoyed the ship owner and perhaps led to litigation.

It is clear that Clarke did not want to annoy. So much for his being a nuisance, then. He further revealed he had 'no knowledge of any surveyor having declined' clearance because of the state of the lifeboats (or, it appeared, for any other reason). If he was covering himself, so too was the Board of Trade. Clarke was sent, in advance, a list of areas his questioning under oath was likely to cover. The stress would be on the adequacy of manning and lifeboats, just these aspects alone, with no mention of any matters below deck.[8]

But regardless of his preparation, Clarke had been trapped and humiliated by counsel from outside the Board's control. Despite his poor showing at the inquiry, however, he kept his job in the Board of Trade Marine Department, although he was soon shunted off to Dublin, where he ended his days in the paper-pushing service of an eventual different state.

* * *

Clarke was not the only one to attempt to make things seem better than they were. The *Titanic's* Fifth Officer Harold Lowe, one of those sent out in a lifeboat by Clarke at Southampton, ridiculously tried to claim at the US inquiry that there had indeed been a fire drill on the *Titanic*, as distinct from a boat drill, before leaving port.[9] Lowe told presiding Senator William Alden Smith of Michigan: 'Fire drill did take place, and it always does take place.' It was prior to the boat drill, he said, elaborating: 'There are so many hoses on each deck, and the water service is on, and the hoses are manned by the men, and the commander sends word along, "That will do for fire exercise," and then we switch off the water.'

But there was already ample evidence that there had been no such fire drill, and Senator Smith grew grave: 'Are you quite sure such an exercise took place?'

Lowe, detecting deep suspicion from the US inquiry chairman, performed a virtuoso somersault: 'Let me see. I may be confusing her with some of the other ships.'

Smith was deliberate, trenchantly telling the witness: 'You are testifying. I want the record to show what you say about it.'

Now Lowe was in abject and full retreat: 'We will annul that, sir, because I am not sure.'

In fact, there never was a fire drill. Nor any further boat drill, although one had been due to be held on the morning of Sunday 14 April, the very day the ship met her nemesis.

Another of the men sent out during Clarke's perfunctory boat drill in Southampton was a sailor named Joseph Scarrott. A practical, no-nonsense seaman, Scarrott firmly denied Lightoller's assurances about all boat equipment 'being brought out on deck every time' for the surveyor.[10] Asked if it was the practice to overhaul boats and examine contents before the ship was cleared, Scarrott commented: 'I have always seen that done in the Union and Castle Line, where most of my time has been, but on the Wednesday we left in the *Titanic* I did not see anything in the boats overhauled at all.'[11]

It was emphatic. He did not see any boat equipment turned out for careful inspection by Clarke in this way. The Board of Trade lawyers were thrown, but Thomas Scanlan, for the National Sailors' and Firemen's Union, asked a penetrating question: 'In the practice of boat drill, was there any inspection made by you or anybody else to see whether the boat was fitted with a lamp and compass and the other proper equipment?'

Scarrott replied plainly: 'There was no inspection made.'[12]

Clarke had been going through the motions. The whole clearance survey was superficial at best, and entirely hollow at worst. And yet the passengers never knew. 'There was no inspection made' – Scarrott might very well have scaled up this one scouring statement to cover everything.

And Scarrott will show us more in due course. His account of the iceberg strike will turn out to be key to understanding why the *Titanic* struck at all – though posterity has missed the reason, as will be explained later.[13]

Scarrott did not want to be aboard the *Titanic* in the first place. He wrote three articles for the *Pier Review* in 1932 about his experiences, beginning: 'Several things happened, especially to me, both before and at the time of sailing, which many people regarded as ill omens. It is a general belief that all sailors are superstitious. Well, I can honestly say that I am one who is not.' When he went to the docks that morning he had as much intention of applying for a job on 'the Big 'Un as we called her', as he had of going to the moon, he wrote. He already had an offer of a job as quartermaster on a familiar Union Castle liner, and was not 'in low water for bees and honey' (in need of money). Yet somehow: 'I signed as AB on Monday 8th April, 1912 (note the total of numbers in the year).'[14] By this he means that the digits nominally totalled thirteen, despite his insistence that he was not superstitious.

When Scarrott went home and told his sister (who may have heard a thing or two) that he had engaged on the *Titanic*, she called him a bloody fool. 'Now this was the first and only time she had shown disapproval of any ship I was going on,' wrote Scarrott. 'In fact she would not believe me until she found I was minus my discharge book.'[15] He did not specify the cause of her misgivings.

'I was under orders to join the ship at 7am Wednesday, April 10th, the time of sailing being 12 noon … I decide I will go, but not with a good heart. Before leaving home I kissed my sister and said "Goodbye," and as I was leaving she called me back and asked why I had said "Goodbye," instead of my usual "So long, see you again soon." I told her I had not noticed saying it, neither had I. On my way to join the ship you can imagine how this incident stuck in my mind.'

Scarrott also commented: 'I had worked aboard the *Titanic* when she came to Southampton from the builders in Belfast and I had the opportunity to inspect her from stem to stern.' Whatever the degree of his scrutiny, he discovered no apparent cause for concern. Yet he was still plagued by doubts: 'Now in the whole of my career of 29 years of going to sea, I have never had that feeling of hesitation that I experienced then, and if I was offered a fortune I could not explain the reason.'

On sailing day, fifteen minutes before noon, he had still not changed from his civilian clothes, noting his own behaviour as odd. The order was given: 'All hands to stations for casting off.'

Scarrott writes in the present tense: 'I am in the starboard watch, my station is aft, and I am still not in uniform. My actions and manners are the reverse of what they should be.'

It was too late for Scarrott to change his mind. The *Titanic* was set to sail.

11

SHORT ON FUEL

THE EVIDENCE

Lawrence Beesley, second-class passenger and science teacher, stayed in a hotel in Southampton the night before sailing. 'I recall that as I sat that morning in the breakfast room, from the windows of which could be seen the four huge funnels of the *Titanic* towering over the roofs of various shipping offices opposite, and the procession of stokers and stewards wending their way to the ship, there sat behind me three of the *Titanic*'s passengers discussing the coming voyage and estimating, among other things, the probabilities of an accident at sea to the ship. As I rose from breakfast, I glanced at the group and recognised them later on board, but they were not among the number who answered to the roll-call on *Carpathia* the following Monday morning.'[1]

Only the South Western Hotel (where Ismay stayed) would have provided a view of *Titanic*'s looming funnels, and it is to there that several of the Harland & Wolff guarantee group decamped for discussion. These were passengers indeed, but men with knowledge; for unlike Beesley, they had been on the trip from Belfast. They would have had compelling reasons to discuss and estimate the 'probabilities' of an emergency en route, whereas any ordinary passenger brashly bringing up the mere *possibility* of an accident would be instantly hushed by their peers for tempting fate. Such mischances should not be dwelt upon, discussed or 'estimated'. And what was there to estimate, unless it was the prognosis and development of a pre-existing condition?

Guarantee group leader Thomas Andrews wrote home from the hotel to his wife, Helen, that he believed 'the ship will clean up all right before sailing'.[2] The phrase 'clean up' may have meant resolving most problems. The day before departure, he wrote: 'The *Titanic* is now about complete and will, I think, do the old firm credit tomorrow when we sail.'[3]

Andrews' secretary, Thompson Hamilton, confirmed that he stayed at the South Western Hotel and wrote after the disaster: 'Through the various days the vessel lay at Southampton, Mr Andrews was never for a moment idle. He generally left his hotel about 8.30 for the offices, where he dealt with correspondence, then went on board until 6.30, when he would return.'[4]

Whether the ship had been 'cleaned up all right' was open to debate, but they were going anyway. At least the exterior was spick and span, the funnels and even parts of the hull touched up by repainting parties following a thorough wash-down after she was coaled.

* * *

In his 1906 book *The Sea Rovers* Rufus Wilson wrote: 'An important feature in the loading of a steamship is her coal.' He elaborated:

It is customary to take a surplus over the actual needs of the voyage, and the bunkers of the vessel are in charge of a special gang of men.

Some vessels load their coal over all, but a majority receive it through openings at the sides. Large V-shaped pockets, running direct to the bunkers, are let down on each side and around them are built stagings on which a couple of men are stationed to dump the coal from huge buckets hoisted by engines from lighters.

On the wharf side the coal is wheeled in barrows up a shelving gangway and turned into the bunkers direct. To load a great vessel requires the services for several days of 125 men, including a boss stevedore and a couple of foremen, with all the appliances of steam and gearing to assist their operations.

The departure of an ocean liner from port was a critical moment for each member of the ship's company, Wilson wrote, before referring to the practice in the Cunard Line, White Star's great rival, and specifically on the *Carmania*. An iron discipline is described: 'All leaves of absence expire twenty-four hours before time for sailing, and this precaution makes it certain that every man shall be at his post.' Quite a contrast with the main competitor. He continues:

At 8 o'clock on the morning of leaving, the sea watches are formally set. The lower fires in the many-lunged furnaces have been started at 10 o'clock the previous night; six hours later the top fires are lighted, and at 6am the operation of getting up steam begins, it being always necessary to have a full pressure of steam at least one hour before sailing.

As the moment of departure draws nearer, an air of suppressed excitement pervades the waiting throng, but there is no confusion among those charged with the ship's conduct and safety.

The *Titanic* had consumed 415 tons of coal during the Southampton stay (through steam-powered generators) for power to run the ship. This expenditure was just over half the estimated 100 tons needed each day the ship would be at sea for 'auxiliary' purposes, such as light, heating, hot water, elevators and winches. She had, in this waiting period, taken on an additional 4,427 tons, cannibalising the supplies of her peers in many cases, because stockpiles of coal had dramatically depleted during the strike and there had been no time to ferry replacement mountains since the dispute ended, four days before. In particular, the bunkers of the White Star liners *Oceanic* and *Majestic* had been emptied in 'brutal hand labour' and transferred to the fleet's new flagship.[5]

Fuel was also pirated from American Line steamers, controlled by the parent company, whose services had been suspended. They included the *Philadelphia*, *New York* and *St Louis*, and these laid-up vessels made for a crowded port, which would soon bring its own problems as *Titanic* took to the sea. Maritime historian John Maxtone-Graham outlines the 'arduous' practical difficulties in raiding no fewer than five ships' supplies. 'Coal heavers had somehow to manhandle barrowloads up through the hull to an upper deck level from which it could be dumped over the side into waiting barges. There were no elevators or lifting mechanisms. Getting sufficient coal aboard *Titanic* would prove challenging.'[6] He also suggests that *Titanic* derived input from 'bargeloads of French coal towed across the Channel, ancient, inferior stuff, much of it with grass growing out of it'.[7]

After what must have been a frenetic week, the servile surveyor Clarke signed the official forms indicating the burden of coal *Titanic* carried ahead of the transatlantic start. Her total was given to him as 5,892 tons, though Clarke had no way of knowing its accuracy – particularly since he had never been below for even a cursory glance. He nonetheless personally certified there was 'enough to take the ship to her next coaling port'.[8]

And yet there could be inaccuracies in official documents. For example, Belfast surveyor Francis Carruthers was later forced in evidence to admit 'clerical errors' in different numbers he had entered in the *Titanic*'s paperwork when four figures on lifeboat accommodation were shown to be in conflict with each other.

After obtaining repeated admission of mistakes at the British inquiry, the redoubtable lawyer Clement Edwards pressed Carruthers as to whether these clerical errors happened very often. The reply was haughty. 'No, very rarely.'[9]

Just because something is written down on a piece of paper that lingers in an archive should not render it impervious to interrogation. In the aftermath of a coal strike there could be every reason – for both supplier and shipping line – to suggest complete normality, despite all the circumstances being obviously extremely out of the ordinary.

In fact, no less a figure than Sir Arthur Rostron, commodore of the Cunard Line and aide-de-camp to the king – whose honours and elevation followed his rescue of the *Titanic* survivors – addressed this question of the coal supply in the context of his understanding of human nature: 'Coal was just a black harvest for many merchants and the dodges they resorted to were often ingenious,' he wrote in his memoirs.[10] 'It may sound a bit incredible, but it is a fact that hollow spaces – wire cages – were sometimes constructed in lighters, with the coal piled around and above them. In others, tubs and packing cases were left lying at the bottom. Which meant the ship was simply not getting the quantity of coal ordered and paid for,' he declared.

'On occasion as much as five per cent of coal has in this way been lost to the ship – and saved by the merchant. I doubt, knowing the breed, whether these twisters, with their ill-gotten gains in their pockets, ever paused to wonder what might happen if, because of their tricks, a ship were left stranded with empty bunkers.'[11]

Even if the *Titanic*'s reported coal stocks are to be taken at face value (and the willingness of other ships to surrender everything they had without some overstatement of their contribution must be in question), the ship still had a fuel leak – through that pernicious spontaneous coal fire in a forward bunker. It constituted an insidious combustion eating its way through whatever tonnage there was.

The author Richard de Kerbrech, an expert in marine steam engines of the period, writes in his book of the tonnage taken for the *Titanic* at Southampton from other sources: 'It is probable she may have been bunkered with an inferior quality coal in addition to the best Welsh that was normally supplied.'[12]

The sister ship *Olympic* was by this stage operating on a daily diet of over 800 tons. As it was a seven-and-a-half day crossing to New York (because the voyage encompassed legs to Cherbourg in France and Queenstown in Ireland before tackling the Atlantic itself), one that involved leaving Southampton on a Wednesday afternoon and getting into New York in the early hours of the following Wednesday – the journey would require at least 6,000 tons. As it so happens, this was the very amount that managing director J. Bruce Ismay swore was aboard the *Titanic* at the time of sailing during his American evidence.

'We only had 6,000 tons of coal leaving Southampton,' Ismay answered Senator George Perkins at the investigation in Washington DC.[13] In comparison, coal consumption of the rival *Lusitania* was 7,000 tons 'each journey' declared her contemporary postcards.

'She [*Titanic*] could carry over 9,500 tons of coal and then not be down to the Plimsoll mark,' added Ismay, demonstrating that the maiden voyager's bunkers were, at best, 63 per cent full when starting off.[14]

Unlike the *Olympic*, which had coaled in the US that month for her return crossing, the *Titanic* did not have sufficient supplies to make the voyage to New York and then return to Southampton, Ismay agreed. But he maintained that there was 'sufficient coal to enable her to reach New York, with about two days' spare consumption'.[15] He suggested that her 'ordinary speed' would mean daily consumption of 620 to 640 tons. This would be at the restrained speed of no more than 20 knots, which the Line had publicly touted she would maintain on the voyage.

But Ismay also hedged his bets, by agreeing: 'On full speed she burns about 820 tons.'[16]

It would be charitable to believe that Ismay simply rounded up to 6,000 tons, when the officially certified amount on board was actually 5,892 – in any case this is the figure shown on Board of Trade documents. And that latter sum is, at least, explicable, according to official entries. 1,880 tons was left aboard on arrival at Southampton from Belfast, plus 4,427 loaded at Southampton, equals 6,307 tons. Less 415 tons consumed during the layover, equals 5,892 tons – the amount said to be on board. But this remained short of what was nominally required for the voyage, and suggests that some electricity and heating economies might have been needed.

Certainly little coal was obtained at Belfast because of the high price, while the *Titanic*, being new, had no reserve stocks; and it is also a fact she did not take on any further coal at either Cherbourg or Queenstown. She was thus operating on the very edge. As the doyen of White Star historians, Jack Eaton, has expressed: '*Titanic* would have precious little coal to spare to get her to New York.'[17]

This state of affairs was exacerbated by the fact that coal consumption increases exponentially above 20 knots, as can be seen by the difference between Ismay's reference to 620 and 820 tons at ordinary and full speed.

A document has recently emerged into the public domain that gives direct commentary on the *Titanic*'s expected fuel consumption. Crucially, it is information in private correspondence from *before* the tragedy – rather than a public pronouncement in its aftermath.

Henry Wilde came aboard as chief officer in Southampton. On 31 March, prior to his signing on the *Titanic*, he wrote a letter to his sister on RMS *Olympic* stationery.[18] Wilde confessed he was 'awfully disappointed to find the arrangements for my taking command of the *Cymric* have altered. I am now going to join the *Titanic* for a time until some other ship turns up for me.'

He then wrote: 'I hope this strike will soon be over and get things settled down a bit. We are paying £2 a ton for coal for the ship *Titanic*, a big price when we burn 900 tons per day.' Wilde wraps up his missive with family wishes.

This arrestingly large consumption figure, much more than Ismay estimates in his sworn evidence, sits on the page with no further elaboration. Yet the surprising estimate of daily coal comes from an officer who was being brought in to bolster the *Titanic*'s upper echelons because of his extensive experience, especially on the *Olympic*. His appointment was at the captain's special request, even if that trod on Wilde's own hopes of a personal command.

It could be speculated that Wilde was estimating 900 tons a day precisely because he understood the Line was paying over the odds for poor quality coal, more of which would need to be burned for the same mileage output. The *Titanic*'s second-in-command, who was tragically lost on the night she went down, thus leaves posthumous testimony to her sailing by the skin of her teeth. With uncontrolled spontaneous combustion also gnawing away on board and about to burst into roaring, open flame, at what point does this state of affairs become reckless and therefore negligent?

12

AWAY AT LAST

THE INTERRUPTED RUN TO CHERBOURG

The new liner's casting off from her Hampshire port was exquisitely ordinary, with little of the celebration that had attended the departure of her sister ship the year before. Then there had been cause for celebration at the heralding of the Olympic class, an intended trio of vessels – in which the second ship could not hope to emulate the fame of the first.[1] *Olympic*'s 1911 maiden entry to New York had seen thousands of spectators line the waterfront of Battery Park and the whole length of West Street. Her local pilot, Julius Adler, enthused: 'She handles like a cat.' The average speed on her voyage was 21.17 knots, and it was noted that the *Olympic* had 'not a great deal' of coal left on arrival. Officers declined to discuss the subject.[2]

Now the *Titanic* hoped for similar rejoicing on the far side of the 'herring pond'. Yet, her send-off from Southampton was distinctly underwhelming. It is only in fable that there was a brass band to see her off at Southampton, with streamers fluttering down among deep and cheering crowds. A photograph taken by Francis Browne shows only about a hundred onlookers on the quay, while postcard images confirm a desultory attendance. Only further down the dock, at its tip, did people congregate and climb into a railway wagon to see the *Titanic* embrace the estuary. But there were no raised hats or wildly waved handkerchiefs. Passenger Lawrence Beesley commented: 'The whole scene was quiet and rather ordinary, with little of the picturesque and interesting ceremonial which imagination paints as usual in such circumstances.'[3]

Beesley at least had the diversion of seeing tardy and firewater-filled firemen racing to board the ship just prior to the ship's departure. The Slade brothers were among them, delayed by a passing goods train. 'A knot of stokers ran along the quay, with their kit slung over their shoulders in bundles, and made for the gangway with the evident intention of joining the ship. But a petty officer guarding the shore end firmly refused to allow them on board. They argued, gesticulated, apparently attempting to explain why they were late, but he remained obdurate and waved them back with a determined hand. The gangway was dragged back amid their protests.'[4]

All this was just an overture, however – because there was more general excitement immediately ahead.

As the ocean-going colossus eased from the quay, tug-lines pulled taut until she was in mid-dock and could cautiously engage engines to move 'all ahead slow'. The French tricolour was struck out on the foremast, indicating her next destination.

'The Southampton town clocks had just struck a quarter past twelve when the *Titanic* moved away from the quay,' wrote Francis Browne (though she had been slated to leave at noon). 'So slowly and gently did she move that, as I leaned over the water, I could hardly realise we were actually in motion.'[5]

The ship exited the Ocean Dock, turning to port, where the hulls of ships huddled against the protection of the Test Quay, named in honour of the river flowing by. This clutter of idle vessels, tied up together, was a product of the coal strike. As the gliding maiden voyager drew alongside the liner *New York*, double-berthed outside the *Oceanic*, there came the sound of snapping tethers from the *New York*, ringing out sharply like rifle reports – mooring ropes parting on the 10,000-ton vessel.

The emptied liner, made susceptible to water movement through her lack of ballast, seemed summoned towards the *Titanic*. On she came, as if under a magic spell.

Tugs rushed to the rescue, while George Bowyer, pilot on the outward-bound *Titanic*, ordered a touch of power astern, solely on the port propeller. That churn of water helped, and the *New York*'s threat to the *Titanic* was narrowly averted, though she swung round in front of Bowyer's bows. A master of port navigation with a megaphone stood stolidly on the quay, it was reported, 'issuing orders across the water as calmly as if he were having his tea'.[6]

It was hardly much of an omen, more a narrow squeak, but Beesley wrote: 'There were, among the passengers, and such of the crew as were heard to speak on the matter, the direst misgivings at the incident.'[7]

Yet at least the passengers had been given their first thrill of the voyage.

Meanwhile, darkly below decks, the full horror of the bunker fire was about to produce a different order of alarm among seasoned seafarers.

The *Titanic* ran on for 100 yards past the ship-shouldered docks, then abruptly stopped when not yet even in mid-river. Images captured some ten minutes later by mystified postcard photographers show the tug *Vulcan* adhering to her port side. This could not have been to remove the local pilot, as he would not be dropped until well past the treacherous Brambles bank and out in mid-channel, near Spithead. So it was a strange hesitation.

Browne wrote later that the tug had come 'to take ashore the workmen and navvies who had been arranging the luggage in the storerooms'. But Browne also recorded that a bugle sounded 'Visitors ashore' before sailing, and no doubt it did so repeatedly, possibly accompanied by yelling, searching stewards. It seems hard to fathom that a whole party of workmen would somehow miss this clarion call to quit.

So Browne's speculation seems wide of the mark. Perhaps workmen had indeed been left aboard and missed the 'all ashore', but baggage handling was always carried out by available crew – and there would have been no need to take off any jobbing luggage sorters because none were employed. Yet that was the explanation given to Browne, and no doubt others, for the utter stillness of the *Titanic* in open water, a scene frozen by photographers, with the *Vulcan* in close attendance. The tug's captain, Charles Gale, said only that he had aimed 'to go alongside and pick up a number of workmen who were about to leave the *Titanic*'.[8]

Chroniclers then and now have recorded that the *Titanic* was an hour late in leaving Southampton, yet this fact somehow evinces no curiosity.[9] She cast off fifteen minutes late, and the threat from what became known as the '*New York* Incident' seems to have taken no more than ten minutes in total (although first-class Canadian passenger Arthur Peuchen testified: 'I should think we were delayed probably three-quarters of an hour by this trouble. Then we moved out of the harbour.')[10]

As the dilatory debutante at last got underway again, the bugler soon sounded *The Roast Beef of Old England* to signal that luncheon was being served. The perplexing stoppage was shrugged off, for the open sea lay splendidly ahead.

* * *

'With the dropping of the pilot, sea routine is promptly taken up,' Rufus Wilson wrote, 'and thereafter on the shoulders of the Commander rests the preservation of the ship and the safety of the passengers and crew,' all of whom he characterised as an army afloat.[11]

Wilson goes on to describe the lot of that army's enlisted men, the infantry of the infernos: 'Distressing at all times is the lot of the poor fellows who man the stokehold,' he wrote, saluting the 'brawny and half-naked' firemen who straightaway began to slave while passengers strolled idly somewhere far above:

Suddenly from somewhere in the darkness comes three shrill calls upon a whistle, and instantly each furnace door flies open, and out dart hungry tongues of fire.

With averted heads and steaming bodies, four stokers begin to shovel furiously, while two others thrust their slice-bars through each door and into the mass of fire and flame. Burying their lances deep in the coals, they throw their weight full upon the ends as levers, and lift the whole bank of fire several inches.

Then they draw out the lances, leaving a black hole through the fire into which the draft is sucked with an increasing roar. Three times they thrust and withdraw the lances, pausing after each charge to plunge their heads in buckets of water. But this cooling respite lasts only a moment at best, for their taskmasters watch and drive them, and each furnace must do its stint.[12]

It was in this meltingly hot melodrama that the fire in a *Titanic* bunker raged.

And it may be that the fire had something to do with the stopping of the ship in mid-river. The thought occurs because the time coincides with concern over its further eruption. One fireman would later describe it as a 'raging hell' when in the Solent, the body of water outside the port.[13]

'When did you start getting the coal out [from the affected three-storey bunker]?' fireman Charles Hendrickson was asked at the British inquiry.

'The first watch we did from Southampton we started to get it out,' he laconically replied.[14]

He was next asked: 'Did it take much time to get the fire down?' The answer: 'It took us right up to the Saturday to get it out.' This was Wednesday and 'the fire was not much out before all the coal was out', three days later.[15] It was clearly an acute threat.

'All the coal' in that particular bunker (designated 'W' in stokehold 10) was 365 tons. To visualise this enormous volume, consider that a single ton would occupy a standard pallet's area to a height of four and a half feet. Alternatively, a ton of coal would easily fill five modern fuel drums. A ton equates to the weight today of more than fifteen average adults.

Once extracted, what was to be done with all that angry coal? It could not be allowed to accumulate. It therefore had to be burnt in the furnaces. Leading hand fireman Fred Barrett, a tough Liverpudlian, bossed a team of eight stokers and four trimmers (wheelbarrow men) in boiler room 5, the second furthest forward, where the burning bunker was a major problem.

'My orders were to get it out as soon as possible,' he said, the urgency underlining the danger understood by his superiors.

When did he receive those orders? 'Not very long after the ship left Southampton.'

Was there anything wrong? 'Yes.'[16]

What was wrong? 'The bunker was a-fire,' barked Barrett in answer. Asked if it was 'fire or only heat', he was absolutely explicit: 'It was fire.'[17]

There was no more smokeless, quiet combustion now, but instead fully fledged and fierce flame. It was a blaze which would have to be tackled by a team of men, day and night, in order to be extinguished. And while orders were to get it out 'as soon as possible', there was no question of 'soon' in this case. The authorities on board, already well aware of rumbling combustion since Belfast, absolutely had to know at this point from careful assessment of the situation that it was not likely to be brought to heel before halfway through the maiden voyage. Yet they went to sea anyway.

'Barrett, in the witness box, appeared to be a strong, clear-headed man, who knew his business intimately,' reported the London *Daily News*.[18] He was making the seriousness of the situation abundantly plain. And his experience of this was first-hand. When on duty he was in charge of seeing the bunker worked out. 'There were between 8 and 10 men doing it,' he said.[19] He also confirmed that they had been playing water on the towering tonnage. 'The hose was going all the time.'[20]

The nightmarish scene in the boiler room can be envisaged: a pooling of water that rapidly evaporated into dense steam, with a moist, clinging slurry underfoot.

'Wet coal had to be avoided because moisture sometimes caused rapid generation of heat and gas, especially when the coal contained a considerable quantity of pyrites (Fool's gold, an iron sulfide impurity),' says Richard de Kerbrech.[21] When water or steam was used to extinguish a bunker fire, 'large volumes had to be used', he continues, otherwise 'water gas' was created, 'which in turn exacerbated an already dangerous situation'.[22] This is because water gas, a mixture of carbon monoxide and hydrogen, is viciously explosive.

Large quantities of water were being used on this particular fire aboard the *Titanic*, one hopes, in part to guard against generation of water gas. This would further underlie the continuous use of the hose, as revealed by Barrett.

Yet how was the water aimed at the fire? It is difficult to see how the hose could have succeeded at the base of the bunker, where the only door was situated. Damping down would have been far more efficient than attempting to 'dampen up'. Clement Edwards, counsel for the Dockers' Union, was put in mind by this to suggest that perhaps 'a hole had to be bored through the bulkhead'.[23] This dramatic bored-hole suggestion was raised during Harold Sanderson's testimony, but no less a figure than the attorney general, Sir Rufus Isaacs, interrupted to declare: 'There is no evidence of that.'

He was entirely correct; 'nothing of the kind' had been said up to that point, as Sir Robert Finlay, counsel for the White Star Line, was similarly glad to point out.

Given a chance to speak again after further rhetorical flurries, Clement Edwards declared: 'Allow me to say, My Lord, that I had this so definitely in my mind when I went over the *Olympic* at the inspection [held by the inquiry in Southampton] that I made special enquiries as to the position where this hole was supposed to have been made.'[24]

So it seems obvious that someone had provided Edwards with this information, erroneous or otherwise. The assertion emerged tangentially. Edwards had conversed with two *Olympic* officers on the point, adding: 'It so happened, My Lord, that two of the men employed by the White Star in helping to clear out the coal had also been employed on the *Olympic*, and had conversed with the officers on the subject.'

Edwards indicated that he had the names of the two men who had previously been on the *Titanic* and who had said as much, albeit he had received this as second-hand information from the officers. They were trimmers (wheelbarrow men), he said, workers literally at the coalface of the bunker. When asked by the commissioner for their names he said, 'They shall be supplied to your Lordship.'

Nothing further was ever heard of the alleged hole and it remains the case that no sworn evidence was ever given of such being bored through a metal wall in order for a hose to play upon the *Titanic*'s bunker fire. But what does seem clear – bored hole or not – is that they were struggling to control the fire below deck while en route to the vast new steamer's first port of call. And it was at this stage of the tragic voyage that first-class passenger Irene Harris received her alarming warning to get off at Cherbourg ('if we get that far') from a visibly distracted man who then carried on down a corridor.[25]

13

THE NEWS LEAKS OUT

PASSENGER INTERACTION

Another White Star liner left the United Kingdom on the same day as *Titanic*. The *Cymric*, under Captain Frank Howarth (which might instead have had Henry Wilde commanding), put out from the Mersey for Portland, Maine. Henry Wills, secretary of the American Manufacturers Export Association, told *The New York Times* that the *Cymric* had a large cabin list. She 'took on all the *Teutonic* people, as she had been taken off [out of service] on account of the coal strike'. Wills was quoting his sister, Mary, who arrived on the ship and sent him a letter, which he entered in the public record. 'We left on the same day as *Titanic*,' she wrote. 'And our course was a very northerly one, on account probably of coal shortage. At all events it was very dangerous. We were in a dense fog for two days, with ice all about us, and it was bitterly cold. The fog horn blew every two minutes.'[1]

Wills told *The New York Times* that he believed it wise to quote from his sister's letter as 'having an important bearing' on the *Titanic* tragedy. One part ran: 'The Captain and crew were most cautious. The Captain did not leave the bridge for 48 hours or more. He picked up a wireless message about the *Titanic*, but as she was a faster boat we could not have rendered assistance.'[2]

It is possible Wills was reacting to the newspaper reports that Captain Smith had not been on the *Titanic*'s bridge at the time she struck. Captain Howarth of the *Cymric* had been feeling his way along in freezing fog, but Captain Smith was racing along in the glacial clear a good distance to the south and felt comfortable leaving his bridge – despite warnings of ice ahead. The marine artist, Norman Wilkinson, whose painting of Plymouth harbour hung over the mantelpiece in *Titanic*'s first-class smoking room, chanced to briefly meet her grizzled commodore on sailing day at Southampton, describing him as having 'radiated Edwardian confidence'.[3] This confidence would prove misplaced.

Of great importance in Mary's letter is the explicit statement that the *Cymric* had a 'coal shortage', yet went to sea on the same day as the *Titanic* – and was risking not only her own passengers but those of the cancelled *Teutonic*. Furthermore, she was sent on a 'very dangerous' northern course (confirmed by wireless position messages during the crossing), which put her in real danger. The White Star Line had received information for weeks that ice was very thick in those latitudes.

Yet, the *Cymric* did not strike or sink, although undoubtedly placed in hazardous conditions. The fact that Captain Smith took a more southern route on the *Titanic*, though similarly embarrassed in regard to coal, may have contributed to his insouciance, it being obviously more distant from the glaciers where icebergs were calved. But all this demonstrates the White Star Line's ultimate disregard (complacency is too mild a word) for the safety of both ships and passengers that April.

For now, however, the *Titanic* had the pleasantly ice-free English Channel to negotiate, though it was generally tricky due to traffic, prone to fog, and no 'milk run' in sailors' parlance. Her course was southwesterly after clearing the Isle of Wight and dusk was descending as she neared the French coast. The *Titanic* arrived in Cherbourg at 6.30 p.m. local time, dusk, picking her way between the Grand and Petit breakwaters.

Some of her would-be passengers, left waiting a couple of hours after the prompt arrival of the boat train from Paris, were frankly furious with her. The *Titanic*'s late appearance hardly augured well for an Atlantic greyhound.

The fashion buyer Edith Russell wrote in 1956:

We sat about on the huge tender [*Nomadic*, now the last fleet vessel afloat]*, specially built the year before for these new White Star ships, and for three hours shivered and waited. It was cold. It had been raining.*

I remember sitting next to Colonel and Mrs John Jacob Astor, who were on their wedding trip, playing with their big dog. The Colonel told me Titanic *had cost ten million dollars to build, and emphasised she was unsinkable, 'a miracle of modern shipbuilding'.*

Finally a murmur went around the tender: 'The Titanic *is in sight.' I saw what seemed like a huge building, with tier upon tier of glittering electric lights. Truly a beautiful and impressive spectacle. The big tender approached the* Titanic *and swung alongside.*[4]

Russell, all of a sudden, wished she were not going aboard. But she was told by Paris agent Nicolas Martin: 'You are just nervous. You are perfectly safe. This ship is unsinkable. You can get off if you want to, but your luggage will have to go on to New York.'

The baggage ascended in the wake of the embarking passengers. Russell wrote: 'I then stood aside and watched for more than an hour a regiment of cooks, bakers, and sailors staggering under the weight of huge wooden boxes they were transferring from the tender to the *Titanic*. I asked one of the stewards what this meant, and he said: "These are rare canned vegetables, fruits of all kinds, and other things to eat … provisions for the trip over, and the return." He added: "We have a pretty good crowd on board, but it is nothing to what we anticipate coming back." I never saw so many boxes in my life.'

Her account of a motley crew doing the ferrying gives the lie to the story told to Francis Browne at Southampton – that the *Titanic* had stopped so the *Vulcan* could take off a dedicated corps of luggage-stowers. There were no such specialists for the French leg.

Postcards issued later of the *Titanic* at Cherbourg depict Russell's tiers of glittering light, as well as smoke pouring from all four funnels. The dark had clearly handicapped the local photographers, who had earnestly desired a daylight arrival, and they were forced to heavily touch up their images. The fourth funnel was a dummy, used for galley ventilation, and did not produce smoke of any colour or consistency.

More than one tender was in attendance. The *Traffic* brought a brimming consignment of third-class passengers, thick-tongued emigrants from all parts of Europe and much of the Middle East. They would have expected much less consideration than the cosseted cabin class, yet would find their shipboard accommodations an unalloyed joy. One crewman at the next port of call, when the Irish embarked, was heard to mutter: 'At least this lot speak English.'[5]

There were passengers going the other way. Fifteen first-class and nine second-class travellers had used the mighty *Titanic* as a mere ferry to France. Also departing, alone and involuntarily, was a creature whose passage had been paid by Marian Meanwell, a sixty-two-year-old dressmaker on her way to visit a daughter in New York. Mrs Meanwell died in the sinking, but a receipt for a canary in a cage (carried across the channel to continental kin) was found in her handbag on recovery from the debris field decades later. The trifling charge also appeared in the cargo manifest.

The use of a 'canary in a coal mine' had been established practice for decades in Britain's pits (underpinned by Acts of Parliament), before it became shorthand for an early warning of toxicity. But this canary, like Mulholland's cat, would go safely down the gangplank.

* * *

Even before the ship arrived in Cherbourg, news of the ominous bunker fire was already leaking out. South African second-class passenger Elizabeth Brown had boarded at Southampton with her husband, Thomas, and teenage daughter, Edith, heading for a new life in Seattle. Subsequently saved (though her husband died), Mrs Brown spoke to the *Post-Intelligencer* on arrival in her destination city. The newspaper quoted her remarks on 27 April: 'The first day at sea, passengers heard reports that the *Titanic* was afire. The officers denied it, but I was told on good authority that there was a fire in one of the coal bunkers and a special crew of men were kept at work day and night to keep it under. I believe this to be true.'[6]

Naturally the fire anxiety of the time would be swamped by the torrent of horrors that burst in later. But Mrs Brown faithfully preserved the memory of a prior preoccupation. At least a small minority of the passengers was aware of a burning concern, which suggests that some crew were ultimately the source of the disclosure and that the blaze was a distinct fear for them, too.

David Haisman, Elizabeth Brown's grandson, spent thirty years in the British merchant service as able seaman, quartermaster, mate and skipper, much of them spent on the North Atlantic where his grandfather had died. His mother, Elizabeth Brown's then sixteen-year-old daughter Edith, had helpfully kept a diary in 1912, which became the basis for a book he wrote.[7] Haisman relates that, according to his mother, the family fell into conversation with a middle-aged man in the second-class library, initially about the touching innocence of the bellboys, all of whom would be lost, despite fruitless efforts by veteran sailor Samuel Rule to inveigle one or two of them into lifeboats. After a period of small talk, the man in the library declared, 'Did you know, since Southampton there's been a fire raging down in the stokehold, and up to this moment they are still unable to put it out?'[8]

The fire had, of course, been present since Belfast, but the conversation was related as having occurred on the third day of the maiden voyage.

The man went on: 'Our saloon steward has a friend who is a stoker on board, and he told him they are still deploying extra men down there to try and keep it under control.'

Elizabeth Brown appeared to have known about the fire within hours of leaving Southampton, but her husband, conscious of her nerves, tried to play it down. 'I'm sure it's under control. Besides, ships being what they are for gossip, it's fairly certain that more people would have heard about it by now.'

Haisman writes: 'The overweight, middle-aged man was not to be deterred. "That may be so, but it doesn't fill one with much confidence in the White Star Line, does it?" His wife, a huge woman, nodded at every word her husband was saying.'

The author comments: 'As a family we always believed what our mother told us over the years. She had no reason to tell us anything other than the truth as she remembered it.'[9]

The Browns had dining companions on the *Titanic* – a family nearly identical to their own, consisting of parents and a young daughter, also bound for western North America, although the Harts were aiming for Winnipeg in Canada, rather than Washington state. The Hart and Brown husbands became shipboard companions, strolling together and making a routine of going for beer in the smoking room each day. The wives talked too, of course, although teenage Edith Brown was rather too old for lisping, seven-year-old Eva Hart.

Table conversation must have included news about the fire since the Browns had learned about it. And the Harts were then informed. Afterwards, Mrs Esther Hart was to lie fully clothed in bed at night on the *Titanic* until an accident indeed occurred, although not of the kind she fearfully imagined. She had, in fact, been uneasy about the whole voyage, filled with dread before it even began and afraid of water. 'Nothing should ever persuade me to undress, and nothing did, although Ben at times got very cross with me,' she soon told the *Ilford Graphic*. 'Each night I simply rested in my bunk, fully dressed and fully prepared, God knows why, for the worst.'[10]

In the same interview she confirmed: 'We were fortunate in having some very nice people at our table. We were in parties of eight in the second saloon, and our party included a lady and gentleman from the Cape, Mr and Mrs Brown, and their daughter, who were on their way to Vancouver [*sic*].'

She added: 'Mr Brown and Ben got on capitally together. They were the exact opposite of each other. Mr Brown was a quiet, reserved man who scarcely ever spoke, and Dadda was fond of talking and so they got on well, promenaded the deck together, had their midday Bass, and smoked their pipes. Indeed, Mrs Brown said that she had never seen her husband take to anyone like he had to my Ben. Oh dear! Oh dear! To think that of the eight at the table, four were taken and four were left.'[11] She and her daughter survived, as did Mrs Brown and her daughter. The men died.

* * *

The *Titanic* left Cherbourg at 8.30 p.m., just two hours after arriving. Shortly after departure, fashionable first-class passenger Edith Russell dined, then took the lift to return to her stateroom. 'I have always liked meeting new people and talking to them, and I remember my conversation with the young boy who was operating that elevator. "I am so proud," he said. "This is my first trip at sea, and they have made me a lift boy. I am only thirteen, you know. It's a bit of an honour." His first and last trip.'[12]

The ship surged into the all-consuming ink of night and sea, ceaselessly fed by muscle and mineral, butting ever forward towards an Irish rendezvous.

14

ARRIVAL IN IRELAND

AND NOTES FROM *MAURETANIA*

Passengers early astir the next morning – and they were many, for the first night at sea is generally a restless one, even when soothed by all the comfort and luxury of a *Titanic* – witnessed the curious 'evolutions' of the liner as she turned and twisted on a 'serpentine' path while steaming north from the Lizard to Queenstown.[1] The postulant priest, Francis Browne, wrote those words – and also explained the snaking twists of her sea-path in the *Irish Independent* on 18 April.[2] Unconsciously echoing the New York pilot who thought the *Olympic* to be as lithe as a feline, he wrote: 'As we made for Queenstown, we had proof that, despite her gigantic size, she was under perfect control. As usual on ships on the first trip, the compasses were being adjusted, so instead of steering a straight course for a time the great ship steamed in "s" shaped curves, answering the helm perfectly.'[3] He was so impressed he took a shot of these wending curves, reproduced in this book, which shows the tight turns the ship was able to make. This is an important point when it comes to the attempted evasion of the iceberg, to be later addressed.

The fumes from the burning coal bunker were meanwhile largely exhausting through the forward funnel, joining the ghostly grey demons generated from the working furnaces.[4]

The morning was crisp in its infancy and Browne next opted for a 'plunge in the great swimming bath, where the ceaseless ripple of tepid sea water was almost the only indication that somewhere in the distance 72,000 horses in the guise of steam engines fretted and strained under the skillful guidance of the engineers'. He didn't, however, envisage the back-breaking labour of firemen and trimmers needed to run these engines. A further half-hour in the gymnasium on the boat deck 'helped send one's blood coursing freely, and created a big appetite for the morning meal'.

As he left for breakfast, Browne received the card of T. W. McCawley, the gym instructor. The cleric was avidly using all the available facilities before disembarkation, when he would take with him his cache of precious negatives. He even snapped a picture of McCawley, posed ironically with hands gripping the oars of a rowing machine. Three days later the physical educator from Aberdeen would stand back from the lifeboats. He refused a lifebelt, lest it interfere with his intended vigorous swimming. He died in the sinking.

Gradually, the Irish coastline neared. 'The coast of Ireland looked very beautiful as we approached Queenstown Harbour, the brilliant morning sun showing up the green hillsides and picking out groups of dwellings dotted here and there above rugged grey cliffs that fringed the coast,' wrote late riser Lawrence Beesley.[5]

The four-funnel first-timer ran towards Fort Camden and Fort Carlisle, twin sentinels on jutting Irish headlands. Her momentum ceased opposite Roche's Point lighthouse, the bow waves dropping off. Enormous cast-iron links of the anchor chain, forged in the foundries of the Black Country, plunged precipitously for the seabed. The raucous noise meant the *Titanic* had stopped. Out came the intake from the seaside town, well over 100 steerage emigrants in the third-class tender *America*, with a handful of cabin class and a curious press contingent in the accompanying *Ireland*. There were also port officials, shipping agents, two surveyors from the Board of Trade (one a surgeon who had shipped with Shackleton) and White Star's own marine superintendent.

As well as passengers, hundreds of sacks of mail were going aboard. Browne watched all this unfold from the boat deck – but another was seen to be observing from higher still. A stoker had climbed an interior staircase to the top of the fourth, dummy, funnel. His sooty scalp and blackened features excited a sensation. To some he was a harbinger of doom, to others he was likely an astonishing piece of evidence of the need to escape that raging fire they had heard about in the somewhere-down-below.

Beesley admitted there had been a fuss regarding the stoker's appearance, but the science teacher was eager to scotch 'a second so-called bad omen' after the worrisome *New York* incident: 'As one of the tenders neared the *Titanic*, some of those on board gazed up at the liner towering above them, and saw a stoker's head, black from his work in the stokehold below, peering out at them from the top of one of the enormous funnels.

'He had climbed up inside for a joke, but to some of those who saw him there, the sight was seed for the growth of an omen, which bore fruit in an unknown dread of dangers to come.'

It was all 'a mass of nonsense in which apparently sensible people believe, or which at any rate they discuss,' he lamented. 'It would seem almost as if we were back in the Middle Ages when witches were burned because they kept black cats. There seems no more reason why a black stoker should be an ill omen for the *Titanic* than a black cat should be for an old woman.'[6]

Yet perhaps the groundwork had already been laid for such expressions of worry, which had been fed by rumour and which in turn stemmed from fact. Beesley, travelling alone, had not heard of the bunker blaze that had been discussed by others. It goes entirely unmentioned in his account. He instead overheard his fellow passengers' grumblings and assumed them to be childish fears.

The press boarded with alacrity and found Captain Smith still presenting his radiant exterior despite the 'tremendous responsibility placed on his shoulders', as noted by the man from the *Cork Free Press* the next day. The journalists heard that the vessel had not been put to the test, thus far, but had been kept at a steady pace of 20 knots. Smith enthused about his new command, mindful of commercial imperatives. 'In an interview, the genial Commander said the machinery of the huge vessel worked splendidly, and there was not the slightest hitch on the way across.'[7]

The same *Cork Free Press* scribe recalled after the sinking:

I warmly complimented the veteran commander on his promotion to the largest steamship in the world. Captain Smith received it in a modest way and quietly remarked that he fully realised his responsible position in having the command of such a luxurious ship with her immense number of passengers.

As he paced the deck of his noble vessel getting everything in readiness for his westward passage, he presented a fine appearance, clad as he was in his commander's blue uniform, but with a well-trimmed beard and standing six feet in height, he made a lasting impression on your correspondent.

Captain Smith, shaking my hand warmly, bid goodbye and sent kind regards to friends on shore. Previous to which your correspondent wished him bon voyage on this, his first trip in the largest and most luxurious steamer afloat.[8]

Smith posed for a photograph outside the bridge with purser Hugh McElroy, who then took pressmen and photographers on a guided promotional tour of the virgin vessel, but not below 'the lower gangway' (E deck).[9] Francis Browne was passing the other way, preparing to get off. 'I met Mr McElroy and Mr [Williamson], Head of the Mail Department on the *Titanic*. "Goodbye," I said. "I will give you copies of my photos when you come again. Pleasant voyage."'[10]

* * *

Besides the mailbags hauled aboard, there was outgoing mail set for Ireland that had been embarked at Southampton. Stokers passed each other ferrying bags up and down, a delegated duty, as had happened at Cherbourg. And it was now that one of their number saw his chance. *The Belfast News-Letter* reported on 17 April: 'It is said that one fireman, *who felt that something was sure to happen* [author's emphasis], deserted at Queenstown.'

It was true. A day later, on 18 April, *The Cork Examiner* ran the following: 'LUCKY STOKER Quits Ship at Queenstown. A young man named Coffey had a lucky escape from being amongst those lost on the *Titanic*. Coffey joined the *Titanic* at Southampton and on the passage to Queenstown decided to get out of her as he did not relish his job. Accordingly, at Queenstown, he stealthily got on board the tender which took the passengers out, secreted himself on board and got clear at Queenstown successfully, and remained here until Sunday morning last when he joined the *Mauretania*.'[11]

John Coffey was twenty-three, a seasoned stoker who had long fired furnaces during his spell in the Royal Navy. An account was given to the Southampton *Evening Echo* many years later by his fellow *Titanic* fireman, Jack Podesta: 'All the White Star boats and Cunard liners outward bound called there (Queenstown) … and it was the custom for we firemen and trimmers to go up on deck and carry the mail from the tender to the mail room [this explains postal chief Williamson's presence on deck as Browne was leaving].

'A fireman whom I knew very well, John Coffee [*sic*] – I was in the *Oceanic* and *Adriatic* with him – said to me, "Jack, I'm going down to this tender to see my mother." He asked me if anyone was looking, and I said no, and bade him good luck. A few seconds later he was gone.'[12]

The indications are that Coffey hid himself under a pile of mailbags taken off the ship. Originally from Queenstown, he may always have intended taking the *Titanic* as a taxi back to his birthplace (he no longer had family in the port, despite Podesta's claim), yet attempting to desert while the ship was anchored offshore was a distinct challenge. Detection would have landed him in the brig or a court on land, with severe penalties at stake. In fact, he subsequently spent time in custody for this desertion, detained in Britain when the *Mauretania* returned to Liverpool on 30 April.

It bears consideration why an experienced stoker should want to stoke no more, that is, until three days later, on the fateful Sunday of 14 April, when he signed on as fireman again but with the Cunard Line instead. So when the *Examiner* reported that Coffey had decided to get out because he 'did not relish his job', it was not that he could not abide stoking in itself. Rather, his antipathy lay squarely with stoking specifically on the *Titanic*.

The *Enniscorthy Echo* also reported the desertion by a fireman 'who felt that something was sure to happen'. Yet how on earth could he be psychic about a far-off iceberg?

It is not known whether Coffey was directly involved in tackling the chaos of bunker W in stokehold 10, which must have further threatened an adjoining bunker, Y, and a bunker running overhead in the starboard roof space of boiler room 6, known as bunker Z. But it was a fireman who had burrowed into mailbags to escape – not a waiter, steward, quartermaster, scullion, pantryman, cook or lamp trimmer.

Coffey thus joins a long catalogue of those representing the exodus from underneath pioneered by Mulholland, Baker, wife-beater Morgan, two worried brothers and a whole army of hands who had taken her round from Belfast. The movements away from the stokehold were many, but multifarious individual motivations must be unlikely. The disappearances speak volumes.

Coffey's grandson, Brian, says his ancestor told New Yorkers on arrival on the *Mauretania* that he had dreamed of the *Titanic* sinking, and thus resolved to leave the ship. 'The Americans loved the story and wined and dined him, taking it all in.'

There were press reports that the *Mauretania* within a few days 'stopped at the spot where the *Titanic* sank in the forlorn hope of finding survivors'.[13] Remarkably, she already had one on board.

In actuality, it turned out that the *Mauretania* was a good distance from the spot where the mighty ship sank – she was dozens of miles directly south (although in the same longitude) when what was termed a vigil was held aboard her by J. Bruce Ismay's opposite number, A. A. Booth, the chairman of Cunard.

The *Mauretania*'s captain for this voyage was William Thomas Turner, later on the bridge of the *Lusitania* when she was torpedoed in 1915. He remarked in his deposition at the *Titanic* limitation of liability hearings that 'a lot of people would not go [on the *Mauretania* in April 1912] because we sailed on the 13th', a Saturday. Turner had received wireless reports of ice and resolved to go substantially south of where the *Titanic* would later strike the ice. He made up his mind on this point though far behind his White Star rival at the time, being over 1,300 miles to the east. It was 'before I heard' of the disaster, Turner emphasised. Yet the ice lay directly on the usual course ahead for all shipping. 'After I heard there was so much ice in the track, I went 65 miles south,' Turner said. 'As a matter of fact … even then I saw an iceberg.'[14]

This same Sunday evening, a New Yorker named Stoughton Walker calmly climbed the *Mauretania*'s rail in full view of other passengers and jumped overboard to his doom. He would not be the last leaper into the North Atlantic that night.

There is another *Mauretania* footnote worthy of mention, apart from her carrying a helpful duplicate of the *Titanic*'s cargo manifest, listing everything from ostrich feathers to shelled walnuts. A fortnight before the White Star maiden voyager's appearance at the Irish port, Captain Turner had failed to embark the Queenstown mails, blaming the weather. He declared: 'The difficulty was increased by the doubt whether, owing to the coal strike, sufficient coal of satisfactory quality would be obtainable at Queenstown to replace the amount used during the stoppage, which might have been protracted.'[15]

* * *

In one of the letters taken off at Queenstown, second-class passenger Kate Buss described suddenly doubling over with some soot in her eye. She did not explain the full circumstances to her family at home in Kent, but a fellow passenger saw what happened and rushed to her aid. It was fortunate that Dr Ernest Moraweck was an eye surgeon, and that the pair had struck up a rapport since Southampton. Kate, who was fated to survive (unlike her benefactor), anticipated eye irritation for the remainder of the voyage.

* * *

One of the passengers who came aboard the *Titanic* at Queenstown was a pretty teenage Irish emigrant named Katie Gilnagh. She was shown to a communal third-class dorm 'near the boilers' (on E deck, evident from a card she retained all her life).[16] Gilnagh wrote in 1966 to the Titanic Enthusiasts of America, telling of occasionally venturing forward in the *Titanic* to climb to the open air. Her letter contained a stunning and overlooked disclosure. 'I think there was something on fire down there because we had to cover our noses whenever we passed by to go on deck,' Katie, by then Mrs Manning, confessed.[17]

The use of 'whenever' implies a continuous situation, applying at all stages of the voyage. Judging by this revelation, the coal-bunker fire was definitely an ongoing, significant problem.

15

CONSULTATION AT QUEENSTOWN

CROSSING THE RUBICON

A remarkable thing happened on board the ship while at Queenstown. A businessman sat down and had a meeting. J. Bruce Ismay was that man, and the perplexing issue with this face-to-face discussion is that, by his evidence, the consultation was arranged to settle the same point that had been settled a day or two before, and which had previously been set in stone by executive decree: namely, the speed of the ship on her voyage.

Ismay, remember, had previously arranged with Chief Engineer Joseph Bell – his long-term delegate to Harland & Wolff during construction – that the new vessel was going to proceed slowly, or so he said. A press release doubly confirmed the point. But Bell was evidently an entirely unreliable man (despite being relied upon heavily by Ismay in the past), because the managing director of White Star now had to have a further meeting with him at Queenstown.

So what did Joseph B. (Ismay) and Joseph B. actually discuss? According to Ismay, the two men were of such like mind that they went over the same familiar and prearranged understanding in relation to modest speed for a wearying third time. Yet there must be the possibility that the talk involved something else entirely, if only for the sake of novelty.

One subject could have been coaling at Queenstown, since the bunkers were at little more than half capacity by that point. Against this was the likelihood that commercial coal in the area was even more unobtainable than before, and if any at all remained it would be of poor quality, as Captain Turner had argued. An unscheduled fuel input would also throw the maiden voyage off schedule and involve hours of delay. Of course, it is more likely – indeed, highly probable

– that the discussion involved the bunker fire eating away at the existing supply, since both men had to have known about it.

Ismay gives the following perplexing explanation for the Queenstown meeting, as recorded in the transcript of the *Titanic* liability hearings:

'Do you remember having a conversation with Mr Bell, the chief engineer, before you left Queenstown?'

'I do.'

'With reference to the coal that was on board, and the speed, that is, that you were going to try her at a certain time on her voyage, and also about when you expected to get into New York?'

'I think I had a conversation with Mr Bell, and I told him that as we would not arrive at New York before Wednesday, there was no object in pressing the ship.'

'Do you remember discussing with him the question of trying her out on Monday and Tuesday to see what her speed would be?'

'That was simply confirming what had already been arranged.'

'You had already arranged that?'

'Yes.' [So why confirm it?]

'With whom had you arranged that?'

'With the chief engineer at Southampton, two or three days before the ship sailed; it was the ordinary practice.' [Why reconfirm ordinary practice, especially when recently reinforced?]

'Who was present at the time of your conversation with Mr Bell at Queenstown?'

'Nobody.' [Bell died in the sinking, like the captain oddly absent from this meeting.]

'Was not your secretary present at that conversation, subsequently lost?'

'I do not think so, but I am not sure.'

'The Captain was not present, was he?'

'No, he was not.'

'Was it at that time it was arranged you were to arrive at the Lightship [New York] *at five o'clock on Wednesday morning, or was it at Southampton?'*

'The whole thing was arranged beforehand. It is a regular rule of the Company that the ships, when they are on the long track, are not to arrive at New York before Wednesday morning, and it was simply confirming what Mr Bell already knew. It has been the practice of the Company for 15 years, I should think.'[1]

Why would he need a private meeting to confirm a fifteen-year-old practice, one that Bell already knew, as the managing director readily conceded? Ismay quite simply has a credibility problem here regarding his meetings and arrangements with Bell. On the face of it, he had no reason at all to hold this meeting on board ship at Queenstown. And the reasons he gave certainly don't add up.

Bell, on the other hand, could have had a compelling reason. What if the impetus for the second meeting, held at the last available point of land, had actually come from the chief engineer? If this were the case, then Ismay would have been lying about the point of the discussion.

If the discussion really was about speed, then the captain would have been involved. It is the captain, after all, in his absolute wisdom and discretion, who determines a vessel's speed at any time, not the chief engineer. Yet the latter could speak about matters exclusively under his own purview, such as progress in fighting a frightening fire since Southampton.

The trouble for Ismay is that he accidentally disclosed contact with Bell at the US inquiry when pressed into evidence as the very first witness. The shipwrecked shipping magnate testified the morning after the rescuer *Carpathia* docked in Manhattan.[2] He was still traumatised, despite being attended by a battery of company lawyers, and his state of mind must have given cause for concern as they sought to stress upon him the need for conservative and cautious responses to questioning.

Within minutes of being sworn in, however, Ismay revealed how he had gone down below and met the chief engineer in the immediate wake of the iceberg crash, revealing a relationship that was totally at odds with the ship's hierarchy. Ismay questioned Bell about the damage and then went back up onto the bridge, the nerve centre where he had earlier stomped in his pyjamas and topcoat to question Captain Smith, who naturally already had his hands full.[3]

It is easy to imagine Ismay's lawyers involuntarily lowering their heads at this admission. Even for a naturally concerned owner, it amounted to invasion and massive interference with the ship's proper chain of command at a crucial time. And it had emerged in public so early in the investigations of the US Senate subcommittee probing the disaster.

By page five of that body's transcript of *Titanic* evidence (which runs to 1,163 pages) Ismay was being startled by a question that tackled his previous assertion that he had been on a voluntary trip as an ordinary passenger.[4]

Chairman Senator William Alden Smith asked: 'Did you have occasion to consult with the Captain about the movement of the ship?'

Ismay rapped out: 'Never.'

Smith put the question another way: 'Did he consult you about it?' and the managing director suddenly stumbled in his prepared argument that he was 'simply a passenger'. He replied 'Never', but then added: 'Perhaps I am wrong in saying that. I should like to say this: I do not know that it was quite a matter of consulting him about it, [or] of his consulting me about it, but what we had arranged to do was that we would not attempt to arrive in New York at the lightship before 5 o'clock on Wednesday morning.'

'That was the understanding?'

'Yes. But that was arranged before we left Queenstown.'

At this point, Ismay had unintentionally opened the door to all his consultations and arrangements, and his testimony had barely begun. Matters led on, and his exquisite pickle was that he always attempted to represent himself as an ordinary passenger, albeit a VIP, and one with no influence at all over Captain Smith.

Yet the *Titanic* had been speeding when she struck the ice, going far faster than the Line had publicly pledged to travel.[5] And coal consumption is, of course, integral to the speed question.

Bearing in mind Ismay's ridiculous attempt at recovery by insisting that he and Bell had only discussed at Queenstown what everyone already knew, which was the need to be exceptionally modest and careful in the ship's speed, it is difficult not to enjoy a question levelled at him during the British inquiry: 'Will you explain that? It is not quite clear why you should discuss the question in Queenstown?'[6]

It is important to recognise here that Ismay had returned home from the US to the British inquiry, and his legal corner men had been able in the meantime to minister to their pummelled prizefighter, one lawyer even joining Ismay's return-journey ship before he landed in England.[7]

This is how Ismay answered that question: 'The reason why we discussed it at Queenstown was this, that Mr Bell came into my room. I wanted to know how much coal we had on board the ship, because the ship left after the coal strike was on, and he told me. I then spoke to him about the ship, and I said it is not possible for the ship to arrive in New York on Tuesday. Therefore there is no object in pushing her. We will arrive there at 5 o'clock on Wednesday morning, and it will be a good landing for the passengers in New York, and we shall also be able to economise our coal. We did not want to burn any more coal than we needed.'[8]

Whoever then saw to it that the ship accelerated beyond her promised speed the whole way, especially on the following Sunday night, it was not Mr Ismay – and indeed he claimed that such a course of action ran directly contrary to the orders and wishes he had patiently and repeatedly expounded. Not that the managing director was going to breathe a word of criticism, mind, of his deceased but impatient captain and his complicit chief engineer.

Ismay maintained throughout that it was his intention to have a little speed test for the *Titanic* only on the Monday, the day *after* the sinking. This would seem to copper-fasten his apparent view that there should be no speeding beforehand, although it would amount to a small sin against the company promise that the *Titanic* would do no more than 20 knots at any point.

It was this – the speed test proposal – that was the magic new ingredient that justified hauling Bell up again at Queenstown for further interview by Ismay. (Not that Bell had any role at all in speed, and not that the test, intended to be for 'a few hours', would have dramatically affected coal consumption.) The idea solved the problem of what this meeting was actually about.

'You have not told us about that?' the attorney general queried in London.

'That was when Mr Bell was in my room on Thursday afternoon, when the ship was at anchor at Queenstown,' Ismay now explained, in contrast to his American evidence. They had discussed the speed test 'at the same time' as the need for moderation in both coal consumption and speed [which is, of course, a direct contradiction]. Ismay was clearly attempting to have it both ways in order to forge an escape route for himself.

The attorney general then asked: 'But what was said about putting her at full speed?'

Ismay answered: 'I said to him then, we may have an opportunity of driving her at full speed on Monday or Tuesday if the weather is entirely suitable.'[9]

He then denied knowing that extra boilers had, in fact, been lit on Sunday morning, the day of the accident, which would have allowed for extra speed long before the planned test. This salient fact had been brought out at the earlier American inquiry, and was again in England.

Seeing where this was going, there were now interruptions: huffing and puffing from legal counsel. The commissioner, Lord Mersey, suggested that prior stokehold testimony about harnessing extra boilers on Sunday morning 'may be inaccurate about the time when these additional boilers were lit … you see, according to the evidence of Mr Ismay, they would not want the additional speed until Monday or Tuesday'.

Sir Robert Finlay (for the White Star Line): 'Yes. And coal being the object at the time, one would suppose they were not lit up quite so hurriedly.'

The attorney general: 'Monday was very close at hand, after all.'[10]

The difficulty with all this was that a swathe of crew members had already given evidence of the vessel surging at 22.5 or 23 knots prior to the catastrophe.

Despite this attempted wagon circling, Ismay's position was hopeless, especially since, on the seventh day of the US inquiry, Quartermaster George Rowe had given evidence of hauling in a rotor device trailed off the stern in the immediate wake of the collision. This device gave the nautical miles that had elapsed since noon. Rowe told the senators: 'As soon as the berg was gone I looked at the log and it read 260 miles. The log was reset at noon.'[11]

Impact was at 11.40 p.m. ship's time. Rowe testified he took the log in within thirty seconds of impact. The distance of 260 miles in eleven and two-third hours means that the *Titanic* had steamed a *continuous average* of 22.3 knots since noon on Sunday. The odometer does not lie.

Rowe repeatedly recounted this mileage in both America and Britain. In the first forum it did not appear to be understood; in the second, the finest brains of the British Bar seemed incapable of basic division, repeatedly managing to underestimate how fast the ship had been travelling.

Ismay was asked again at the subsequent liability hearings if he knew they were firing up some extra boilers on the Sunday. He said: 'I had no knowledge at all as to what was being done below.' This despite the fact that he had brought the chief engineer up to his room at Queenstown. 'I have no knowledge at all with regard to the speed of the ship.' He knew of no slowing down or speeding up, nor anything else in the stokehold (and he was astonishingly never asked by anyone, at either inquiry, about the fire in the coal bunker). 'I say I had no knowledge with regard to the speed the ship was making.'

But why summon Bell to his room and hear him there in private – with or without his secretary present? It seems very likely that something other than exquisitely boring, pre-confirmed arrangements were on his mind as the *Titanic* lay in her Queenstown limbo.

* * *

The Cork Examiner recorded the moment the *Titanic* weighed anchor irrevocably, giving it as 1.25 p.m. She was proceeding on her first Atlantic crossing. 'To the battle of the Transatlantic passenger service the *Titanic* adds a new and important factor, of value to the aristocracy and the plutocracy attracted from East to West, and [from] West to East,' the newspaper trilled. 'In the fight during the coming season, there will be a scent of battle all the way from New York to the shores of this country – a contest of sea giants, in which the *Titanic* will doubtless take high honours.'[12]

The London *Daily News* recorded that she 'left Queenstown in charming weather. On the passage from Southampton to Cherbourg, and thence to the Irish port, her huge engines worked most smoothly, and although not driven at a high pressure, recorded twenty knots.'

The *Cork Constitution* begged to disagree with the *Examiner* on when, exactly, the anchor ascended. 'Her time of departure was 1.20, which, considering the heavy embarkation, was a rapid despatch, and was in keeping with the excellent arrangements always made at Queenstown.'[13]

The differences as to the precise moment of departure might blind us to overall agreement. It is clear that both time and speed were uppermost considerations for the newspapers, reflecting reader (and thus passenger) appetites, conditioned as they undoubtedly were by shipping line publicity.

Yet in this case it was the very act of leaving that was momentous. There could now be no going back.

16

UNDERTAKING THE ATLANTIC

GETTING OFF

Among the mail taken off at Queenstown (along with fireman Coffey) was a letter from the chief officer of RMS *Titanic*. Henry Wilde wrote to his sister, Ada, on ship's stationery. Only days before he had described the vessel as 'wonderful', but he was more confessional in this last note, datelined at the final port of call. Wilde confided: 'I still don't like this ship ... I have a queer feeling about it.'[1]

He was perfectly placed to detect what the captain's expression and demeanour actually indicated, once the press had been sent on their radiant way with his ringing encomiums for this new command. Wilde, who was Captain Smith's sought-after support, must have been aware of the fire – though other officers claimed in evidence not to have known (despite rumours reaching the passengers and being freely discussed among the crew).

How dangerous exactly was that outbreak? The *Cairnrona* was just one example where a similar outbreak had occurred. In her case, they began working out the bunker, quarrying coal urgently away. Notably, in light of what Clement Edwards claimed he had been told in the *Titanic*'s case, the chief engineer of the *Cairnrona* had ordered a hole cut in the bulkhead, the better to hose water on the fire's seat.

The official report following that case, which instructed ships never to put to sea with spontaneous bunker fires, declared: 'Steps taken by the chief engineer to get at the source of the heating, namely by clearing the coal out of the trunkway in the bunker and by playing a hose for about two hours through a hole cut in the side of it, were inadequate.' Evidently so, for the bunker exploded.

In March 1912, a month before the *Titanic* sailed, there had been large American press attention paid to the formal scuttling of the remains of the USS *Maine* off Florida after she was raised from Havana harbour the year before. The *Maine* sank in Cuba in February 1898, when 260 men (three-quarters of those aboard) were killed in a sudden explosion. The press seized on the idea that she had been destroyed by a mine and the incident led to the Spanish–American War ('Remember the *Maine*, to hell with Spain!').

The US Navy, however, quickly concluded that the cause had been a spontaneous coal fire, which ignited 'firedamp' gas, instantly taking the ship's magazine with it in a devastating blast far bigger than any mine could have caused. Detailed re-investigation by Admiral Hyman Rickover in 1976 determined the cause to be prolonged heat from a bunker fire against a bulkhead, behind which were shells and munitions. A National Geographic TV documentary in the twenty-first century proved this argument with a bunker wall built to original specifications.

Nonetheless, the nineteenth-century instant press idea of a mine, followed by whipped-up patriotism, happened to suit some. The *Maine* became a symbol of the United States to such an extent that her transplanted mast is today the rallying point for the Changing of the Guard at Arlington National Cemetery. Her captain, Charles Sigsbee, survived and became a hero, and his views would be eagerly sought on the *Titanic* disaster, which may be one of history's deeper ironies.

Over the years, it is likely that very many steamships were sunk by spontaneous coal fires and their associated detonations, certainly many more than is known to history since the vessels involved never made port. The White Star Line had itself experienced a strange disappearance that haunted the company for nigh on twenty years. The cattle boat *Naronic* was built in 1892 and described as the finest and safest vessel ever launched. She was the largest freight steamer afloat and left Liverpool on 11 February 1893, promptly disappearing.

J. Bruce Ismay was briefly asked about the *Naronic* at the US inquiry. 'She was never heard of after leaving Liverpool,' he told Senator Smith, adding she had been destined for New York. 'She was practically a new ship when she was lost.'[2]

Speculation at the time included the idea that the culprit was an iceberg, but modern research compiling all hydrographic data and reports extant for the

North Atlantic makes clear that 1893 was a year of very little ice in the shipping lanes. Nor had the weather been unduly rough on the voyage and there had been no other vessel posted 'overdue', which might have suggested that a collision was to blame.

J. Bruce's father, Thomas Henry Ismay, formed the view that the *Naronic* had been lost from hitting a 'floating derelict', but neither he nor an official inquiry could determine anything for certain. One floating derelict that confirmed the ship's loss was an overturned lifeboat, bearing the name *Naronic*, found by the *Coventry* on 4 March. It was logged in a position 138 nautical miles northeast of where the *Titanic* would strike an iceberg in 1912.

Some seventy-four people, including seventeen cattlemen, had been on board, along with 700 steers. No ice had been reported within 100 miles. She had 1,100 tons of coal on board and burned fifty tons a day. The press was mystified, pointing out she had nine bulkheads and that her captain, William Roberts, 'was one of the most competent commanders in the White Star service', having twenty years' experience with the Line.[3] Evidently, however, she had gone down quickly.

In January 1913 *The Lookout*, the magazine of the Seamen's Institute of New York, opined: 'Could the particulars of this [*Naronic*] disaster have been made known through wireless telegraphy, then not in use, the object lesson might possibly have served to avert the more terrible one of the *Titanic*.' Indeed.

The not-knowing in the case of the earlier loss is total, but while the scale of what is not known about the *Titanic* may be significant, it is certainly far from absolute. The idea that everything was honestly laid bare in evidence, however, must be challenged – especially since Second Officer Lightoller later wrote that it was 'necessary to keep one's hand on the whitewash brush', and probably meant other hands too, in the nautical parlance of crewmen as 'hands'.[4] What was at stake, after all, was the survival of the Line itself and every livelihood attached to it.

There is no evidence the *Naronic* sank from a coal-fire explosion, just as there is no evidence that she sank from striking an iceberg, a derelict, or by any other cause. What is clear is that her loss had no effect on White Star navigation on the North Atlantic.

* * *

The last man off the *Titanic* before the ice hit the hull was the specialist White Star pilot at Queenstown, John Cotter. He was not called to give evidence and died of a bowel obstruction five years and one day after the maiden voyager went down.

Two others to disembark there were Eber Sharpe, the Board of Trade surveyor stationed at Queenstown, and Captain James McGiffin, who was White Star's marine superintendent at the port. Sharpe entered the witness box (for two minutes), but McGiffin went uncalled. The former answered 'Yes' to the question whether, when she departed, the ship was, in his opinion, 'seaworthy, in safe trim, and in all respects fit for her intended voyage?'[5] Sharpe then provided statistics for passengers in different classes and the number of crew, next agreed shortly with Lord Mersey that it was a very lucky thing for the fireman Coffey to have deserted, and finally gratefully stepped down.

The failure to call McGiffin, however, is particularly noteworthy – given that the Line's marine superintendents at Liverpool (Charles Bartlett) and Southampton (Benjamin Steel) both appeared. White Star did not maintain such a position at Belfast, since it was not a port of call in its network. Why was the Queenstown manager not sworn in? Perhaps because he was not entirely happy with what had gone on – a theory bolstered by his resignation from the White Star Line later in 1912.

McGiffin had served on board the White Star liner *Medic* to Australia and New Zealand with *Titanic* officers Charles Lightoller and William McMaster Murdoch, the former saved and the latter lost in the sinking.[6] On 1 January 1984 McGiffin's son, James Oliphant McGiffin, wrote to American researcher Diana Bristow that First Officer Murdoch had been his father's 'closest friend'. He disclosed: 'Lightoller told my father in Queenstown that Mr Bruce Ismay kept pressure on Captain Edward Smith to keep the *Titanic* to her maximum speed of 22–23 knots in order to create new record time for the southern track crossing of the Atlantic. This Captain Smith did, in spite of ice warnings from other ships in the area.'[7]

Elsewhere in this decades-old letter, James wrote: 'My father seemed to have no knowledge of a fire aboard the *Titanic* when she arrived in Queenstown. He, as Marine Superintendent, would have been informed, but in discussing the disaster in later years made no mention of a fire.'

In a 1977 audio recording he recalls: 'I was six years and four months old, and I remember it quite distinctly. While we were at Queenstown, the officers on these vessels used to come up for lunch. But on the *Titanic* occasion, I don't think they came up. I don't think Lightoller and Murdoch came. But when they were aboard *Olympic*, and Captain Smith was captain, they used to come up quite frequently. Most of the White Star liners that called at Queenstown, we were invited and quite often used to have lunch aboard. We went right over the vessels, and looked into all the compartments, including the engine room. Quite interesting. I remember all the details quite vividly.'

His brother, Bill, was recorded in 1983, and though only four years and nine months old at the time, had this to say: 'I was only a nipper. I understand both Lightoller and Murdoch bounced me on their knee. I remember my father was in tears and that is indelible in my mind to this day. There was an unfortunate dash across the Atlantic, which came with terrific cost to everyone … That was the *Titanic* disaster. [It is] indelibly on my mind, as on Jim's. In my father's case, I saw him cry. I never saw him cry before in my life. Isn't it funny how something like that hits you and sticks with you all your life?'[8]

There is a sense that the marine superintendent kept much bottled up. After quitting the White Star Line, his family began a slow slide into poverty. McGiffin died on 13 January 1936, aged seventy, never having committed anything to paper about his *Titanic* recollections.[9] It seems likely, however, that the Line at least sought a report from him, as had the Board of Trade with Maurice Clarke. If such a report was ever made it would seem to be no longer extant. In any case, the subsequent inquiry choice of Sharpe giving evidence over McGiffin is singular to say the least. As a result, we are left with press reports of Captain Smith's demeanour at the final port of call and no insights from the colleague who intimately knew both the master and his brother officers, being the man to whom any problems in running the ship were supposed to be reported.

* * *

And so the introductory service of White Star's second super-liner continued along the Irish coast away from Queenstown, passing the Daunt Rock and thereby starting the clock for the transatlantic crossing. Soon the ship approached the Old Head of Kinsale, where eagle-eyed lighthouse keepers ran out signal flags.

Quartermaster Rowe, the crewman who would later testify to 260 miles steamed since noon on the night she expired, related in a June 1968 letter:

We left Queenstown just after lunch on April 11th and at 2 pm I relieved Bob Hichens at the wheel. A little later we were passing the Old Head of Kinsale. I was instructed to keep her steady on her course.

The junior officer was taking a bearing when [the] *lighthouse would be abeam, when he gave the word, or stood up and told the Chief, who was Mr Wilde, that there was a signal flying at the station and the Chief told him to look it up in the International Code book, which read either Good Luck or Success. It was a two-flag sign. We replied with a two-flag signal: Thanks.*

The flags were bent [tied] *onto the halyards and hoisted by Hichens and the junior officer. The signal ashore was pulled down and Hichens pulled ours down till it was almost within reach, when the tack* [that is the small piece of rope that is part of the flag] *parted and the flag went flying away to leeward at the end of the halyards.*

Wilde now ordered a surprising helm manoeuvre and the ship was swung from her course by Rowe at the wheel. 'I turned the ship about, under the instructions of the chief, and so retrieved the flags …' (It was a sharp turn, no doubt.)

As well as the potential 'omen' with the flags, Rowe noted another strange occurrence: 'Just one more thing: there was not a single seabird followed us leaving the Fastnet Rock.'[10]

Passenger Lawrence Beesley begged to disagree. He wrote in his 1912 book: 'The gulls were still behind us when night fell, and they screamed and dipped down into the broad wake of foam which we left behind; but in the morning they were gone: perhaps they had seen in the night a steamer bound for their Queenstown home and escorted her back.

'All afternoon we steamed along the coast of Ireland, with grey cliffs guarding the shores, and hills rising behind gaunt and barren. As dusk fell, the coast rounded away from us to the northwest [*sic*; should be northeast], and the last we saw of Europe was the Irish mountains dim and faint in the dropping darkness.'[11]

The Times published news from France that 'one of the last vessels to sight the *Titanic* was probably the Boulogne steamer trawler *Alsace*, which passed the liner on Thursday April 11, off the south-west coast of Ireland'. The voice of the establishment scolded: 'The trawler appears to have been rather dangerously near to the *Titanic*, passing so close in fact that she was splashed with spray from the *Titanic*'s bow.' According to the report, 'The fishermen cheered the liner, and their salutations were responded to by the officer on the bridge.'[12] More likely, however, they cursed that liner with shaken French fists – and were told, in turn, exactly where they could go.

17

THE BLUE CONCOURSE

AIMING FOR AMERICA

Second Officer Lightoller knew all about fire at sea, even if he subsequently denied knowledge of the one aboard the *Titanic*. Nineteen years previously the undoubted hero of 1912 had been third mate on a four-masted barque, the *Knight of St Michael* on the 'Western Ocean', as British officers were apt to call the Atlantic.

'We were loaded with an unromantic cargo of coal, and with the everlasting working of the ship, there had evidently been just sufficient friction to cause it to heat up, and eventually catch fire,' Lightoller wrote in his memoirs. 'Had we possessed boats to carry us all, it would not have been so bad, but situated as we were, if she did go up, there wasn't a ghost of a chance for a quarter of us,' he added, unconsciously conjuring the boats-for-all brouhaha that engulfed the *Titanic*'s aftermath.[1]

The barque had no passengers and a crew numbering fewer than 100, but the danger, once detected, was instantly known to all. 'It was the only subject we could discuss with any degree of naturalness,' he lyrically portrayed, which might serve to throw his staccato *Titanic* denials into some relief.

'Look at it any way you liked, we'd about as much chance of surviving as the sailors' proverbial snowball in the lower regions ... Neither was there much likelihood of rest during the day, or sleep at night, with a potential volcano immediately underneath one, and level betting that if you did sleep, the chances were you'd wake to find yourself rising on the rim, getting a good start heavenward.'[2]

An echo of Esther Hart and her inability to sleep can be detected here, but the *Knight* passed through and came to a landfall bay. The crew 'attacked the fire at its base ... and got it sufficiently under control for all hands to get to work, and dig down night and day, until they had got a trunkway clean through the lower hold.

'We hammered up the ends of several lengths of three-inch iron piping, after drilling it full of holes. These we drove down into the coal in different places, and then tucked on the business end of a fire hose.'[3]

They next limped to port and 'six days swinging anchor, with always an eye on our slumbering friend down below, giving him an occasional sousing with the hoses'. The surveyor next came along, and was – naturally – shown all the damage.

In the *Titanic*'s case, however, nothing was said to the outside world and the command structure was similarly determined that not a word be breathed about the 'potential volcano' to either the *beau monde* of the saloon or the demimonde of steerage.[4] New York journalists were nonetheless able to find *Titanic* fireman survivor John Dilley (whose real name was Christopher Shulver) when about to voyage home on the Red Star liner *Lapland*. The Londoner was quoted from the quayside:

From the day we sailed the Titanic *was on fire, and my sole duty, together with eleven other men, had been to fight that fire. We had made no headway against it.*

Of course the passengers knew nothing of the fire. It started in bunker [sic; *he means boiler room*] *No. 6. There were hundreds of tons of coal stored there. The coal on top of the bunker was wet, as all of the coal should have been, but down at the bottom of the bunker the coal was dry. The coal at the bottom of the bunker took fire, and smouldered for days. The wet coal on top kept the flames from coming through, but down in the bottom of the bunker the flames were a-raging.*

Two men from each watch of stokers were told off to fight that fire. The stokers, you know, work four hours at a time, so 12 of us was fighting the flames from the day we put out of Southampton until we hit the iceberg.[5]

Dilley admitted further: 'The stokers were beginning to get alarmed over it, but the officers told us to keep our mouths shut. They didn't want to alarm the passengers.'

The facts seeped out to some, of course, but other passengers may only have experienced the side effects of what was happening down below. The deposition of passenger Imanita Shelley has previously been quoted as to how the heating system for the second-class cabins 'refused to work' and those in steerage had the same trouble.[6] This may appear to be a minor matter, but there were no reports of any faulty heating system among the first-class passengers. Instead, Edith Russell referred to her stateroom's 'warm radiator casting a soft glow, everything so cosy'.[7]

Shelley said she was told that only three cabins had been 'reached by the heat' in second class, and these were stifling. The occupants had supposedly complained to the purser, 'who had ordered the heat shut off entirely'.

Another man who shut off heat on board his ship was Captain Arthur Rostron of the Cunard liner *Carpathia*. He did so when summoned by wireless to the rescue of RMS *Titanic*. The garlanded saviour wrote in his autobiography: 'One of the first things I did, naturally, was to get up the Chief Engineer, explain the urgency of matters and, calling out an extra watch in the engine room, every ounce of power was got from the boilers and every particle of steam used for the engines, turning it from all other uses, *such as heating* [author's emphasis].'[8]

This was no latter-day embroidery; surviving orders from Rostron preserved in the Library of Congress show the instruction to cut heat, and it was reported in the *New York Tribune* the day after the *Titanic*'s shipwrecked were landed. A steward from the *Carpathia* (unnamed) said Captain Rostron 'had shut off the hot water all over the ship and turned every ounce of heat into steam, and the old boat was as excited as any of us'.

Heating used coal; thus the denial of heat meant the *Titanic* could maximise 'every particle' for 'every ounce of power', both in terms of speed and mileage obtainable, against the background of a nagging fire. So it can be suspected that the heating for the lower orders was cynically cut off in order to conserve coal for her crossing, given the low coal stocks known to be aboard, meaning they prioritised the ship's progress. Businesses can, and do, mistreat their customers in pursuit of corporate goals.

And a smart passage was clearly the goal. 'From noon Thursday to noon Friday, we ran 386 [actually 484] miles,' wrote Lawrence Beesley in his schoolmasterly way. From Friday to Saturday the sum ran substantially more – 519 miles.[9] The day is a little longer than twenty-four hours when sailing westbound, but this was an average speed already of 21 knots, meaning they were casting cautious pre-publicity to the salt wind in the ship's wake.

'The second day's run of 519 miles was, the purser told us, a disappointment,' Beesley revealed, possibly in some astonishment. What had become of initial claims about coal conservation and at no point exceeding 20 knots, he may have wondered. Second-class purser Reginald Barker then pessimistically told him 'we should not dock until Wednesday morning [i.e. on advertised schedule] instead of Tuesday night, as we had expected'.

Here, it must be asked, did the second-class purser apparently know more of the ship's innermost intentions than the managing director of the White Star Line, who had supposedly held so many meetings and consultations about the need for restraint? The answer must surely be no. Instead, this middle-ranking member of crew was revealing a widely shared plan for an eye-catching early arrival. The *Titanic*, already lean, would use every ounce of power to impress.

* * *

The coal situation would generate another effect, as noted by Lawrence Beesley. Every morning thus far, he had risen to see the light behind the *Titanic* in an eastern sky of circular clouds, which faded from pink to white as the sun rose. He had never before been out of sight of the shores of England, but now he could 'stand on the top deck and watch the swell of the sea extending outwards from the ship in an unbroken circle until it met the skyline with its hint of infinity'.[10]

Then the Dulwich College science teacher detected something:

It was interesting to stand on the boat deck, as I frequently did, in the angle between lifeboats 13 and 15 on the starboard side ... and watch the general motion of the ship through the waves.

I timed the average period occupied in one up-and-down vibration, but do not now remember the figures. The second motion was a side-to-side roll, and could be calculated by watching the port rail and contrasting it with the horizon as before.

The almost clock-like regularity of the two vibratory movements was what attracted my attention. It was while watching the side roll that I first became aware of the list to port.[11]

A list to the port side meant the ship was not on an even keel, despite having on board many 'trimmers', whose job was to take coal from the bunkers to the furnaces, but to do so methodically, so that the ship would be trim – balanced – in the water. Instead she was heeled to her left-hand side when looking forward towards the bow.

It is not clear from his book when Beesley initially discerned this list, whether on the first or second full day at sea, but he raised it with his new friend, purser Barker, on the third. 'I then called the attention of our table to the way the

Titanic listed to port (I had noticed this before), and we all watched the skyline through the portholes as we sat at the purser's table in the saloon.

'It was plain she did so, for the skyline and sea on the port side were visible most of the time and on the starboard only sky. The purser remarked that probably coal had been used mostly from the starboard side.'[12]

The all-knowing Barker was 'probably' privy to this secret, too – that a round-the-clock squad of trimmers was digging out the content of the forward starboard bunker affected by the spontaneous coal fire. The vessel was not being kept trim for an overriding reason: the pressing need to extract the coal from the out-of-control conflagration that threatened the ship.

Beesley's dispassionate observation – and he did not know about the bunker fire at any point – is incontrovertible proof that the fire was of a deadly serious nature. His diagnosis, shared with his table as Elizabeth Brown must have shared news of the fire with hers, was confirmed and endorsed by the second-class purser. It corroborates the account of fireman John Dilley. All the coal extraction was taking place on the starboard side in a desperate race against the fire itself, causing the vessel to lean to her heavier port side.

Beesley, innocent of the full implications, still managed to identify a possible danger that this list would cause. He muses in his book: 'It is no doubt a common occurrence for all vessels to list to some degree; but in view of the fact that the *Titanic* was cut open on the starboard side, and before she sank listed so much to port that there was quite a chasm between her and the swinging lifeboats, across which ladies had to be thrown or to cross on chairs laid flat, the previous listing to port may be of interest.'[13]

Once again, then, the fire is proven to be a grave threat to the *Titanic* and its perilous presence is bringing about the most intense countermeasures on board.

First-class American passenger Norman Chambers corroborated Beesley's account. He told the US inquiry that 'as the ship had a list to port nearly all [Sunday] afternoon', he decided to remain on board following the collision, since the ship now had a noticeable new list to starboard.[14]

What Beesley witnessed mid-voyage, however, is of great importance. The port-side list had become increasingly noticeable and would continue to be pronounced until the very instant of the near-midnight impact with an implacable ice mountain. The *Titanic* would thus be lifting her most vulnerable side to that icy ogre when navigation and nature met in shocking collision.

18

THE MYTH OF
'EXCEPTIONAL STRENGTH'

WEAKNESS IN WAITING

The stubborn fire was not only a danger in itself, as evident from Lightoller's description of the *Knight of St Michael*, but also had implications for the structural integrity of the ship – both because of its intensity and, crucially, its location. The fire was in the second boiler room from forward (i.e. No. 5 – they were counted backwards from the bow, No. 6 being the furthest forward, No. 1 being the aftermost, closest to the stern). It was originally detected in bunker W of boiler room 5, investigators accepted – although fireman John Dilley begged to differ, insisting it began in No. 6.[1] Boiler rooms 5 and 6 were separated by steel bulkhead E, running across the ship from port to starboard. Bunkers W and Y were located on either side of this bulkhead, in boiler rooms 5 and 6 respectively. Heat on one side of a bulkhead will threaten to ignite coal in the opposite bunker, so it seems certain that both bunkers would have had to be worked out on board the *Titanic*.

W, the starboard bunker in No. 5 boiler room, was a rectangular space three storeys high, holding 365 tons of coal. Its forward wall was a main collision bulkhead for the *Titanic*, and one of its side walls was the hull of the ship herself. There is evidence that the blaze was directly affecting that forward bulkhead, E, as shall be described in due course, yet there is no direct surviving evidence as to any effect on the side wall, meaning the skin of the great liner that would be dramatically punctured as the berg barged in. The use of the hull as one wall of the boiler room was arguably a design flaw in the case of spontaneous coal fires, which were known to weaken metal.

Senator Jonathan Bourne of Oregon asked J. Bruce Ismay at the US inquiry whether he was familiar with the boiler rooms of his great vessel. Ismay was explicit: 'No, sir; I had never been down in the boiler rooms.'[2]

Bourne asked Ismay about plans submitted to him for the design of the ship. He wondered if the question had come up of 'bulkheads between the [bunkers] and the skin of the ship'. The senator, who himself had been shipwrecked thirty-five years before, was not unsympathetic.[3] A Harvard-educated industrialist with mining and mill interests, Bourne appeared to have a strong grasp of technical questions.

When Ismay replied that it had not come up for consideration, Bourne pressed him: 'Your attention has not been directed, then, to that point, as to whether the ship could be made more nonsinkable by having airtight or watertight bulkheads between the boilers [sic] themselves and the skin of the ship?'[4]

'No, sir,' said Ismay. 'That matter was never discussed. You mean to make the coal bunkers watertight?'

Senator Bourne refined his question: 'Yes; I mean the coal bunkers.'

Ismay grasped the point but appealed to the strength of just one of the walls of the bunker – the bulkhead – even though it was not this wall that made direct contact with the iceberg. 'No, sir; that was never discussed. Of course we have bulkheads in the boiler rooms, right across the ship.'

The use of the hull as a side wall to a coal bunker was an acknowledged weakness.[5] *Carpathia* Second Officer James Bisset wrote emphatically in his memoirs: 'Very strangely she [*Titanic*] did not have a "double skin" in the sides of her hull, as the *Mauretania* and the *Lusitania* had, for bunkers … That expense had been saved in the *Olympic*, as also in her sister, the *Titanic*. These new White Star mammoths were built with single hulls … the publicity that these big ships were unsinkable was tragic optimism.'[6]

Soon after the *Titanic* disaster, her sister ship *Olympic* was withdrawn from service for structural improvements, to make her yet more 'unsinkable'. That word itself would be quietly scuttled. When she reappeared, the second layer of necessary protection identified by Senator Bourne had been incorporated. The *Olympic* now had an inner hull, 'double sides as well as double bottom', and was now 'virtually two ships in one' according to lavish 1913 advertising.[7] The new 'inner skin', so labelled on different decks, was shown in cutaway drawings of the vessel. Diagrams also demonstrated that transverse bulkheads had been carried up higher than in the *Titanic*, the two structural reforms 'augmenting the flotation capacity and enhancing to the utmost the safety of the vessel'.

The *Sphere* magazine ran a photograph of the space between the hull and the 'new inner lining', which it said was 'calculated to add very considerably to the vessel's buoyancy'. It was thus the 'New *Olympic*', most definitely not the old and co-compromised sister to the *Titanic*, and 'will be everything that human foresight has devised for the safety of passengers and crew'. Truly she was 'the greatest production of the premier British shipbuilders – the highest achievement of their long and fruitful experience in constructing many of the largest steamers of recent years'. There was no mention that one of those large steamers had gone down just the previous twelvemonth.[8]

The *Titanic* actually did have one level of insurance against sinking, but it was only a double bottom, extending seven feet above the keel.[9] It would have guarded against a grounding event and keel rupture, but it did not extend at all, leaving the sides with just a single layer of metal to keep out any colliding objects and the swamping seas that could come with them. She was a single-skin ship with bulkheads not high enough to cope with widespread flooding.

While double-skin ships are the norm today (and even mistakenly appeared in some cutaway *Titanic* illustrations in 1912), the reality was that the North Atlantic and the ship's interior were separated only by one thin band of steel in the *Titanic*'s case. Seen in cross-section, that separation would be about the width of a polysyllabic word in this book. Specifically, the steel plate for the *Titanic* at the waterline plane, the turn of the bilge and bottom plates, was just one inch in thickness. Therefore, the breadth of hull plating at boiler rooms 6 and 5 (both penetrated by the ice) would also have been a single inch, except where plates overlapped and were riveted together.

By contrast, the forward internal bulkhead separating the boiler rooms was fifty-six-hundredths of an inch, or barely more than half an inch thick. It also tapered – that is, it grew thinner – as it ascended. At F deck, the top of the bulkhead's forty-four-foot wall, the thickness was but thirty-hundredths of an inch.[10]

Both the bulkhead and outer skin of the ship were made of mild steel of low carbon content (0.15 per cent). It was the normal steel used in shipbuilding of the day, and the *Titanic* was neither more nor less unsinkable in that respect than many another vessel.[11] Naval architect Thomas Andrews referred to her fabric as steel to 'ordinary requirements'. What this means is that if the fire compromised the structural integrity of forward bulkhead E – as firemen later testified it had – then it is possible the same blaze, depending on its location, might also have affected the metal of the hull, albeit to a lesser extent.

The precise bed of the fire within the bunker was never discovered or specified. If it was located in the centre of the quantity of coal, then the effect on the hull would be less than on the bulkhead, because of the former's greater metal thickness. If, on the other hand, the concentration and greatest intensity of heat was located close to the outer skin, the hull, the debilitating effect on the strength of that steel would have been commensurately increased. Hull weakness in this crucial area, bumped and knocked by the iceberg as it passed along from its first contact further forward, cannot be accurately assessed because the true seat of the fire is unknown.

University of Birmingham metallurgist Martin Strangwood suspects the effect on the hull would have been much less than that on the bulkhead in any case, because the cold of the outside water would have conducted heat away. 'If the hull had been compromised in the same way as the bulkhead, then fracture would have been far more on collision … and so the sinking would have been much more rapid [than proved to be the case].'[12]

But the second skin, the doubling of the *Olympic*'s sides with another sheath of interior metal, demonstrates that hull weakness exacerbating collision damage was known about – given that it was later addressed. And it is further established by the comments of Harland & Wolff naval architect Edward Wilding in evidence to the *Titanic* limitation of liability hearings. He first agreed that inner skins were 'known to the shipbuilding art' before 1912, and indeed were present in the pioneering *Great Eastern* steamship of 1850.

Wilding was asked: 'You then, at the time the *Titanic* was being built, deemed inner skins a desirable protection against certain emergencies, did you not?'

The builder faltered in answering: 'If we considered it …' not finishing his reply before declaring: 'You are asking me a leading question, and in a form in which it is not easy to answer.'

Asked to give 'the best answer you can', Wilding managed to come up with a frail defence: 'My difficulty in answering is that it is very difficult to separate my knowledge now from my knowledge then.'

'You weren't called upon to express your judgment at that time?'

'I wasn't called on to judge that point at that time.'[13]

Wilding's mention of the *Great Eastern* brings another important point to light. Although a major innovation, that ship was so truly cellular that those aboard had to ascend from one compartment to a top deck and then descend to the next compartment. Hampered in movement, the design became infuriating. Openings were needed and subsequent ships would provide such passages, for both crew and passengers alike. The *Titanic* had in fact two great thoroughfares running fore and aft, known to the crew as 'Scotland Road' and 'Park Lane'. Watertight doors could be closed within.

If structural integrity was routinely compromised in such a manner, there were also considerations of cost and weight to all metal scantlings. Additional layers brought not only a higher outlay in themselves, but the additional permanent weight created a built-in drag on profitability, because the heavier a ship, the more coal needed to propel her through the water – just as the chrome-laden, sagging-chassis American automobiles of the 1950s were dubbed 'gas guzzlers'.

The *Titanic* went with ordinary steel and mostly standard specifications. Passengers were either misled or deluded themselves over her alleged superiority, with Lawrence Beesley factually wrong when he opened his 1912 book with this statement: 'All her structure was of steel, of a weight, size, and thickness greater than that of any ship yet known: the girders, beams, bulkheads, and floors all of exceptional strength.'[14]

Every consideration involved compromise … until the fact of the *Titanic* disaster meant a necessary new trade-off to ensure the continuing confidence of the paying public. It was this: no continuation of some of the old trade-offs.

* * *

On 8 July, after the inquiry had concluded, *The Times* carried a letter on page 18 from Andrew Scott, secretary of *Lloyd's Register*, the Bible of British shipping:

Sir, — In view of the reports which have appeared in the Press in connexion with the inquiry into the loss of the S.S. Titanic, to the effect that the vessel was built considerably in excess of the requirements of Lloyd's Register, I am directed to say that these statements are inaccurate.

On the contrary, in important parts of her structure the vessel as built did not come up to the requirements of Lloyd's Register for a vessel of her dimensions.

A damning assessment.

* * *

The forces of commerce saw a doubling in the *Olympic*'s insurance charge even after her refit, with *The Times* noting it 'was generally expected that as an outcome of the *Titanic* disaster a large increase would be made in the premium', but still marvelling that it had been so compounded despite the hull 'being greatly strengthened by having a double skin fitted, and the vessel therefore presumably a far better risk than she was before'. The *Daily Telegraph* noted in parallel to this: 'Underwriters are now to pay claims in excess of £300,000 only, instead of £150,000.' White Star had no choice but to meet the terms demanded.

Of course indemnity against all eventualities found its greatest expression in 'boats for all'. They were soon to be piled on willy-nilly, cramping all space on boat decks that had previously been 'sun decks', with only a light decoration of escape craft for subtle reassurance as passengers enjoyed the promenade.

There were, however, reservations from some quarters about these new regulations. The *Weekly Irish Times* of October 1912, serves to make the point:

The House then entered upon consideration of the Titanic *report and Mr Leslie Scott, speaking for the shipping owners, strongly condemned the new regulations issued by the Board of Trade.*

For years, he declared, the Board was all behindhand with its regulations, and now it was rushing ahead too fast, and its proposals would render a very large number of vessels unseaworthy, by making them top-heavy.[15]

The sheer number of lifeboats making the need for their use more likely was certainly a novel argument, but it shows that the shipping industry was irked and impatient with changes demanded in the aftermath of the disaster.

Attending to the previous lack of lifeboats was a visible response, but ships remained vulnerable on their flanks – as had been demonstrated by both the sinking of the White Star liner *Republic* (after her gouging by the *Florida* in 1909) and by the collision of the *Olympic* with the Royal Navy cruiser HMS *Hawke* in the Solent in September 1911. The one-inch steel of *Olympic*'s hull may have been thicker than an internal bulkhead, yet the plating still appears wafer-thin to the casual observer of photographs showing the massive triangular hole in her starboard quarter that resulted from the collision.

It is true the encounter also badly damaged the *Hawke* – her bows were crumpled up – yet deep penetration had been made in the *Olympic*, which also sustained a teardrop-shaped cavity below the waterline with a 'diameter of about 30 feet', caused by the armoured warship's ram. The latter would prove 'extremely expensive' to remedy.

The remarkable aspect of this ruinous coming together, which took the *Olympic* out of service for two months, was that it somehow seemed to confirm the myth of inviolability for these vessels. The *Titanic*'s older sister returned to port under her own steam, was fitted with a stopgap of wood and thereafter was dispatched to her builders in Belfast for hull reconstruction. Back in her original waters, she was berthed close to the *Titanic*, which was still fitting out. Only two days before the *Hawke* collision, the maiden voyage of the *Titanic* had been announced for 20 March – not April – and this earlier date was advertised in passenger lists and other documents. But the diversion of resources to address the *Olympic*'s damage resulted in a three-week delay, inadvertently rescheduling the *Titanic* for introduction to an iceberg.

There would be knock-on losses for the Line through lost passenger revenues foregone for both ships, but it was the *Olympic*'s repair bill that was most alarming. One report authoritatively headlined the 'Enormous Outlay Necessary' to renew her mangled metalwork. The *Belfast Weekly Telegraph* explained: 'There is no doubt that first estimates of the sum required for the repair of the *Olympic* will be wholly dashed, and instead of £20,000, as originally stated in some quarters, something like eight times that amount will have to be expended.

'The damage sustained above the waterline was severe, but slight as compared with what was subsequently discovered down below, and it is a matter for congratulation that the vessel got back to Southampton.'

The newspaper remarked on the tip of the excess that could be borne by insurers, up to £20,000, making for 'a substantial payment being required from them'. It declared: 'The owners ran the vessel at their own risk to the extent of £150,000, any excess of that sum being covered by insurance, and for some time the underwriters entertained no suspicions that they might be called upon to meet a claim.'

White Star would doubtless endeavour to recover the final probable cost of £170,000 from the Admiralty (owners of the *Hawke*), but 'such a large sum illustrates the tremendous risks which shipowners and underwriters have to face in these days of ocean-going leviathans. On the other hand, had the *Olympic* been of smaller dimensions she would have been lost altogether.'[16]

19

INTERFERENCE BY ISMAY

IRRESISTIBLE TEMPTATION

The *Titanic* forged remorselessly ahead on the weekend days that ought to have formed the middle block of her voyage from Southampton to New York. The digging-out of affected bunker W meant a huge quantity of coal was excavated onto the plates of boiler room 5. Bunker Y, on the far side of the bulkhead, in boiler room 6, was not immune to the commotion. It could not have been left as it was, packed with coal, because of the danger of heat transfer starting sympathetic combustion in that compartment, too.

The coal quarried out of W, at least, could not be left there in the boiler room. Neither could it be transferred to any other bunker or compartment for fear of spreading the fire. It had to be burned. This is what was called for in the standard operating procedure for containing such blazes. There was, naturally, increased speed from burning the coal. The *Titanic* had been gradually accelerating into Saturday 13 April, from 21 to 22 knots, and then to 22.5 knots the following day until 'doing about 23 knots' at time of impact.[1]

Necessity could have become a virtue. If the spontaneous coal fire and an urgency about getting that fuel extracted and expended meant that speed rose sharply over the originally intended rate of progress, then perhaps it could be turned into a public relations coup, especially as the weather had been fine and clear since the start of the Atlantic crossing. Winds were light, visibility good and the sea calm, with swells at a minimum.

It may only gradually have dawned on J. Bruce Ismay that this necessity, and even the light original loading of coal caused by striking miners, could play its part in a maiden voyage sensation. The fire might then turn out to be a 'blazing in disguise'. One all-out push could get the liner into New York the day before she was due, even if it risked living on the scrapings of coal dust by the end. A Tuesday evening arrival would capture the imagination of the American press and its readership, bestowing laurels on the Line that could ensure a steady patronage. He may have thought: let the ship be unleashed and let her run as hard as she likes.

The speed element thus would have shifted from unintentional by-product of accelerated bunker evacuation to the intended end-product of an inaugural crossing.

It was the concept of actively sought haste that would trip up Ismay during the British inquiry, when his inexplicable meetings with Chief Engineer Joseph Bell were once again broached. One of the managing director's cross-examiners in London was Leonard Holmes for the Mercantile Marine Services Association. He started: 'You have told us [that] at the conversation between you and the Chief Engineer, the Captain was not present?'

'He was not.'

'And that you had no conversation with him [Captain Smith] during the voyage about speed?'

'Absolutely none.'

'Then will you tell us how it was he was to become aware of your decision to increase the speed on the Tuesday?'[2]

It will be remembered that Ismay had claimed he and Bell had planned a speed trial for the Monday or Tuesday, even though the *Titanic* was showing an impressive turn of speed long before.

The witness now answered: 'I think the [Chief] Engineer would probably have spoken to him.'[3] But this is an utterly ridiculous answer and traps Ismay in false testimony – Bell had no role in determining speed and was at all times subservient to the captain. He could not have been left indirectly to tell Smith what to do.

Ismay must have squirmed when he was now asked: 'Did you make any arrangement with the Engineer about that?'

He answered simply: 'I did not.'[4]

Holmes drove home his advantage. 'Then as far as you know the Captain was not aware that you were going to make this increase in speed?'

'No.' [Another ludicrous answer.]

'Do you know under whose instructions those extra boilers were put on, on Sunday morning?'

'I do not.'

'Is that a thing the Chief Engineer would be likely to do on his own account?'[5]

The transcript does not allow us to see pauses, nor to hear tone of voice, but Ismay – who claimed to be an ordinary passenger, with no influence over the captain on the navigation of his ship, now had to somehow legitimise the usurpation of the master's function by the chief engineer, a man whose job meant that he was necessarily isolated below decks and could never judge prevailing conditions for prudent speed.

'I should say so,' answered Ismay, thereby undermining his shipping line's hierarchy just as much as if he had improperly influenced Smith. He is caught either way.

The next question may have been asked by Holmes in a charitable tone of voice, but its copper-fastening of Ismay's double bind was devastating. 'At all events, you had no conversation with the Captain about it?'

Ismay replied: 'Absolutely none.'[6]

Yet if he had spoken to the chief engineer about putting on more boilers without the captain's knowledge, then this action amounted to gross interference with Captain E. J. Smith's command of the ship. No master could tolerate such treatment.

Another lawyer, acting for the National Sailors' and Firemen's Union, had already taken Ismay to task. Earlier in that session Thomas Scanlan asked: 'Now, Mr Ismay, I want to ask you this question: What right had you, as an ordinary passenger, to decide the speed the ship was to go at, without consultation with the Captain?'[7]

The commissioner, Lord Mersey, interrupted: 'Well, I can answer that – none; you are asking him something which is quite obvious; he has no right to dictate what the speed is to be.' Yet the presiding judge would not make this finding in his report.

Scanlan suggested Ismay could have acted 'as a super captain', one 'who can say to the Chief Engineer of a ship what speed the ship is to be run'.

The commissioner commented: 'I do not know that he did. You know the Captain is the man who must say all those things.'

Scanlan replied: 'I dare say, My Lord, but I think it is important that this conversation and this decision was not arrived at with regard to the speed of the ship in the presence of the Captain, but was arrived at in a meeting between this gentleman and the Chief Engineer.'

However, Lord Mersey dismissed the dilemma: 'Never mind, we will not argue about it. The question you put to him is answered by me. You take my answer that he had no right at all to do anything of the kind.'

But again there was no such official finding on this issue – and thus no blame attributed.

In the course of his interrogation, Ismay changed his story that only Bell and he had been present for 'the conversation with reference to speeding up'. He now claimed that his secretary, William Henry Harrison, had been in attendance. Harrison had not survived, leaving a widow, Ann, who never remarried.[8] We must assume that Ismay's account was made of malleable material.

The managing director was also asked about the conflicting aims for the United States arrival. 'Who suggested that it was possible for you to arrive in New York on Tuesday?'

'Nobody,' he firmly replied.[9] He had not said it, he expected the bench to believe, but it would be incredible, given the general gossip, if it had not come to his ears, whoever had been saying so.

Yet the increasing speed at which the ship was travelling meant that this belief undoubtedly ran throughout the entire ship. First-class passenger Edith Russell wrote in 1956:

On Sunday, April 14, it was brilliantly sunny, but so intensely cold that it seemed the only sensible thing to do was to stay in bed to keep warm, which I did until 4 p.m. I then went out on deck and noticed a large crowd of men passengers looking down at the water being thrown up from the propellers.

The foam whirled in a great cascade, made blood-red by the rays of a glorious setting sun. I remember commenting to a group of people standing there about this beautiful and awesome waterfall, and then I walked forward in the ship and was never to see any of these people again.

There was much remarking on the intense cold and most of the men said they had heard notices were posted that we were in the icefields. However that did not seem to make very much difference. We were going full speed ahead and would positively arrive in New York on the following Tuesday, as it was intended the ship should make a record trip.

And with this calm sea and perfect weather there was no reason why we should not do so.[10]

There are many accounts from on board of an early arrival being in prospect (the burning of coal from the affected bunker playing its part). Some of these expectations were even attributed to Ismay himself, despite his subsequent protestations and his claim that he had told the now dead chief engineer at Queenstown: 'It is not possible for the ship to arrive in New York on Tuesday, therefore there is no object in pushing her.'

Elizabeth Lines was a fifty-year-old New Yorker who was travelling home in first class on the *Titanic* with her daughter, Mary. She had seen J. Bruce Ismay when he lived in New York, recognised him and confirmed his identify with her table steward. The crewman also confirmed the identity of the white-bearded gentleman wearing a ship's uniform who sat with Ismay at luncheon on the Friday and Saturday – Captain Edward John Smith. On Saturday, the two men, seated close to Mrs Lines, were discussing the day's run since Friday noon, giving a mileage of 546 and a speed of 22 knots. The distance achieved was publicly available information (and frequently wagered upon by passengers). It was being 'talked all over the ship', she told the liability hearings in 1913. 'I had already heard it from the sailors.'

Mrs Lines declared: 'I heard a conversation on Saturday afternoon, the thirteenth of April.' Captain Smith and Ismay had adjourned to the first-class reception room and she was 'very near' at the next table. They would remain in conversation for at least two hours, and she was present throughout. 'At first I did not pay any attention to what they were saying, they were simply talking and I was occupied, and then my attention was arrested by hearing the day's run discussed, which I already knew had been a very good one.

'It was Mr Ismay who did the talking. I heard him give the length of the run, and I heard him say "Well, we did better today than we did yesterday, we will make a better run tomorrow. Things are working smoothly, the machinery is bearing the test, the boilers are working well." They went on discussing it, and then I heard him make the statement: "We will beat the *Olympic* and get into New York on Tuesday."'

She repeated the statement five more times. 'Those words fixed themselves in my mind.' She did not hear Captain Smith say anything, but Ismay was 'very positive, one might almost say dictatorial'. She saw the captain nod his head a few times.

'They seemed to think a little more pressure could be put on the boilers and the speed increased so that the maiden trip of the *Titanic* would exceed the maiden trip of the *Olympic* in speed. Mr Ismay gave the runs made on certain days by the *Olympic* on her maiden voyage and compared them with the runs made by the *Titanic* on the first days [of hers]. I did not hear him defer to Captain Smith at all. His voice sounded very emphatic.'[11]

In cross-examination Mrs Lines revealed that Ismay had brought down his closed fist on the arm of the chair when declaring his aim and ambition.

Both Mrs Lines and her daughter were saved, and there is no obvious ulterior motive for her contradicting Ismay, who was emphatic to the British inquiry that there was no conversation with Captain Smith, 'absolutely none', during the voyage as to speed. Mrs Lines' allegation supports what the White Star marine superintendent in Queenstown was said to have been told by Second Officer Lightoller in the aftermath, that the *Titanic* was attempting to post a record crossing for the White Star Line.

Another first-class passenger, Emily Borie Ryerson, who encountered Ismay the day after Elizabeth Lines, told the same hearings she couldn't remember his exact words but the impression left on her mind was that 'we are going to get in and surprise everybody'. A Tuesday night arrival was mentioned, rather than Wednesday morning, as scheduled. 'I don't know whether he used the word "record," but that was left on my mind.'[12]

* * *

Yet ice warnings, dim flecks of fresh threat to the auspicious prospects for the maiden voyage, were already coming to the bridge on Saturday 13 April, the same day that Mrs Lines heard Ismay and Smith's discussion on increasing the speed. Ismay had not yet seen any such warnings, and there is no indication he was told about them, but there can be no doubt Smith was aware of these.

The final report from the British inquiry chose only to list the ice warnings broadcast on Sunday, the day she struck, yet shipping all over the North Atlantic had for days been encountering ice north of 41 degrees latitude and west of 49 degrees longitude, with warnings entered in wireless ledgers known as PVs. The French liner *Niagara* struck ice on 10 April, dented some plates and sent out a distress call, later cancelled. The Allan liner *Corsican* bumped ice on 12 April and was lightly damaged. In late March the *Romsdal* had discerned a steamer trapped in ice and indicating distress. She could have been the British *Erna* or Norwegian *Kamfjord*, neither of which were ever seen again. They joined the *Mountoswald* and other ships on the missing list that spring.

Not many vessels had wireless, but those that did could broadcast warnings of their chill encounters. Others had to wait until they put into port before notifying the Hydrographic Office of past sightings, and a bewildering array did so, perhaps prompted in part by news of the most devastating loss, that of the *Titanic*, received on arrival.

It is certain the *Titanic* received ice warnings up to the Saturday night, as they were already on the officers' noticeboard and marked on the chart, although none of them were deemed in a position likely to pose a problem. Captain Smith had even been provided with the latest information prior to leaving Southampton, including 'reports of obstruction to navigation' listing the last location of submerged hulks and derelicts.

Some ice messages were likely also missed, however, because the *Titanic*'s wireless chose to break down in mid-voyage, as the sole surviving operator reported. Harold Bride wrote: 'The night before the disaster [senior operator Jack] Phillips and myself had a deal of trouble, owing to the leads from the secondary of the transformer having burnt through inside the casing and made contact with certain iron bolts holding the woodwork and frame together, thereby earthing the power to a great extent.

'After binding these leads with rubber tape, we once more had the apparatus in perfect working order, but not before we had put in nearly six hours' work.'[13]

Even if he had not yet been told of any ice warnings, it seems obvious that Ismay was irrepressible in transferring his 'pushing' impulse to the ship. His senior employees had to balance his desires against navigational considerations. They did their work, of course, hoping for the best in a different way than he did. Some may even have guessed that the die was being cast.

20

GAUGING SPEED, TIME AND DISTANCE

A CANCELLED BOAT DRILL

A strange entry appeared in the shipping columns of *The New York Times* on Monday 15 April. It was the third one down on page eleven, beneath a headline 'By Wireless', listing messages sent to the Marconi station at Sandy Hook, sentinel of the city. The entry read: 'SS *Titanic*, Southampton to New York, 1,284 miles E. at 2.15 am, due 16th, 4 pm. White Star Line.' The sixteenth was Tuesday and 4 p.m. would be exceptionally early to be getting in.

Here was a published statement of intent, although it was overlooked by the later senatorial inquisitors. The time of 2.15 a.m. cannot relate to Monday, the day of the newspaper, because the ship would already have been almost sunk, famously going down at 2.20 a.m. by her own ship's time. It instead reflects time of receipt on early Sunday morning in New York, which would in be the vicinity of 4 a.m. on the *Titanic* in her eastern location. (Other catalogued messages from different ships gave 10 a.m. and 10.30 a.m., proving they were Sunday morning times of local receipt printed in Monday's paper.) These parameters would mean the *Titanic* maintaining a speed of just under 21.5 knots to arrive in New York on Tuesday at 4 p.m.

On the news pages that Monday, however, the same paper was clamouring: 'New Liner *Titanic* Hits Iceberg', with the subhead 'Big *Titanic*'s First Trip – Bringing Many Prominent Americans and Was Due in New York Tomorrow'. The 'tomorrow' was Tuesday, based on the earlier wireless advice to Sandy Hook. By her official schedule, however, the *Titanic* was only due to arrive on Wednesday morning.

Further crucial evidence as to the ship's distance from New York only emerged in 2015, with the auctioning of a *Titanic* dinner menu from the last meal served aboard. It sold for $118,000. The menu was signed by five male first-class passengers, one of whom would be lost a few hours later. A gentleman among the surviving quartet carried off the card in a jacket pocket. In the menu's margin, under the signatures and scrawled addresses of Spencer Silverthorne, George Graham (lost), Edward Calderhead, James McGough and John Flynn, are the words '1160 miles out'. There is no accompanying time to which this relates.

There are contradictions between the apparent morning and evening figures of 1,284 and 1,160 miles to New York respectively, because there is only 124 miles between them. This would be a lapse of only five and a half to six hours at the *Titanic*'s rate of progress, bringing us to somewhere around 8 a.m. rather than 8 p.m. It seems someone was over-confident with the newspaper. What is beyond doubt, however, is that *The New York Times* and menu distance both incontrovertibly relate to Sunday and each is consistent with a Tuesday (after-noon or evening) arrival at the White Star piers on the west side of Manhattan.

Passenger Lawrence Beesley recorded a comment by second-class purser Reginald Barker at Sunday lunch: 'I don't suppose we shall do more than 546 now', referring to the daily run.[1] But two days' run at that rate, to lunchtime on Tuesday, would give 1,092 miles towards her destination.

Clarity comes with consideration of the wreck location, discovered in 1985. The remains lie in 41° 43' N, 49° 56' W, and the distance to New York is just over 1,080 miles when she is put back on the course being travelled before she struck. This would imply, with the testified rate of speed, that the final dinner menu was signed three and a half hours prior to the predicament, or shortly after 8 p.m., in the first-class dining saloon, being passed around the table after the various orders had been given to a waiter.

The *Titanic* was travelling between 22 and 23 knots, most likely the latter, when the berg was finally discerned. A speed of 22.75 knots would have been sufficient on the remaining mileage from the wreck to Manhattan to get her in on Tuesday night, despite all that Mother Nature could throw at her, a term the press would likely have employed in their exultation. But most probably, once the area of danger was behind her, the *Titanic* would have further increased her speed, accelerating for a sustained period on the Monday (and probably again on Tuesday).

Moreover, the *Titanic* had a design advantage that would have aided her efforts to better the *Olympic*'s maiden voyage arrival, although the elder sister had herself arrived since on Tuesday night in New York, the passengers staying aboard to disembark after breakfast. Some American newspapers reporting on the ship's 10 April departure from Southampton included the following final paragraph: 'The *Titanic*, while its engineering principle is the same as that of the *Olympic*, is expected by experts on navigation to make faster time because of a slight difference in the curvature of the propeller blades.'[2]

To newspaper readers at home in England, then, the White Star Line was extolling modesty in progress, but to its American audience, which could hardly care less about a British coal strike, was openly hinting at ambitious speed. The *Titanic* was thus assuredly speeding in order to impress, despite ice warnings.

It helped the Line afterwards that the sole surviving wireless operator, Harold Bride, twice told the British inquiry that he was unable to remember any messages at all before the fateful Sunday. The ones they had received were beyond recall, whether or not they related to ice in the ship's path, and any *Titanic* transmission to Sandy Hook – though it would have been sent in Bride's own night watch – went unmentioned.

The maiden voyager had a powerful wireless set that had astonishingly reached Tenerife in the Canary Islands and Port Said in Egypt while at Belfast – over 1,600 and 2,000 nautical miles respectively.[3] The apparatus was more powerful at night because of atmospheric conditions and it could have projected such 'freak' distances, as Bride termed them. More commonly, however, messages were bounced onward, ship by ship, in leapfrog style.

Operator Bride did manage to recollect that some 250 Marconigrams had been sent during the voyage up to the dread event, but threw no further light on them. Direct contact with Cape Race in Newfoundland (for onward transmission of accumulated passenger messages) was only established on Sunday evening, he insisted.

The New York Times Sandy Hook message is an orphan then, and cannot be linked directly to the *Titanic* (whatever about the White Star Line in New York), bearing in mind Bride's claim the wireless had suffered a fault, even though recent research strongly suggests this happened on Friday night, rather than the Saturday night of Bride's memory. All this being said, however, there is no disputing that the *Titanic* received specific ice warnings on Sunday. The British inquiry catalogued a large number of these warnings, culled from the wireless logs of other ships, because the *Titanic*'s records had gone down. While she may, even then, have missed others similar, these cautions, in normal circumstances, would probably have caused her to slow down from a very rapid rate of steaming, were her guiding spirits on the bridge (and elsewhere) of a mind to be prudent.

However, these alerts did not cause the *Titanic* to moderate her speed, nor to significantly divert from the area of the ice that they clearly foreshadowed. The question arising from this is whether it was sheer bravado that prompted persistence in full steam ahead, or whether on-board problems (as might be caused by a bunker fire, leading to a high rate of fuel depletion and consequent high speed) meant that the *Titanic* simply could not meaningfully respond to these warnings.

What is known for definite is that in the build-up to the collision with the berg Captain Smith cancelled a boat drill that the crew had expected to be held on the Sunday morning. Sailors, stewards, firemen and others were supposed to muster at the boats at 11 a.m. on Sunday and it was standard practice. Such lineups and inspections were performed on the Sabbath when bound outward and homeward in White Star liners, but not on this ship on this particular date – when both would go down in history. The master dropped the muster without explanation, and speculation as to his reason has existed ever since. Perhaps the high speed had a role, yet it is tragic to think how this basic practice could have helped in the emergency that unfolded a few hours later. At least the crew would have been familiar with their lifeboat stations.

'We were to muster on Sunday at 11 o'clock for the fire and boat drill, and it did not come off,' cook John Collins told the US inquiry.[4]

Steward George Crow insisted he had seen two notices, in different places, announcing a Sunday boat muster. 'The fog horn or siren is blown for boat drill. All men proceed to boats. The captain, after the men are in readiness, inspects all men at the boats and sees if all men are present. In some cases he orders boats to be lowered and put back into their sockets if satisfactory at the time. If not, repeat. That is the custom of the American Line.'[5]

There had been no drills at all on the *Titanic* at sea, and as for an explanation for the muster cancellation, Crow could give 'none whatever'. The church service, normally presided over by the captain, would have finished comfortably before the scheduled exercise, Crow added.

Second-class passenger Madeleine Mellinger, aged thirteen on the *Titanic*, told the Canadian Broadcasting Corporation in 1968: 'A strange thing that Sunday morning: Mother and I were coming home from church. We'd gone right down on E deck, and all of a sudden, some doors opened! I didn't even know they were doors; and these gentlemen came through with all their gold braid …

'[Mother] said: "They must be officers," and then somebody said, "That's the Captain!" and that was Captain Smith and his retinue. They were inspecting the airtight compartments.'[6]

Fireman Fred Barrett was asked in London: 'Is it usual on liners to call all hands, including stokers, to muster for boat drill?' He replied: 'About twice a trip – once going to New York, and once coming back.'

'Are firemen called too, on these occasions?'

'Yes.'

'And there was no such practice or no such muster on this voyage?'

'No.'[7] (He also mentioned three further boilers had been lit below at 8 a.m. on Sunday.)

There was no adverse weather, and it hardly seems disinclination on the master's part. Captain Smith had been photographed inspecting long lines of crew mustered beside the boats when in prior command of the *Majestic*. It may be that the boat muster was deemed a distraction from what was now the sole goal of the voyage, posting a smart time and allowing sweated labour no relief from that overriding aim.[8]

* * *

Fireman John Thompson and trimmer William McIntyre were interviewed in a ward as they recovered in St Vincent's Hospital in New York. They told reporters they were finished with White Star and would not re-engage because they had been compelled to work so hard. In an interview in the New York *Evening World* Thompson declared:

From Queenstown out, all the firemen had been talking of the orders we had to fire her up as hard as we possibly could. We were to make as quick a passage as possible, the orders ran, and were to beat all records on our maiden trip. I heard that these orders came from the engineering department, but bless you, we men didn't have time to talk about where those orders came from. We were carrying full pressure. From the time we left Queenstown until the moment of the shock we never ceased to make from 74 to 77 revolutions. During that whole Sunday we had been keeping up the 77.

It is customary on the big liners to give little breathing spells to the men, but there were no such spells on the Titanic. *We never had a chance to let up for a moment when on duty, for Mr Farquharson was always at our heels, telling us to work harder and faster.*

The first three days out, I was in the engine room and then transferred to the stoke room. I watched the gauges, and they were always getting higher, showing that we were increasing our speed all the time.

Whenever anyone from the engine room came in the stokehold, we always asked about the speed. In fact that was the only thing we talked about. Then on Sunday they put on those additional boilers. That doubled our work. They carried 215 pounds of steam all the time. The boilers could not stand any more.[9]

Thompson told another newspaper: 'The work in the stokehold was terrific. It was so hard that some of us decided we didn't want any more of it and not to go back on the *Titanic*. Usually they give a man a chance to get his breath and to smoke a cigarette, but Second Engineer Ferguson [*sic*; Senior Second Engineer Farquharson was mistakenly cited as 'Ferguson' in some reports] was after us all the time and we had no chance to let off work.'[10]

On the Saturday he saw Farquharson 'chalk up on the blackboard the number of revolutions. He made it 77 and that would be about 22 knots. The next day the engineers got two more boilers working [actually three] and the speed was increased. I was told that the ship was making close to 23 knots when she hit.'

The same article also reported: 'Thompson expects to be called to testify before the Senate committee in Washington.' This never transpired.

Instead J. Bruce Ismay announced almost immediately in his US evidence (perhaps reading from prepared remarks): 'I understand it has been stated that the ship was going at full speed. The ship never had been at full speed. The full speed of the ship is 78 revolutions. She works up to 80. So far as I am aware, she never exceeded 75 revolutions. She had not all her boilers on. None of the single-ended boilers were on.'[11]

He thus flatly contradicted Thompson's remarks about 77 revolutions and more. Yet Ismay would abjectly concede two years later: 'I had no knowledge at all as to what was being done below.'[12]

21

THE SINFUL SABBATH

WARNINGS IGNORED

Bunker W was fully evacuated by Saturday evening, its huge tonnage of fuel vanished. But work might still have been going on with bunker Y, of 307-ton capacity, on the far side of bulkhead E, both on the starboard side. Leading hand Fred Barrett, in charge of a squad of firemen, regarded them as the one bunker, which happened to have a bulkhead running through it. 'There is a watertight compartment running right through the centre of the bunker,' he said in London, repeatedly referring to a bulkhead through the middle of the coal bunker, defying the designers' designation as separate bunkers W and Y. To his mind the bunker was 'partly on one side of the watertight bulkhead and partly on the other'.[1] By the time of collision, he testified, 'the bunker was empty', thereby implying that both sides had been evacuated.[2]

Charles Hendrickson, a fireman, said: 'It took us right up to the Saturday to get it out,' and Barrett agreed it took the whole of Saturday.[3] 'The fire was not out much before all the coal was out,' said Hendrickson. He finished the bunker out with three or four other men. Afterwards, 'you could see where the bulkhead had been red hot,' Hendrickson declared, repeating the assertion: 'You could see where it had been red hot; all the paint and everything was off. It was dented a bit.'[4]

Asked if bulkhead E, running through two bunkers, was damaged, he answered: 'Yes, warped.'[5] Barrett confirmed the bulkhead was 'damaged from the bottom'.[6] He explained: 'The bottom of the watertight compartment was dinged aft and the other part was dinged forward.'[7]

Once the fire was out, Chief Engineer Joseph Bell told him: 'Builders' men wanted to inspect that bulkhead.'[8] This meant the guarantee group from Harland & Wolff in Belfast, led by naval architect Thomas Andrews.

It must be remembered that leading hand Barrett was always on duty in boiler room 6, whereas bunker W was located in boiler room 5 – usually nothing to do with him. This strengthens the likelihood that bunker Y, in number 6, was also evacuated of coal because of the threat of fire. Moreover, the builders would have wanted to inspect the bulkhead on both sides, including bunker Y in Barrett's bailiwick. Incredibly, this visit by the builders' men was not further investigated by the British inquiry, which was where it was disclosed.

Yet next comes confirmation that a team came down to carry out a structural inspection. We are lucky to have Barrett's testimony – he was only saved because he made it up on deck. In London he was asked if he had seen any engineers once he gained the open air on the night of crisis. He replied, 'when I went up [topside] I saw one of the builders' men'.[9] He could only have recognised one of the shipyard's guarantee group, who were saloon passengers, if they had previously descended into Barrett's own netherworld to see this warped, damaged, dented and dinged bulkhead for themselves.

It would be unfair to ask firemen whether the effect of the prolonged blaze contributed to the sinking, but they were deliberately put on the spot anyway. They had no technical or metallurgical knowledge, but were jobbing labourers whose livelihoods depended on the willingness of a shipping line to hire their muscle. So it would be both honest and wise on their part not to answer such a question in any meaningful way, no matter what their private opinion. Just as it was a subtle form of intimidation, artfully disguised as frankness, to ask them.

The president of the Wreck Commissioner's Court in London, Lord Mersey, peered down at Fred Barrett from on high and asked: 'Did the fact that there was fire in that bunker in any way conduce to the collision as far as you know? Had it anything to do with it?'[10] Mersey notably said 'collision,' rather than sinking.

Barrett, knowing his station in life, answered, 'I could not say that,' which would be true of the collision, *per se*. Mersey next asked: 'Do you think that the fire had anything to do with this disaster?'

The leading hand, who would tell of a 'wave of green foam' pursuing him as he dashed for an escape ladder in boiler room 5, was judicious in evading the question: 'That would be hard to say, my Lord.'[11]

Trimmer Thomas Patrick Dillon, who remembered working under orders to clear out a bunker affected by fire, was similarly asked: 'Would you call it a serious fire?' He answered that he did not know, but confirmed in his next answer it had taken some time to put out.[12]

Hendrickson, too, was lined up: 'You are not a professional expert, and would not be able to express an opinion as to whether that had any effect on the collision?' He answered a leading question with the words: 'I could not say that.'[13]

It would be absurd to rely on the non-committal answers of lowly firemen to questions attempting to fix them with a responsibility not theirs, and which could cost them dear, as constituting evidence that the fire was not serious, solely because they had not publicly declared its contribution to the catastrophe. These men did not specify their personal beliefs one way or the other, and the evidence indicates they were anxious to skirt the question – without being a willing party to any suppression or dismissive commentary of the type given by White Star director Harold Sanderson. The lawyers for the employers of these firemen, and the employers themselves, were looking on from the well of the court.

Edward Wilding, naval architect with Harland & Wolff, was put into evidence, and was at least qualified to comment. But his attitude was equally as defensive and downplaying as that of Sanderson, although he did make an important admission. Tommy Lewis, representing the British Seafarers' Union, asked Wilding late in the inquiry: 'You remember the evidence with regard to the fire in the bunker?'

'Yes.'[14]

'It was stated by one witness, I think Hendrickson, that the fire caused the bulkhead to be red hot. If that is correct, would that make the bulkhead very brittle?'

Wilding complained: 'What do you mean by "very brittle"? It does not convey anything very definite to me.'

Lewis persisted: 'Well, exceedingly brittle, so that a blow would cause damage much easier than if not brittle?'

Wilding now gave ground: 'It depends on the force of the blow. It would not be brittle like a piece of sheet glass, but it might be more brittle than in an undamaged condition.'

He was asked to confirm that admission, more brittle than in an undamaged condition, and replied: 'It might be a little more – yes, somewhat more.'[15]

The bulkhead (and possibly the ship's side) would have been subjected to temperatures up to 1,000 degrees Celsius, according to Dr Guillermo Rein of Imperial College, London's dedicated science university. He based his conclusion on experiments using spontaneous coal fires over long periods conducted in his lab in the college: 'What the bulkhead does is, the hottest part bulges outward in a convex manner. The computer prediction is that [during a spontaneous fire] two areas to the side of the convex blister actually bulge inwards, in a concave way. There is a bulge out and a part that bulges inwards. You have effectively a wave across the bulkhead, like a corrugation.' So a computer model in 2016 confirms independently what fireman Fred Barrett described in 1912, evidence of which Dr Rein was unaware. Barrett said: 'The bottom of the watertight compartment was dinged aft and the other part was dinged forward.'[16]

On being shown this comment, Dr Rein said: 'That's precisely what we are predicting in the simulation. It means the range of temperatures is also confirmed. Which means that the size of a fire is also confirmed as being in the order of magnitude of 1,000 degrees Celsius. It is confirming the whole story.'

Dr Martin Strangwood, a Birmingham University metallurgist, says the intensity of that temperature – confirmed after the fact by its effect on the bulkhead – would also have affected the molecular structure of the steel and its very integrity: 'The strength will change. How much it can resist cracking will change. At high temperatures it's going to be one quarter of the strength that it has at room temperature. That is why it deformed so much. So if you have a gradual build up of water against it, the load or force against the steel is high enough to cause a crack. And then the brittleness of the steel means that single crack spreads right across in an instantaneous and very catastrophic manner.'[17]

Strangwood's declaration that the deformed bulkhead would have lost three-quarters of its original strength as a result of the fire and its sustained super temperature stands in stark contrast to Wilding's grudging admission that the post-blaze bulkhead would be 'a little' or 'somewhat' more brittle.

Moreover, the by-then weakened bulkhead would have also lost the buttressing fortifications of hundreds of tons of coal on either side, amounting to more than 670 tons at capacity. It is no longer a formidable rampart, but has been reduced to a frail and isolated wall just fifty-six-hundredths of an inch thick. Soon it will have to deal with the shock attack of a torrent of rampaging seawater, backed by hundreds of tons of volume, the total weight of water ominously building by the second.

In the meanwhile the *Titanic* furnaces had been gorged on coal and the ship was streaking for New York, impelled by the drive to empty the combustible caverns 'as soon as possible' to eliminate Second Officer Lightoller's 'potential volcano'.[18]

* * *

The idea that the fire on the *Titanic* fanned the flames of her speed is not a new one. In 2004 Geological Society of America and Ohio State University Professor Robert H. Essenhigh said attempts to control the coal fire on board could have been the reason why the *Titanic* was hurling herself upon an area festooned with icebergs. He summed up the essentials of the argument to *Science Daily*: 'Because of a miners' strike, there wasn't originally enough coal on the ship for sailing at full speed and the original plan was to sail at half-speed and take it easy.' But he also noted the standard method to control and eliminate spontaneous coal fires on steamships was to shovel coal from the bunker into the furnaces more quickly, hence speeding the ship.[19]

The *Titanic* was therefore turbocharged, and the drive from the stokehold unleashed the idea of a publicity push for New York. In effect, the coal fire acted as propellant and accelerant for the latent ambitions of Ismay.

This chain of events did not dawn on the investigating subcommittee of the Senate, however, which has been criticised for its scattergun approach and 'lubberly' questions, implying its members did not know one end of a ship from another. But the stepping stones that had led to a shuddering, juddering disaster were at least perceived in other quarters in 1912.

Even the *Topeka State Journal* in Kansas, a newspaper landlocked in the centre of the continental United States, could make the connection. It reported on 22 April: 'The White Star liner *Titanic* was on fire from the day it sailed from Southampton. Its officers and crew knew it, for they had fought the fire for days. This may explain in part the speed at which the doomed liner was rushing across the Atlantic.' It attributed direct cause to a 'story told for the first time by the survivors of the crew, who were sent back to England on the Red Star liner *Lapland*,' adding it 'was only one of the many thrilling tales of the first and last voyage of the *Titanic*'.

Not only had the newspaper hit the rivet on the head with regards to the likely origin of such speed, but it also neatly encapsulated why the cause of the catastrophe, in all senses, had been overlooked – there were other tales more thrilling.

The senators themselves had fallen victim to a 'need for speed' syndrome, having acted impulsively to get on board the *Carpathia* the night she docked with survivors, arriving in Pennsylvania Station from Washington DC by special train. 'They went into conference immediately with the officers of the Line,' reported the *Sun*.

Earlier that day, the chairman of the investigating panel, William Alden Smith, met hurriedly with President William Howard Taft and Attorney General George Wickersham. Both men wanted a prompt production of answers. Senator Smith said it himself: 'The passengers will of course describe the horrors of that awful night, but the subcommittee is particularly anxious to get the facts of the collision from the surviving officers and crew. They should be able to tell more about the reason for the great loss of life.'[20]

The American inquiry was brief, despite Smith staving off attempts to procure even more succinct proceedings, and it fell into the trap of hearing the horrors and 'facts of the collision', leaping to that point without much consideration of the period prior to acute imperilment. It also wandered down rabbit holes relating to corporate interest and other ships, rather than paying attention to what firemen survivors had plainly said on landfall in New York.

The senators may have been caught up in their own 'rush to judgement', as the British press sniffily said (amid protests of the 'monstrous proceedings of a foreign parliament enquiring into the loss of a British ship on the high seas')[21] and after only eighteen days of hearings, Senator Smith (who had previously crossed the Atlantic with his namesake captain) felt fully equipped to report.[22] In a florid speech to the US Senate he made no mention of the fire but referred to the 'mystery of indifference to danger' on the captain's part.[23] 'With the air literally charged with warning signals and wireless messages, the stokers in the engine room fed their fires with fresh fuel, registering in that dangerous place her fastest speed.'

Overconfidence may have 'dulled the faculties so normally alert', he imaginatively guessed, while noting that 'prizes await the fleetest skipper' and that 'the very presence of the owner and builder unconsciously stimulates endeavour'.[24]

In the end it was all rather uncertain, contradictory, weak and lily-livered. White Star could only have been delighted.

22

FOREWARNINGS OF FATE

BACKED INTO A CORNER

Specific ice warnings received on the Sunday of the cancelled boat muster began with one to Captain Edward Smith at 9 a.m. from the *Caronia*:

Captain, Titanic. *– Westbound steamers report bergs, growlers and field ice in 42° N. from 49° to 51° W., 12th April. Compliments. – Barr.*

Smith acknowledged receipt, no doubt mentally noting that this information about ice was two days old. But its literal and metaphorical drift still threatened his ship and Fourth Officer Joseph Boxhall recalled that the ship's chart was marked as a result.

Sailor Joseph Scarrott, whose sister had called him a bloody fool for engaging on the *Titanic*, had become of sunnier disposition now that they were 'racing along'. He wrote in the *Pier Review* twenty years later: 'For the time of year, the weather is remarkably fine for this part of the Atlantic. The sky is cloudless and the sea as smooth as glass, the only wind being that made by the movement of the ship, but the temperature is rather cold.'

At 1.42 p.m. a wireless message from the *Baltic* was received. It ran as follows:

Captain Smith, Titanic. *– Have had moderate, variable winds and clear, fine weather since leaving. Greek steamer* Athinai *reports passing icebergs and large quantities of field ice today in lat. 41° 51' N., long. 49° 52' W. Last night we spoke German oiltank steamer* Deutschland, *Stettin to Philadelphia, not under control, short of coal, lat. 40° 42' N., long. 55° 11' W. Wishes to be reported to New York and other steamers. Wish you and* Titanic *all success. – Commander.*

Smith again acknowledged. Three minutes later, at 1.45 p.m., a message from the German steamer *Amerika* was sent to the Hydrographic Office in Washington:

Amerika passed two large icebergs in 41° 27' N., 50° 8' W., on the 14th April.

The *Titanic* heard this message, which showed ice to the south of her intended line. It was now abundantly obvious that ice lay across her western course.[1] However, Lord Mersey would later find of this particular message: 'Being a message affecting navigation, it should in ordinary course have been taken to the bridge. So far as can be ascertained, it was never heard of by anyone on board the *Titanic* outside the Marconi room.'[2] This official verdict on the *Amerika* message is terse and restrained, but it does not mean the wireless operators jealously guarded an ice message; it signifies rather that there was no conclusive statement that it had been received on the bridge.

As we already heard from first-class passenger Edith Russell, she found the Sunday so cold that 'it seemed the only sensible thing to do was to stay in bed to keep warm'. She did so until the afternoon. Another first-class passenger, seventeen-year-old Jack Thayer, opined: 'It looked as if we were in for another very pleasant day. I spent most of that day walking the decks with my Mother and Father. We had short chats with many of the other promenaders, among whom I particularly remember J. Bruce Ismay, Thomas Andrews, and Charles M. Hays, President of the Grand Trunk Railway of Canada.'

He added: 'It became noticeably colder as the afternoon wore on. I remember Mr Ismay showing us a wire [Marconi message] regarding the presence of ice and remarking that we would not reach that position until around 9 pm.'[3]

So here is apparent proof that Ismay had received a physical paper copy of an ice warning. That it was the one from the *Baltic*, which also noted that the *Deutschland* had run short of coal, was shown by passengers' evidence. It had been presented to him by no less a figure than Captain Smith, and Ismay was flaunting it.

Mrs Emily Borie Ryerson, whose husband was drowned, later told how 'Mr Ismay, whom I know very slightly, passed me on deck. He showed me, in his brusque manner, a Marconigram, saying, "We have just had news that we are in the icebergs." "Of course, you will slow down," I said. "Oh, no," he replied, "we will put on more boilers and get out of it."'[4]

Ismay vehemently rejected this account. 'I deny absolutely having said to any person that we would increase our speed in order to get out of the ice zone, or any words to that effect.'[5]

While the story was initially told second-hand, Mrs Ryerson personally confirmed it at the liability hearings.[6] It was further corroborated by another first-class passenger, Grace Scott Bowen, who saw Ismay 'come up and speak to Mrs Thayer and Mrs Ryerson, and sit down on the end of a steamer-chair and talk to them for some minutes; he had a white slip of paper in his hand, which he appeared to show to them. He said we were among the icebergs; and some of us said that was why it was so cold (but I don't mean, necessarily, he said so), and that the *Deutschland* had sent a message she was out of coal, [but] we weren't going to bother about that.'

She heard the detail of the discussion reported by Mrs Ryerson soon afterwards. 'I can't remember whether she said because they wanted to make this a record trip, or because they wanted to see how soon we could get in. I should say she said a record trip and didn't want to be delayed. She didn't say Mr Ismay said they were going to start up the boilers in order to go faster, [but] that was the impression.'[7]

Canadian saloon passenger Arthur Peuchen told the Ryerson story immediately on landfall (while Ryerson herself was under medical seclusion), adding: 'The proximity of icebergs was well known to Mr Ismay on Sunday, the day of the accident, but he refused to sacrifice speed for safety.'[8]

Ismay's version of this event in the inquiry evidence started: 'I was on A deck. I was talking to some passengers, and he [Captain Smith] handed me this [*Baltic*] message, and I looked at it casually ... He said nothing at all. He simply handed me the paper and I looked at it and put it in my pocket.'[9]

The managing director did not speak to passengers about it at that time, he maintained. It was the first message the master had given him, but he had 'crossed with Captain Smith before, and he has handed me messages which have been of no importance at all'.[10]

It was 'for information', Ismay declared, as if there were no hint Smith was looking for advice or seeking to issue his own warning by passing it on. Ismay said he was given it at 'ten minutes to one', or eight minutes after it had been received by Marconi and handed to the captain.[11] This was a prompt onward transmission – did it mean Smith had immediately sought out Ismay?

The White Star chief next went to lunch. It was in the afternoon that he 'spoke to Mrs Thayer and Mrs Ryerson', but he could not recollect what he said. 'I think I read part of the message to them about the ice and the derelict – not the derelict, but the steamer that was broken down; short of coal she was.'[12]

Was this, then, Captain Smith's real intention? To convey the dangers of running out of coal? It was the only aspect of the *Baltic* message that distinguished it from any other ice warning. Never enjoying a glut of fuel, the *Titanic* had been expending it to a shocking degree.

Ismay insisted he did not understand from the Marconigram that there was ice across the ship's track. Asked if he attributed any importance to the ice references, he replied: 'I did not; no special importance at all.'[13]

But if it was of no importance, why read it aloud to passengers?

At the limitation of liability hearings, Ismay said: 'I do not think the telegram made very much impression on me with regard to the ice. What I was more impressed about was the steamer being broken down.'[14] But Ismay had previously agreed that the *Baltic* message indicated that quantities of ice and bergs were 'on the track' they were following.[15] It meant they would soon encounter thick floes, but it did not strike him as serious because 'the only thing for the Commander to do would be to take steps to avoid the field ice. Therefore, it did not concern me.'[16]

Ismay always maintained that he did not interfere with the navigation of the ship. Yet perhaps the message meant they were on the horns of a dilemma – without enough fuel for a major detour, but with ice lying in wait if they persisted in high speed.

Hours went by, and if Smith had been expecting guidance or a decision, he was out of luck – he heard nothing from Ismay. The captain eventually requested the return of the message after 7 p.m. and Ismay gave it back. It was now his turn to be wordless in doing so. This back-and-forth exchange of the piece of paper thus brought no practical result, other than to allow Ismay to read an extract to two ladies – not for the purpose of bravado, he would have investigators believe, but merely for their information.

So why didn't the captain slow down as he approached the potential ice? Steamship coal expert Richard de Kerbrech comments: 'Well, if she was to slow down, to increase the speed again you have to open up your boilers and pile on more coal at that time, which would increase your consumption. I think probably the likelihood is they weren't going to slow down, but just crack on, at top speed, through the ice.'[17]

Why not divert? This is what Ismay claimed he wanted: 'steps to avoid the field ice'. However, having reached top speed, at least in part because of the spontaneous coal fire, the *Titanic* likely didn't have the coal reserves to do anything other than maintain her pace, staying on the shortest route for sheer economy. Otherwise beckoned the embarrassing fate of the *Deutschland* – with the ship out of fuel and drifting aimlessly (even if on ice-free seas).

De Kerbrech observes: 'Just consider, she's on her maiden voyage, carrying a gaggle of millionaires who've got arrangements and shares to look at when they get to New York. They weren't to foresee the striking of the iceberg, but they could foresee not arriving in New York because they ran out of coal. And that would be damaging to the prestige and public relations of the White Star Line.'[18]

At 4 p.m. Edith Russell at last surfaced and went out on deck. There she noticed the large crowd looking down at the water being thrown up from the propellers. Top speed was not only being maintained, but momentum was building further.

Dusk drew in; the *Titanic* was plunging southward to 'the corner', the point where she would alter sharply westward – and head directly for iceberg alley. Lord Mersey described what happened next, as darkness descended: 'At 5.50 p.m. the *Titanic*'s course (which had been S 62° W) was changed to bring her on a westerly course for New York. In ordinary circumstances this change should have been made about half an hour earlier, but she seems on this occasion to have continued for about ten miles longer on her southwesterly course before turning, with the result that she found herself, after altering course at 5.50 p.m., about four or five miles south of the customary route.'[19]

Captain Smith, almost assuredly on his own account, made a miniature diversion, virtually the smallest possible. He was giving the ice a safety margin of only 'four or five miles'.

This could be the most significant clue of all, its importance overlooked ever since. Did Captain Smith make his tiny detour not because of 'overconfidence' (why then divert at all?) but rather because it was the calculated maximum of his only available discretion? He was, after all, doubly hamstrung by high speed and whittled coal. Here, potentially, lies the answer to the mystery, signposted by the extreme economy of effort in avoiding the known danger. Smith must have felt he simply didn't have the resources to go a hundred miles down and a hundred miles back before resuming a straight line to New York.

Ismay had left him in a pretty pickle.

23

CONVERSATIONS AND CONTRADICTIONS

DINNER GUEST SMITH

The *Titanic* now turned the corner, the wheel rolling over and being held there, the rudder responsive at its own extreme and the vessel herself sweeping stylishly in a starboard arc, bubbles of phosphorescence in the water beneath. Many missed it as they had begun the extended Edwardian process of dressing for dinner. Fashion buyer Edith Russell knew some of the department store agents aboard, who were returning from scouting missions to the 'continent', and found herself with an embarrassment of choice. 'I was taking with me not only my own wardrobe, but many orders executed for business firms and private clients.'

Even as her train pulled out of the Gare St Lazare for Cherbourg, the dapper Monsieur Laurent, head tailor of Paquin, famous couturier of the Rue de la Paix, had rushed to her compartment window, accompanied by underlings, thrusting in two huge snowy boxes tied with tapes. Irresistible transport and intruding whiteness are the motifs of her story.

On this evening, she prepared as usual: 'I dressed in a white satin evening gown as there was a gala dinner. The men were in their evening clothes and all the ladies in full dress,' she recalled. 'But I wish to say there was no dancing. British ships do not, or did not at that time, permit dancing on the Sabbath. Nor was there excessive drinking … It was a calm, well-behaved group of people. I distinctly remember the lounge, a very beautiful spectacle; everyone sitting in evening clothes, the orchestra playing.'[1]

The *Titanic* was being boosted through the blackness at a rate of at least 22.5 knots, heedless of what was known to lie ahead. The boilers lit in the morning were now feeding into pushing power output. And it would seem the final boilers had also been connected, even if they would not be able to contribute for several hours yet.

Fireman Alfred Shiers finally disclosed what had never been admitted before at the end of October 1913, after he had left the White Star Line, and behind closed doors. His interview and sworn deposition were in preparation for a civil suit in the United States. The twenty-nine-year-old Southampton stoker was examined privately at the Law Courts in London by Thomas Scanlan MP, in the presence of barrister G. G. Phillimore and, crucially, Henry Duke KC, counsel for the White Star Line. Other lawyers and notaries also attended, while Charles Hersee took shorthand stenography. No member of the public was present.

'In the night, on our watch, they were lighted; on the Sunday night,' Shiers plainly declared of three extra main boilers, making a distinction between these and others previously lit on the Sunday morning.[2]

He was asked about it again, for certainty's sake. 'The engineer came through and told us they were connected up at 7 o'clock,' Shiers said firmly. (In contrast, the morning boilers had been yoked to the straining effort at 8 a.m.)

To make the point crystal clear, counsel Thomas Scanlan MP asked a third time: 'Do you know when the three additional boilers that you have spoken of were connected up?' And Shiers could not have been more specific: 'At 7 o'clock in the night.'

The fireman had now spoken of three main and five auxiliary boilers being harnessed, and yet knew nothing of the ship's speed. Mr Duke, for White Star, objected to his being asked whether there was any other purpose for lighting additional boilers than increased speed. 'That is a leading question,' he fumed.

The query was put another way. For what purpose might they be fired and lit? Shiers now banishes all suspicion that his testimony could be that of an ex-employee with a score to settle. He replied: 'I could not answer that question. I do not know', although the reason was surely obvious. He went off duty from boiler room 4 at 8 p.m.

The pulsating pace of this maiden voyage velocity left Captain William Thomas Turner plainly aghast. He was following in the *Titanic*'s wake as master of the *Mauretania*, one of the twin fastest vessels on the North Atlantic, against whom White Star had supposedly chosen not to compete, concentrating instead on comfort and luxury. 'Since I have been master of these ships I have always slowed down when I got in the vicinity of ice or when ice was reported,' Turner testified.[3] Captain Smith's command, on the other hand, was to remorselessly speed up.

In the same circumstance as the *Titanic* Turner would have slashed his speed to 10 knots, he said. White Star's wonder ship was going considerably more than twice as fast.

Turner, generally adjudged to be brusque, was not of a mind to do Captain Smith any favours when he entered evidence, although he freely admitted he did not know the man, or even 'the first thing' about any Olympic-class ship. Asked whether it was prudent to proceed at a speed of 20 knots with ice reported ahead of his vessel on a calm, clear night, Turner refused to close ranks. 'Certainly not,' the seasoned mariner boomed. 'If a couple of hundred, or a thousand miles off, you can go ahead; if it is close, you cannot. It is foolish to do so. We had ice reported on the track when we were a thousand miles from it. We went ahead full speed until we got near to it.' By 'near' he meant fifty miles away, yet Captain Turner in April 1912 also knew he would be in the ice region ahead in clear and precious daylight.

The dangers of ice were known to Atlantic navigators for ages past, he insisted, certainly 'ever since I have been going to sea'. Even the comforting idea that ice was abnormally far south when in the vicinity of 41 degrees latitude in April was a notion unceremoniously punctured by Turner. 'They [icebergs] have been down as far as 39 and 38 [degrees], I think.' In other words, over 225 miles south of where the *Titanic* struck, although Smith allowed himself those four or five miles of grace.

The captain of the *Mauretania* was asked what he would do if not far east of the reported threat, but instead in the vicinity of 50 degrees longitude. Turner recognised the assumed scenario was discarding all possibility of diversion. 'In a case like that you are amongst the ice,' he said. 'Stop your ship or slow her down.'

Would it not be reasonably safe for such a vessel to proceed at 20 knots or upwards in such circumstances? So came a gentle query as he stood in the witness box. Turner goggled. 'Certainly not; 20 knots through ice? My conscience!'

The exclamation mark stands out violently in the transcript. Captain Smith, however, was carrying out his commitment to hold course, wedded to someone's iron will in continuously climbing speed.

'We were steaming along at 22 or 23 knots, not reducing speed at all, in spite of the many warnings of the presence of ice from other ships during the afternoon and evening. We were out for a record run,' summarised passenger Jack Thayer.[4] 'It had become very much colder. It was a brilliant, starry night. There was no moon and I have never seen the stars shine brighter; they appeared to stand right out of the sky, sparkling like cut diamonds.

'I have spent much time on the ocean, yet never seen the sea smoother than that night; it was like a mill pond, and just as innocent looking, as the great ship quietly rippled through.

'I went onto the boat deck – it was deserted and lonely. The wind (our 22 knot progress through the still air) whistled through the stays, and blackish smoke poured out of the three forward funnels. It was the kind of night made one feel glad to be alive.'[5]

At 7.30 p.m. a wireless message had been delivered to the bridge. It was from the *Californian*, describing conditions on the Boston track an hour earlier:

6.30 pm apparent ship's time; lat. 42° 3' N., long. 49° 9' W. Three large bergs five miles to southward of us. Regards. – Lord.

In a later report to the Marconi company, *Titanic* junior operator Harold Bride wrote: 'I took it just as written, namely on a chit of paper … to the officer-on-watch on the bridge. [He] was at the time standing in the wheel house on the port side and had in front of him a little table on which I placed the report, attracting his attention by banging the chit down.'[6]

A fifth ice warning, and arguably the most important, was received in the Marconi room of the *Titanic* at 9.40 p.m.:

From Mesaba *to* Titanic *and all eastbound ships. Ice report[ed] in lat. 42° N. to 41° 25' N., long. 49° to long. 50° 30' W. Saw much heavy pack ice and great number large icebergs. Also field ice. Weather good, clear.*

Lord Mersey, somewhat superfluously, found: 'This message clearly indicated the presence of ice in the immediate vicinity of the *Titanic*.'

He wistfully trusted, however: 'If it had reached the bridge [the message] would perhaps have affected the navigation of the vessel. Unfortunately, it does not appear to have been delivered to the Master or to any of the officers.'[7]

This seems like a qualified attempt to absolve the ship's command on Mersey's part, yet there is nothing at all to indicate that Captain Smith would have undergone an eleventh-hour conversion and turned from the path of perdition. The possibility exists that the message did indeed come to one of his officers' hands, but they were already tied. Whether or no, the content spoke to a 'great number' of 'large' icebergs, both these notions being relative and subjective, making this message just the mealy opinion of a middling cargo vessel.

Senior surviving officer Charles Lightoller later did his best for Captain Smith, painting the picture of a solicitous seafarer. He claimed the master appeared on the bridge during his watch, at about 8.55 p.m. Fourth Officer Joseph Boxhall joined in, saying: 'The first I remember seeing of Captain Smith was somewhere in the vicinity of 9 o'clock, but from 9 o'clock to the time of the collision, Captain Smith was around there the whole of the time.'[8]

Lightoller had a conversation with the captain which lasted 'about 25 minutes or half-an-hour' from Smith's arrival on the bridge at five minutes to nine, he testified in London.[9] Unfortunately the recalled substance of the exchange does not suggest it could possibly have stretched to twenty-five minutes. 'We then commenced to speak about the weather,' Lightoller related.

[Smith] *said, 'There is not much wind.' I said, 'No, it is a flat calm as a matter of fact.' He repeated it; he said, 'A flat calm.' I said, 'Yes, quite flat; there is no wind.' I said something about it was rather a pity the breeze had not kept up whilst we were going through the ice region* [notice how Lightoller did not say 'about to go through']. *Of course, my reason was obvious. He knew I meant* [they would then be able to see] *the water ripples breaking on the base of the berg. ...*

We then discussed the indications of ice. I remember saying, 'In any case there will be a certain amount of reflected light from the bergs.' He said, 'Oh, yes, there will be a certain amount of reflected light.' I said, or he said – blue was said between us – that even though the blue side of the berg was towards us, probably the outline, the white outline would give us sufficient warning, that we should be able to see it at a good distance, and, as far as we could see, we should be able to see it. Of course, it was just with regard to that possibility of the blue side being towards us, and that if it did happen to be turned with the purely blue side towards us, there would still be the white outline.[10]

Lightoller had introduced the idea of a blue-sided or dark berg, one that had calved or cracked, capsized and then shown a face saturated with seawater to an onrushing ship, making it difficult to detect. Even if he hadn't actually raised it with Captain Smith, it was useful conditioning of his listening inquisitors.

Despite this alarming idea of the undetectable berg, Lightoller said the conversation with the master ended with the White Star commodore declaring: 'If it [the situation] becomes at all doubtful let me know at once; I will be just inside [the chart room].'[11]

It was already doubtful.

Lightoller somehow failed to tell the captain his own calculation (to which he separately testified) that they would come up to the reported ice at 9.30 p.m. – a point imminent with the end of the conversation.[12]

That frontier came five to ten minutes after the captain showed a sudden disinclination to discuss matters further, turning his back and walking off, muttering those dubious remarks. Perhaps the 'doubtful' conversation is itself doubtful, as the master's many qualities could not have included bilocation – he was reportedly seen below decks in the same time frame that Lightoller and Boxhall put him vigilant and alert about the bridge.

French-American first-class passenger George Rheims, a wealthy business-man, told the liability hearings he saw Captain Smith with Ismay that night after dinner. 'It must have been 9 or 9.15 [p.m.],' Rheims said. '[They were] taking coffee outside the dining room with a party of people.' He had seen the captain there ten minutes before. Now Smith and Ismay were talking together.[13]

Eloise Hughes Smith, who lost her husband, made a sworn deposition on 20 May 1912 saying a dinner party was 'given by Mr Ismay to the Captain and various other people on board'.[14] She was positive no one was intoxicated when she left at 8.45 p.m., passing through the room where 'people sat and listened to the music and drank coffee and cordials after dinner'.

Imanita Shelley made a similar legal statement: 'Certain first-class passengers had asked if the ship was to be slowed down whilst going through the ice belts and had been told by the captain that, on the contrary, the ship would be speeded through.'[15]

And a third female passenger had made an even more damning affidavit on 11 May. Daisy Minahan, who lost her brother in the sinking, declared:

When we entered there was a party already dining, consisting of perhaps a dozen men and three women. Captain Smith was a guest. Captain Smith was continuously with his party from the time we entered until between 9.25 and 9.45, when he bade the women good night and left. I know this time positively, for at 9.25 my brother suggested going to bed. We waited for one more piece of the orchestra, and it was between 9.25 and 9.45 (the time we departed), that Captain Smith left.

I read testimony before your committee stating that Capt. Smith had talked to an officer on the bridge from 8.45 [sic] to 9.25. This is positively untrue, as he was having coffee with these people during this time. I was seated so close to them that I could hear bits of their conversation.[16]

If Captain Smith was not on the bridge but was entertaining when his ship streaked into an icy obstacle course, then it was grossly irresponsible on his part. If he also personally parroted Ismay's line – that the ship would be speeded through – as alleged by Imanita Shelley, then it destroys Lightoller's assiduous efforts to suggest the captain of the *Titanic* would have taken precautions in any emerging 'doubtful' conditions. Instead he would have colluded in the outrageous risks being undertaken.

24

TO THE EDGE OF THE FIELD

APPOINTMENT WITH ICE

Time moved on, the passengers going about their business. 'About 9.30, having some letters to write, I went up to the drawing room and incidentally chatted with a little lady from Los Angeles,' wrote Edith Russell.[1] Her friend was Virginia Clark, whose husband, Walter, now sauntered amiably along and said he was going to the smoking room to play Bridge. Russell described the wife's tart retort: 'Play all the Bridge you want to,' she said, 'but under no circumstances do I want you to come down and waken me. I want a good night's sleep.'

Walter played Bridge, while the ship's bridge played with him and everyone else on board. His would be the longer sleep, his body unrecovered.[2]

Also in the smoking room a little later was the French-American businessman George Rheims, whose brother-in-law, Joseph Loring, would be also marked lost. The ship's speed was foremost on their minds. 'We were trying to figure the speed of the boat to see what the run would be next day,' he recalled. A venerable steward approached and confided: 'Gentlemen, you might figure on a bigger run!' They asked the reason, and he answered with evident pride: 'Because we are making faster speed than we were yesterday.'

Rheims declared: 'My brother-in-law said, "What do you know about it?" He said: "I got it from the engine room." My brother-in-law said, "That doesn't mean anything." He said, "Gentlemen, come out and see for yourself."'

They went into the passageway and the steward told them: 'You notice the vibration of the boat is much greater tonight than it has ever been.'

Rheims recorded how 'we did notice the vibration, which was very strong that night, and my brother-in-law, whose stateroom was right underneath the passage, said: "I never noticed this vibration before; we are evidently making very good speed."'[3]

They went back inside, and may have contemplated backing the *Titanic* towards a new daily mileage record when it came to the keenly contested betting pool.

* * *

A year after the disaster the Countess of Rothes suddenly froze at a gala dinner, carried instantly back to the horror of that April evening.[4] Her clammy fear was caused by the music where she now dined on land – the Barcarolle from the *Tales of Hoffman*. Number 183 on the White Star playbook was the last piece played after dinner by the *Titanic*'s orchestra on the night of lifeboats. The flashback triggered a trembling fit at her table. She had to sip water and compose herself, using a napkin to dry the unbidden cold sweat that broke out on her brow. Certainly the piece intrudes with chill strings and tentative, mournful cello, before a tingling crescendo breaks into a warmly washing waltz. *Belle nuit, o nuit d'amour, souris à nos ivresses … Beautiful night, o night of love, smile upon our raptures …*

As the melody sweetly played for passengers aboard the *Titanic*, down below, in the fiery depths of the ship, men of glistening backs bent to the shovel and the scrape of coal, slinging great shots into molten mouths that seared the skin as they worked, a ringing soundscape overlaid with bellowing commands and the thunderous falls of tipped barrows. The needles of the pressure gauges shimmered and wavered in the heat, as if leaning as the men did, like metronomes; reaching, lifting and slinging. And somewhere the steady undercurrent of the engines, the *thrum thrum thrum* of the propellers.

At 10 p.m. Lightoller was joined on the bridge by his relief, the new officer of the watch. William McMaster Murdoch, first officer, took a few minutes to adjust his eyes to the pitch dark. Then Lightoller left. As he went about his rounds, it is possible he heard music coming from parts of the ship other than first class. Seaman Scarrott writes: 'The sailors who are not on special duty are at leisure and are having a sing-song in the forecastle, all merry and bright.'[5]

All the way aft, under the stern, there was similar delight in the third-class common room. In a letter home to a friend in the Athlone Pipe Band, Irish passenger Eugene Daly described scenes of jollity. 'We were having a great time of it that evening in steerage. I played the pipes and there was a great deal of dancing and singing.'[6] Another Irishman, Danny Buckley, confirmed in a similar missive: 'We had a great time on the *Titanic*. We got a very good diet and had a very jolly time dancing and singing. We had every type of instrument on board to amuse us.'[7]

Second class sounded the most austere, with only an evening hymn service, accompanied by plangent piano. Second-class passenger Lawrence Beesley was curious to hear many of those present request hymns touching on ocean dangers. 'I noticed the hushed tone with which all sang the hymn "For those in Peril on the Sea",' he recalled, though its proper name is 'Eternal Father, Strong to Save'.[8]

This solemn but deeply satisfying affair was called to an end when it was noticed stewards had been patiently standing at the back a long time, waiting to serve coffee and biscuits. The casual congregation, suitably edified by their self-organised efforts, now broke up and engaged in polite chatter. Beesley eventually made his excuses and went to his bed in D56, the two-berth cabin he had to himself. It was a quarter to eleven. After undressing and climbing into the top berth, he eagerly read his book by the electric light. He was actually reading two, the other borrowed from the ship's library, the page marked by the declaration card offered to passengers that day, another intimation of early arrival: 'Form for non-residents in the United States. Steamship *Titanic*: No. 31444 D.'[9]

But his concentration was not entirely on his text. 'During this time I noticed particularly the increased vibration of the ship, and I assumed that we were going at a higher speed than at any other time since we sailed from Queenstown. Now I am aware that this is an important point, and bears strongly on the question of responsibility for the effects of the collision; but the impression of increased vibration is fixed in my memory so strongly it seems important to record it.

'Two things led me to this conclusion – first, that as I sat on the sofa undressing, with bare feet on the floor, the jar of the vibration came up from the engines below very noticeably; and second, as I sat up in the berth reading, the spring mattress supporting me was vibrating more rapidly than usual: this cradle-like motion was always noticeable as one lay in bed, but that night there was certainly a marked increase.'

The science teacher puzzled it out some more: 'The vibration must have come almost directly up from below, when it is mentioned that the saloon was immediately above the engines, and my cabin next to the saloon. From these

The *Cairnrona* should never have put to sea with a coal bunker fire, declared a 1910 inquiry involving F. C. A. Lyon (*inset*), who later sat on the *Titanic* investigation. (Author's collection; inset: courtesy of Southampton City Archives)

The *Titanic* at Belfast. Affected by a national coal strike, her capacity, conflagration, consumption, course and collision are all inextricably linked. (Courtesy of Steve Raffield)

Captain Edward John Smith of RMS *Titanic*. (Author's collection)

Right: Senior surviving officer Charles Lightoller. (Author's collection)

Below: His widow Sylvia, who told *Titanic* secrets to a granddaughter. (Courtesy of Patrick Stenson)

First officer William McMaster Murdoch (*left*), said to have been alone on the bridge, and Fourth Officer Joseph Boxhall (*right*), who was on duty but claimed to be in his cabin before impact. (Courtesy of *The Sphere* (Murdoch); author's collection)

Titanic fireman Charles Hendrickson testified that the bunker fire began in Belfast. (Taken from the *Daily Sketch*)

Mrs Elizabeth Brown learned of the outbreak and of men working day and night to fight it. (Courtesy of Dorothy Kendle)

Katie Gilnagh, who boarded as a teenager (*left*) at Queenstown and had to cover up because of fumes, a fact she revealed half a century later. (Author's collection)

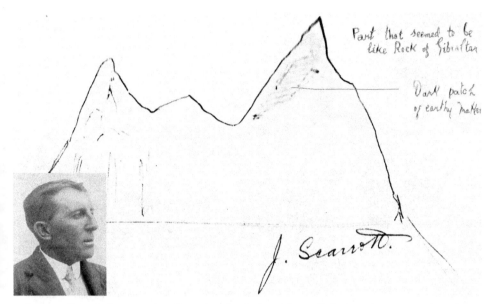

Part that seemed to be like Rock of Gibraltar

Dark patch of earthy matter

J. Scarrott.

Seaman Joseph Scarrott (*inset*), looked back from the well deck and saw an iceberg like the Rock of Gibraltar with its length to starboard. He personally signed a drawing of what he had seen, which was printed in 1912. (Taken from *The Sphere*)

A Gibraltar-like berg photographed in the locality from the Cunard liner *Carmania* prior to the *Titanic*'s collision. The picture appeared in the *Philadelphia Inquirer* confidently headlined 'Iceberg which sank *Titanic*.' (Taken from the *Inquirer*)

New York art professor Lewis Skidmore drew a twin-humped berg on the advice of survivor Jack Thayer aboard the *Carpathia* on 15 April. (Courtesy of the *New York Herald*)

Damage to the *Olympic* in 1911. Her collision with HMS *Hawke* showed she had but a thin single skin. *Inset:* Board of Trade surveyor Maurice Clarke, who cleared the *Titanic* to go to sea. (Author's collection; inset: taken from *The Graphic*)

Graffiti in a transatlantic stokehold. Fireman Joe Mulholland (*inset*) told of slogans on the *Titanic* and trouble in her innards on the delivery trip from Belfast to Southampton. (Author's collection; inset: courtesy of Southampton City Archives)

Francis Browne's photograph of sharp S-turns that conclusively demonstrates the *Titanic*'s responsiveness. (Courtesy of the Society of Jesus, Dublin)

Mrs Henry B. Harris (*left*), who was alarmed by a strange man urging her to get off at Cherbourg if she valued her life; Edith Russell (*centre*) and Chief Engineer Joseph Bell. (Courtesy of the US National Archives (Harris); author's collection (Russell); *Carlisle Journal* (Bell))

White Star Line chief J. Bruce Ismay in a Kaiser-like portrayal. He must have known about the fire. (Taken from the *Illustrated London News*)

Fireman John Coffey deserted the ship in Queenstown because he 'felt sure something was going to happen'. (Courtesy of Southampton City Archives)

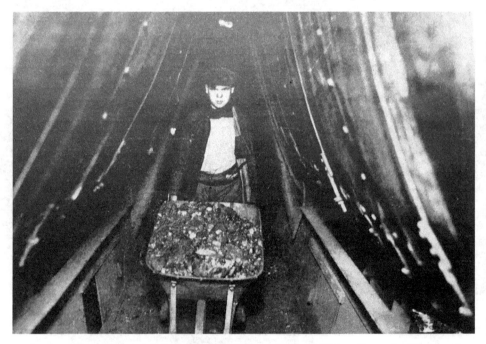

A trimmer wheeling coal in a pass between two boilers. (Taken from the *Illustrated London News*)

Right: White Star marine superintendent at Queenstown Captain James McGiffin was not called in evidence and resigned in 1912. (Courtesy of Maureen Landreth)

His counterpart at Southampton, Benjamin Steel, who was notified of the blaze but kept it secret. (Author's collection)

RMS *Titanic* at Queenstown on Thursday 11 April 1912. (Author's collection)

White Star director Harold Sanderson acknowledged a bunker fire had blazed since Belfast. (Courtesy of Wilton Oldham estate)

Lookout Fred Fleet, who rang warning bells from the crow's nest and was next forced to telephone the bridge. (Courtesy of the Library of Congress, LC-DIG-hec-00939)

Titanic firemen survivors at the Seamen's Institute in New York. Tall Fred Barrett has his hand on John Dilley's shoulder. (Taken from the *New Yorker Staats-Zeitung*)

Bulkheads were surprisingly thin even after the *Titanic*'s sinking. Eight seen in sequence at the building of her sister ship, *Britannic*, in 1914. Watertight doors were to be mounted in the gaps. (Courtesy of *Engineering* magazine)

An experimental tank built at Wallsend-on-Tyne to probe bulkheads after the *Titanic* disaster shows 'the vertical stiffeners and plating bulged outward by the pressure of water, and the angle bar stiffeners bent and showing signs of fracture'. (Courtesy of *The Engineer*, 17 April 1914, p. 426)

Stoker John Dilley insisted that the uncontrolled fire was never extinguished on the *Titanic*. (Courtesy of Southampton City Archives)

John Bigham, Lord Mersey, was brought out of retirement to sit on the *Titanic* inquiry. He later presided over the *Lusitania* and *Empress of Ireland* inquests, both of whose faulty verdicts suited the British establishment. (Author's collection)

Senator William Alden Smith of Michigan, who chaired the US Senate subcommittee hearings into the disaster. He was suspicious of an attempt to rush the *Titanic*'s crew home to Britain. (Courtesy of the Library of Congress, LC-DIG-ggbain-02672)

Right: The *New York World* highlights the uncontrolled outbreak and attempts to ensure the silence of the *Titanic*'s crew. (Front page, Saturday 20 April 1912)

Below: Chief Officer Henry Wilde (*left*) and an extract of a letter written by him from the *Olympic* on 31 March about paying £2 a ton for coal and burning 900 tons a day. He died in the sinking. (Photo from the *Illustrated London News*; extract courtesy of Henry Aldridge & Son)

TITANIC'S SEAMEN CLOSELY GUARDED IN LAPLAND'S HOLD

White Star Officials Place Watch to Keep Interviewers Away From Survivors.

BOATS' CREWS REMAIN.

Many in Tears and Poorly Garbed as They Are Herded Aboard Tug to Depart.

Approximately 160 of the 306 members of the Titanic's crew who survived were sent back to England to-day on the Red Star liner Lapland, which sailed from Pier No. 61 at 10 o'clock. The sailors went as passengers in the steerage. Few of them wore uniforms, the majority having been furnished civilians' clothing by the White Star line officials.

Unusual efforts were made by the Red Star line officials to prevent the Titanic's survivors from talking. The mo-

FIRE IN TITANIC'S COAL HOLD RAGED UNABATED 5 DAYS

Stokers in Relays Unable to Halt Blaze, Ready to Give Up Sunday.

TOLD TO KEEP SECRET.

Stoker Asserts Plan Was to Call Fireboats Here to Drown Out Flames.

The White Star liner Titanic was on fire from the day she sailed from Southampton. Her officers and crew knew it, for they had fought the fire for days.

This story, told for the first time to-day by the survivors of the crew, who were sent back to England on board the Red Star liner Lapland, was only one of the many thrilling tales of the first and last voyage of the Titanic.

The Titanic sailed from Southamp-

I hope this strike will soon be over & get things settled down a bit we are paying £2 a ton for coal for this ship & the 'Titanic' a big price when we burn 900 tons a day

Union leader Tommy Lewis (*left*), who was asked to help raise *Titanic* crew, only to later become a thorn in the side of the British inquiry; so too was Clement Edwards, MP, who frequently clashed with the bench. (Lewis courtesy of University of Birmingham; Edwards from Denbighshire *Free Press*)

Emily Borie Ryerson (US passport photo) told of Ismay predicting a Tuesday night arrival to 'surprise everybody'. (Courtesy of the US National Archives)

Philip Franklin, White Star's principal in New York, who received a flurry of messages from the *Carpathia* issued by Bruce Ismay (in the background). (Courtesy of the Library of Congress, LC-DIG-hec-00937)

Alfred White is a crucial end-time witness to a critical bulkhead failure at 1.40 a.m., hearing the chief engineer cry out in despair. (Courtesy of Doris Dowling)

Captain Turner of the *Mauretania* testified that full speed was utterly unconscionable in a known ice area. (Courtesy of the Library of Congress, LC-DIG-ggbain-19067)

Lookout Archie Jewell (*left*), the British inquiry's first witness, said in a letter written from New York: 'If the watertight doors had worked she would not have went [*sic*] down.' Thomas Whiteley (*right*) said he had a 'foreboding' before the *Titanic* ever left Britain. (Taken from the *Daily Sketch* (Jewell); *New York Herald* (Whiteley))

Steward James Witter and Stewardess Annie Robinson. The former met the ship's carpenter, John Maxwell, who said bulkhead doors were 'not holding', meaning: 'she's going down'. Robinson saw the same man 'bewildered' by the flooding. (Taken from the *Illustrated London News*)

George Cavell told of the *Titanic*'s boilers being pushed beyond their design limits for steam pressure. (Courtesy of Southampton City Archives)

Leading fireman Fred Barrett fled No. 5 boiler room when there was 'a rush of green foam'. (Courtesy of Southampton City Archives)

THE LATE MR. T. GRAY, C.B.,
MARINE DEPARTMENT OF THE BOARD OF TRADE.

Marine artist Norman Wilkinson's image of a steamer encountering a sailing ship dead ahead. Rules devised by Thomas Gray (*inset*) required both to go to starboard, passing on the port side of each other. This stricture applied even in the case of unidentified obstructions and was obeyed by other vessels in the vicinity that awful April night. The rule, usually dependable, sealed the fate of the *Titanic* in 1912.
(Taken from the *Illustrated London News*)

two data, on the assumption greater vibration is an indication of higher speed – and I suppose it must be – then I am sure we were going faster that night than we had done before.'[10]

The vibration of high speed would have been at its worst in the lower reaches of the stern. Third-class passenger Katie Gilnagh wrote: 'Quite a few women were seasick and later some could not get out of bed when the engines stopped because they were so sick. The ship had been going so fast that we could not sleep with the rocking back and forth.'[11]

* * *

J. Bruce Ismay also went to bed around this time in his altogether more salubrious B deck suite with private promenade, having presided over a splendid dinner. They were reaching the area of the ice that night, he knew, and in the morning the passengers would marvel to him at how his vigorous new vessel had knifed contemptuously through.

So much for Ismay's forthcoming Monday or Tuesday speed test (a possible invention of a clever lawyer, explaining the Bell interviews and subtly suggesting moderation throughout). It was now that the *Titanic* raced at her highest rapidity. Thus the test was unnecessary, while Ismay's subsequent testimony that she 'never had been at full speed' was strictly untrue. There had *already been* a speed test! It took place on the delivery voyage, from Belfast to Southampton. Harland & Wolff naval architect Edward Wilding revealed the fact in forgotten or neglected testimony from 1913. Wilding, who had been on board for that leg but got off at Southampton, announced that a speed of 23.25 knots had been achieved that trip. At the liability hearings in New York, two years after the disaster, he described a working Wednesday in the Irish Sea when they pushed her to the limit: 'During April 3rd when running south, we obtained a speed of about 23¼ knots for several hours.'[12]

Wilding was with Thomas Andrews, who made the maiden voyage with the guarantee group, and they would certainly have outlined their success to Ismay at the South Western Hotel in Southampton. It could only have further stoked his alacrity for an impressive first crossing. After all, he now knew what she could do.

This night, however, Ismay dropped off dreamily to sleep beneath a quilted coverlet.

Sailor William Lucas, on the other hand, was in the forecastle crew quarters at the bow. He and his mates were playing the card game 'Nap', or Napoleon – a kind of poor man's Bridge – while other seamen dozed in bunks ranged about the dormitory. Lucas was wearing two of the blue 'White Star' jerseys because of the cold. He was his 'own thermometer'.[13]

Elsewhere, another instrument was at work. Chief Marconi operator Jack Phillips was hunched at his key, transmitting passenger messages to lonely Cape Race, a thin finger of Newfoundland several hundred miles away, just now in range. The blue spark in the transmitting room spat and rasped across the points gap, agitating the invisible 'ether' that rippled out its dot-and-dash reportage, bringing with it boasts to relatives, hotel bookings and staccato requests to be met in Manhattan.

Phillips was irritated when incoming traffic assaulted his ears. It was the Leyland liner *Californian*, eight times smaller and destined for faraway Boston, impudently chattering: 'Say, Old Man, we are stopped and surrounded by ice.'[14]

Phillips angrily jabbed back at the 'jambing' as they called it, from the elegant French for putting your foot in it. 'Shut up, shut up, I am working Cape Race,' he retorted. The chastened *Californian* dutifully clammed. Mollified, the senior man on the larger ship resumed his lordly right of way.[15]

Below deck, the bakers were firing their morning loaves.

Captain Smith was in his chart room, doing whatever unconcerned captains do. 'His responsibility never ends, not even when asleep,' wrote Rufus Wilson of an Atlantic master in 1906. 'Sometimes the dangers which beset him forbid any attempt at sleep, and hour after hour the Captain must stand upon his high bridge, exposed to all manner of storms. Often does a Commander come into port from a perilous voyage, during which for two days and nights he has not left his bridge, except four or five times, only for a few minutes.'

Captain John Alexander Fairfull, of the Allan liner *Tunisian*, reported speaking to the *Titanic* by wireless, sending 'Good luck,' to which came the reply, 'Many thanks; Goodbye.'[16]

The area both ships had entered was treacherous, as proven by the *Tunisian*'s cautious approach: 'When 887 miles east of St John's, [*Tunisian*] entered a huge icefield, through which she carefully picked her way for 24 hours, then stopped all night, eventually turning sixty-two miles south. No fewer than 200 icebergs were seen. The Commander was on the bridge for a thirty-six hour spell.'[17]

Dedicated vigilance was undoubtedly required.

Elsewhere on the maiden voyager, stewards now hovered in the first-class smoking room, waiting to finish up while mentally cursing the diehards. And in the reading and writing room, the ladies' equivalent of the *fumoir*, Edith Russell, late riser, stubbornly continued penning correspondence to fashionable friends.

'I had been writing some time when the library steward called: "Lights out, please, it's 11:30," and I handed him a number of letters, telling him that I did not have my purse with me but I would pay for the stamps the next morning. I took a couple of books from the library to read.'[18] Evidently she was still not tired.

Meanwhile, Mrs Esther Hart, who had been to the second-class hymn service, lay on her bunk, fully dressed and awake, fretting once more.

Quartermaster George Rowe was on the poop deck, pacing up and down to stay warm in the sharp outside air. Quartermaster Alfred Olliver was on the compass platform, high up between the second and third funnels. Second Officer Charles Lightoller had gone to bed. Fourth Officer Joseph Boxhall would say he was just leaving his cabin, although it was his period of duty on watch. First Officer William Murdoch, on the bridge, peered into the impenetrable black.

Robert Hichens, steady at the wheel, occasionally flicked his eyes to the compass, and may have allowed his mind to wander, perhaps to the strange incident of the signal flags at Kinsale. Able seaman Joseph Scarrott, having no special duty, walked the decks and descended into the forward well, sheltered from the worst of the whistling wind. He was now approaching No. 2 hatch; just ahead was the foremast. On that foremast was the crow's nest, and in that metal box, ninety-five feet above the arrowing wedge of the bow, stood the lookouts, Fred Fleet and Reginald Lee.

Scarrott came to the edge of No. 2 hatch and stopped. The air hissed with the rush of passing air. All the way aft, Quartermaster Rowe saw 'whiskers round the light', ephemeral hairs of ice in the atmosphere.[19] It was very still, save for the steady *thrum, thrum* behind.

All the way forward, in front of the blind bridge, a deathly destiny gradually manifested itself beneath stern stars. It grew with ripe expectancy. And in the crow's nest, a gloved hand suddenly shot up – reaching for the frosted rope of a bronze bell.

25

WAS IMPACT INEVITABLE?

TOWARDS AN ASTONISHING ANSWER

We are left with precious little evidence about the collision itself. A select number of people beheld the *Titanic* iceberg, but just a handful prior to collision. Of the actual eyewitnesses to those crucial moments, only a tiny few survived. Helmsman Hichens, for instance, was wholly enclosed and effectively blind, sealed off with Sixth Officer James Paul Moody [lost] in the interior wheelhouse. So although Robert Hichens lived, he never saw the berg.[1]

Those who did see it included the lookouts who made the initial sighting, Fred Fleet and Reginald Lee, but in the later investigations on both sides of the Atlantic they maddeningly proved to be almost pathologically unhelpful. Nobody who was said to be present beforehand in the command centre both saw the approach to the iceberg and was subsequently saved.

Information about the ice-evasion efforts is very scant, and thus our understanding of the coming-together is beggarly. An extraordinary feature of the *Titanic* investigations on both sides of the Atlantic is that they simply did not determine why the vessel struck the iceberg in the first place. The tendency at the 1912 inquiries, and ever since, was to take the crash as a given and to proceed from there. It was a trap the Americans fell into after giving up on the lookouts, and investigators in London largely followed suit.

The US inquiry was outrageously and lamentably frustrated by the studied refusal of the crow's nest men to offer any time and distance when it came to initial detection of the berg. The same inability to assist continued in London, along with shoulder-shrugging attempts to obscure what had happened through excuses such as a 'black' berg, highly localised haze, or freakish weather conditions of the 'once in a century' variety. But impulsion into an iceberg is the reason why 1,500 people died, quite apart from the speed leading up to it.

Years later lookout Fred Fleet drew the berg as being on the horizon at 'first sight'. In his evidence in 1912 he admitted it grew from being 'not very large when I first saw it', 'small' or even 'very small' to being 'a great big mass' on impact. In London he repeated it was 'a small object' when first seen, and even agreed to it being 'a very small object'.[2]

Yet when asked by the commissioner: 'Could you give us some idea what it looked like when it came? Was it a great big mass that passed you or was it a small mass that you could see?'

'Well, a great big mass.'[3]

So what is that transformation in terms of time and distance? It would seem extremely substantial, because the berg has gone from being 'small' to 'a great big mass'.

Fleet agreed at the US inquiry when it was put to him that the berg 'grew in size' between seeing and reporting and the smash. 'It kept getting larger as we were getting nearer it.'[4] This effectively destroys the common but childlike idea that the berg was struck because it was 'seen too late' to avoid (even with added berg darkness). The lookouts were watching it for a long time – too long for there to be insufficient reaction time.

Despite this, Fleet refused to help the inquiries on distance and time elapsed between sight and shock. There can only be one reason for him doing so: because the berg was in fact seen by him at sufficient distance and in plenty of time to be avoided.

In London he was asked: 'Was this a good night for seeing; would you describe it as a clear night, or a night in which it was difficult to see?'

Fleet: 'It was not difficult at all.'[5]

Failure to avoid the berg in such circumstances is, very plainly, negligent navigation. The claim that it was seen too late cannot stand. It thus becomes inescapable that there was some massive failure involving the bridge or wheel-house on the *Titanic*, which went totally unexplained at the inquiries.

So what happened to bring about the ship's destruction?

* * *

Accident investigators will usually trace back the moments before a collision to see what happened, but with the *Titanic* this is naturally more difficult. The waters have closed. All that remains is limited testimony, and it is unlikely that every witness assertion is true evidence, especially when so much was at stake in this tide of human affairs. Lightoller and Ismay in particular had a powerful motive to paint a sanitised version of events, because any finding of negligence could sink the whole line, while there can be little doubt that a small number of key personnel could be prevailed upon to prevaricate, pervert or play down for corporate purposes. So what was sworn in evidence may be trusted by a court but may not be true in all respects.

For the White Star Line, looking to its own survival, it was crucial that testimony show the captain was not on the bridge. Having the *Titanic*'s master off the bridge for the unfolding crisis would materially assist an 'Act of God' defence in subsequent proceedings. In contrast, a commander on the bridge and consciously defying safety and sense in ice at night would wreak severe reputational harm and cause passenger concerns about captains in other White Star ships. It might have been the lesser of two evils to leave a Senate chairman baffled by the 'mystery of [Smith's] indifference to danger', having left the bridge, than to see him actively presiding over reckless navigation. That scenario would also prompt questions as to why he was doing it.

At the subsequent inquiries, wheelsman Hichens (who later intimated that he had secrets to tell) testified that, promptly upon collision, 'the skipper came rushing out of his room'.[6] Plausible and accepted ever since, Hichens was one of only two survivors thought able to state the captain's whereabouts, but neither of these was in a convincing position. Hichens was in an enclosed and dark wheelhouse located behind the bridge, while the other, Fourth Officer Joseph Boxhall, said he was walking to the bridge at the time of the collision and only got there when the damage was done, at which point he saw Smith, the captain having supposedly emerged from his quarters.

A further puzzling aspect is the account of Boxhall, who was on duty and should have been on watch – yet managed to be off the bridge at the exact time of trouble (although 'most of the time I was on the bridge').[7] He was thus also unable to shed light for the inquiries on when the iceberg had arrived in view and how far away it had then been. Saying he was temporarily absent would allow him to escape difficult questions, such as those about steps taken to avoid their doom.

The fourth officer testified that even though it was his watch (in a spell of duty when ice was expected, and with the captain retired for the night), only the first officer and lowly sixth were forward, the latter unseeing, being housed with the helmsman. Both of these officers drowned, however, and were not available to any earthly court.

Boxhall should have been on the bridge. He claimed he was heading there, from the officers' quarters, when the impact occurred. He gave no plausible explanation for his absence in 1912 (and was oddly not interrogated about it), but remarked in a BBC broadcast in 1962 that he had been having 'a cup of tea' in his cabin before getting up to wander back to his post. Yet he would surely, in ordinary course, have had that cup of tea brought to him as he stood watch. This excuse for his absence seems utterly risible. But Boxhall's not being on the bridge might afterwards have been deemed strategically necessary.

Imagine instead that Boxhall had indeed been attending there, and not walking along the deck on the starboard side. His non-walk would then explain problems with his stroll story, such as uncertainty over whether he had seen the iceberg or not (despite his being present to starboard as it passed by at close quarters), and the inherent contradictions within his time frame.[8] There are, in fact, significant anomalies in much of Boxhall's evidence. For instance, he described the berg in America as a 'small black mass, not rising very high out of the water', contrary to passenger and crew accounts of an ice mountain as high as the boat deck.

In fact, ice toppled into the forward well deck, where seaman Joseph Scarrott was standing beside No. 2 hatch. Scores upon scores of people saw it deposited there. But Boxhall insisted the berg was not 'above the [C deck] rail', which was less than thirty feet above the waterline.[9] If this was the case, how could ice get into the well deck? And he himself related in London: 'I took a piece of ice out of a man's hand, about as large as a small basin … I took it from him and walked across the deck to see where he got it. I found just a little ice in the well deck covering a space of about three or four feet from the bulwarks right along the well deck, small stuff.'[10] Small or not – Edith Russell said passengers ran forward, picking up bits of ice and snow 'which lay scattered along the deck … the ice crunching beneath their boots. Someone said: "Why, they are walking on a solid ground of ice"' – it had nonetheless tumbled inboard. By noting this, Boxhall directly contradicts his own claim that the berg was 'very, very low in the water'.[11]

If his estimation of its size is untrue, is the berg's proclaimed blackness also false? Quartermaster Rowe saw the iceberg from aft as 100 feet high and distinctly white. It looked like 'a windjammer with all sails set', he said.[12]

There are other contradictions in Boxhall's account – his walk forward is too brief for all he claimed occurred in its duration. Covering those twenty yards should have taken 13.33 seconds (male adult average walking pace: 1.5 yards per second), yet the clanging lookout bell, long wait until the juddering whack, and then the berg sliding by, all took place within it. Or so he said. Boxhall insisted in America that he had no knowledge they were in the vicinity of ice, but in London said earlier ice warnings 'conveyed to my mind that the ship would shortly be in the region of the ice'.[13] Other inconsistencies could be cited, but it seems that he was adopting a minimalist approach to disclosure (he was suffering from pleurisy in America, which made for sympathetic treatment).

But why are there so many contradictions here? Could the command remnants have agreed to massage the facts after such a traumatic experience? Lightoller appears to admit as much with his 'whitewash' comment and there was certainly plenty of time for conferring on the rescue ship *Carpathia*, which took three days to put back to New York.

Potential proof of such a cabal was shown by passenger Arthur Peuchen when he expressed annoyance at being called before a 'committee' of ex-*Titanic* officers to answer why he had been 'stirring up' fellow survivors.[14] The press reported his complaint on arrival, but in sworn evidence Peuchen's anger had cooled and he claimed 'the second officer [Lightoller] sent for me on board' for an unrelated reason.[15] Yet a committee was clearly in session before one ever sat on land.

Perhaps not everyone was accessible or pliable – or even deemed relevant enough by the controllers to be brought in on their attempts to whitewash. To widen a small circle would be a risk in itself. Thus we can assume that not all hands wielded White Star's brush. And in fact there are tantalising traces of what might really have happened in the moments before the collision.

26

PRESENTATION OF ICE

UNCLEAR BUT IMMINENT DANGER

Does it matter which way a ship should go in order to avoid collision?

In the case of a driver facing an oncoming tractor-trailer or articulated lorry, he or she knows that the length of the vehicle ahead will all be behind its driver. Yet icebergs don't observe the rules of the road. They can present in any form. And if one is encountered in the dark, with only the forepart of an obstruction initially visible, it cannot be assumed the body or load is all to the rear. It may be floating side-on, and if so, how can those on board the ship know to which side deadly length may extend? To the left or right? To port or to starboard?

The lesser-known *Titanic* lookout, Reg Lee, was asked by the attorney general: 'Can you give us any idea of the breadth [of the iceberg]? What did it look like?'

Lee answered: 'It was a dark mass that came through that haze and there was no white appearing until it was just close alongside the ship, and that was just a fringe at the top.'[1]

The lookout had been specifically asked about breadth. But he may genuinely not have known at the time. It was a guessing game, being dark. He could just make out the white fringe.

Both inquiries shrugged away the monumental inconsistency of collision on a clear night with good visibility and a long lead-in. They should have listened to a 'bloody fool', Joseph Scarrott, who gave a much clearer picture of the iceberg in his evidence. This tough-minded able seaman kept his head long after his close encounter at No. 2 hatch. He would single-handedly fight off a rush at lifeboat 14, flailing with the boat's tiller before Fifth Officer Harold Lowe arrived brandishing a Browning pistol to restore order.

Scarrott saw the berg. He testified in London: 'I went and looked over the rail there and I saw an iceberg that I took it we had struck. It would be abaft the beam then – abaft the starboard beam.'[2] He said it was as high as the boat deck, thereby becoming another to contradict Boxhall.[3]

'What was the shape?'

'Well, it struck me at the time that it resembled the Rock of Gibraltar looking at it from Europa Point. It looked very much the same shape as that.'[4]

Lord Mersey asked: 'Like a lion couchant?'

Scarrott agreed. 'As you approach Gibraltar – it seemed that shape. The highest point would be on my right, as it appeared to me.' He was now looking back from the forward well deck; thus the highest point – the lion's head – was nearest the starboard side of the ship. Scarrott helpfully drew a picture of what he saw and signed his name. It is indeed much like the Rock of Gibraltar seen from Europa Point.

But how did it appear to lookouts Fleet and Lee before impact?

Obviously it was the horizontal flip of what Scarrott saw when looking backwards. Therefore when the ship struck, the iceberg's entire length was off to starboard. Scarrott's precise drawing means that, as the ship steamed towards the iceberg, the major peak was ahead, with the length of the berg extending to the right (see picture section).

Which way to go – to port or starboard? It may seem the ship's command would have to gamble, not knowing the extent of the obstruction in front of them. But now comes a truly horrifying fact, not brought up at either inquiry. Standard operating procedure, when faced with an object dead ahead, was to go to starboard. The way to avoid collisions in 1912 was to travel to the right in any emergency, and to do so decisively. Yet doing so in this case would be fatal with the berg drawn by Scarrott, because he demonstrated that its mass extended in that direction.

The international maritime 'Rules of the Road', which sought to take the gamble out of collision avoidance, ordained that everyone in imminent danger of head-on accident must avoid to the right, even if the object ahead could not be identified. If the obstruction proved to be under governed power of human hand, it would make a reciprocal turn. If not, the manoeuvre would still hopefully result in the evasion of a static object. Only if the obstruction had extreme length to the right, would the dangerous situation clearly become much worse instead of being relieved, as became the case with the *Titanic*.

With this chilling realisation, the next question goes to the reliability of

Scarrott's iceberg description and his eyewitness portrait of a 'Rock of Gibraltar' presenting as it did.

In fact, other eyewitness accounts back up his description. American passenger Charles Stengel told of seeing icebergs all around when daylight came the morning after the sinking. He told the US inquiry: 'There was one of them, particularly, that I noticed, a very large one, which looked something like the Rock of Gibraltar; it was high at one point, and another point came up at the other end, about the same shape as the Rock of Gibraltar ... it was an enormous, large iceberg ... I should judge it was 250 feet high at the highest point.'[5]

The day after the *Carpathia* docked with *Titanic* survivors, the *New York Herald* quoted her passenger Fred Beachler: 'The large black iceberg which caused the disaster stood out like the Rock of Gibraltar.' Another *Carpathia* passenger, Alfred Crocker, wrote a letter to the *Cincinnati Enquirer* (dated the very day of the disaster) mentioning 'the immense iceberg standing like the Rock of Gibraltar'. Esther Hart, *Titanic* second-class passenger, told the *Ilford Graphic*: 'Moving slowly and majestically along by itself, *a mile or so in length* [emphasis added], in form like pictures of Gibraltar I have seen, was the monster iceberg, the cause of all our trouble.'[6]

Alfred Shiers, leading hand fireman, was asked in 1913 how he identified in the morning the iceberg *Titanic* hit the night before. He answered: 'By the shape ... like the Rock of Gibraltar.' It was 'the biggest one there', he added, referring to other menaces seen in the morning.

Titanic steward Alfred Theissinger concurred. 'About half a mile away was a massive iceberg. It looked like the Rock of Gibraltar.' But it is what he said next that is arresting: 'It was fully three miles long, and extending out [from] the huge cliff was a section seemingly three to six feet above the water. It was into this that we had run, and this that tore the plates from the bottom.'[7]

Some passengers opined as to width or length. Arthur Peuchen said bergs seen in the morning were 'of a width I should think of 300 feet and 400 feet long'.[8] Imanita Shelley spoke of a large mass 'stretching oh-so-far lengthways', and Edward Dorking of 'a great white spectre ... at least four or five times as large as the *Titanic*'.

Dr James Kemp, *Carpathia* passenger, 'describes the iceberg which sank the *Titanic* as being 400ft. long and 90ft. high'.[9] Artists who happened to be on the

Carpathia, Lewis Skidmore and Colin Cooper, both drew double-hump bergs broadly reminiscent of the Rock.

Better evidence would be a photograph. And it is remarkably the case that someone on the Cunard liner *Carmania* photographed a 'Gibraltar' berg in the right location days ahead of the disaster. Headlined 'Iceberg Which Sank the *Titanic*, Photographed From Deck of *Carmania* Shortly Before Fatal Accident to White Star Liner', the picture appeared in the *Philadelphia Inquirer*.

Captain Daniel Dow said the *Carmania* entered ice at 1.30 p.m. on Thursday 11 April, and at 3 p.m. passed within a quarter-mile of this berg, which he estimated as of forty million tons. There were twenty-five large bergs within a comparatively small area, and the *Carmania* proceeded 'dead slow' in daylight. 'Captain Dow never left the bridge for a second during the hours he was feeling his way through the ice.'[10]

On the face of it, the *Carmania* berg would appear to fulfil Theissinger's profile of the villain, having a shelf extending out from the towering cliff. (Such as would support claims for a parallel 'grounding', i.e. running over a projection or spur, for which there is a degree of oral assertion.) While Dow didn't give a position for it, another captain did. The *New York Tribune* reported: 'What is thought to be the iceberg which sent *Titanic* to the bottom was sighted by the Greek liner *Athinai* eleven hours before the White Star liner crashed into it. Captain John Couloucoundis ... described it as being *half a mile long* [emphasis added] and 150 feet in height.'

'This particular berg,' according to Captain Couloucoundis, 'was the shape of the Rock of Gibraltar. I am sure this is the one the *Titanic* struck, for at noon on Sunday, as my log shows, our position was latitude 41 46 and longitude 49 41. You will observe that our latitude was exactly the same as the *Titanic* when she sent out her cry of distress, and our longitude was almost exactly the same.'[11]

In fact, the position dovetails beautifully when drift is tracked back from the position of the wreck on the seabed today.

* * *

The gloved hand that reached for the cold-stiffened bell-pull in the crow's nest of RMS *Titanic* rang out three distinct clangs on Sunday evening, 14 April. Senator Duncan Fletcher asked the owner of that hand: 'What do three bells mean?'

Lookout Fred Fleet replied: 'Oh, three bells: that means a vessel, or whatever it is, right ahead. It indicates anything right ahead; any object.'[12]

Three bells struck, obstruction dead ahead. One bell for an object to port (left), two bells for starboard (right). But it is Fleet's phrase 'a vessel, or whatever it is', that is most revealing. Time cannot be wasted trying to determine the obstruction's nature, form or identity. It might be an iceberg and it might be a sailing ship, like Quartermaster Rowe's windjammer.

The maritime Rules of the Road, laid down in a pamphlet of 1867 by Thomas Gray, assistant secretary of the marine department of the Board of Trade, ordained that steamships were to pass each other red-to-red. A vessel's red light was on her port side, with green to starboard. Each vessel was required to move to starboard, making an avoidance manoeuvre to the right, in order to pass on the port side of the other. They would show each other their red light, meaning they could not collide.

Sailing ships, however, did not uniformly carry sidelights, which were seen as the accoutrements of the encroaching steam age.[13] Nor did derelicts (floating hulks or wreckage), nor did icebergs. Nonetheless there had to be a rule to ensure the most good. Thus, even when met by an obstruction without light ahead, the safety principle was to alter to starboard in all cases. Never to port.

Right up to the *Titanic*'s time, and for a period afterwards, the wheel was put over to the opposite side of where it was intended the ship should go. Thus 'port your helm' meant to put the wheel over to the left in order to go to starboard (right). Yet witnesses said the command given on the *Titanic* was 'Hard-a-starboard!', meaning the wheel was put to the right, with a sharp ship's turn to port.[14] No doubt *Titanic* moviegoers will recall that they starboarded the helm. 'Hard-a-starboard!' is in the evidence. They supposedly tried to go to port, to the left, but it was too late. The ship still scraped an iceberg that extended a very long way to starboard.

Well, that's what they *said* they did.

But the witness evidence is highly incomplete. Consider Fleet's account, in which he effectively admitted seeing the iceberg a long way off. His crow's nest colleague, Reg Lee, said the berg 'might have been half a mile or more' away when seen. Even at 23 knots, this would have given a minimum of a minute and a half to avoid it, a luxurious margin.[15] Had the *Titanic* chosen straight away to move to port, they would surely have escaped. But they would have been breaking an ingrained rule. It bears repeating that standard operating procedure, when faced with an object dead ahead, was to go to starboard. Not to port.[16]

Thus 'Hard-a-port!' (going to starboard) was the officially laid-down manoeuvre in threatened head-on collisions, as warned about by three strikes of a bell from the crow's nest. A single order of 'Hard-a-starboard!' would have caused collision under the Rules of the Road. There is an object dead ahead; it could be another oncoming vessel. To do opposite to the rule – while the other applied it – would guarantee destruction. If one's vessel happened to survive such foolishness, she would be saddled with blame and compensation for another's damage or sinking, quite apart from guilt and liability over injury or loss of life. The captain or officer who deliberately ordered the opposite move to that laid down in the Rules would have their certificate (operating licence) confiscated and would likely never get it back. The regulation was not open to interpretation – it had to be rigidly applied, even in doubtful cases. Thus, with an object ahead (no matter what it might be), the automatic response must be: 'Hard-a-port!'

Now the trouble in the *Titanic*'s case, as Joseph Scarrott has shown, is that hard-a-port helm presents the ship with an extended ice cliff as it progresses to starboard. In this scenario, by the time it is realised that she is heading at speed for the middle of a wall, the evasion order absolutely must be countermanded if disaster is to be to avoided. The order only then becomes 'Hard-a-starboard!', starboarding the helm (wheel) to send the ship back again in the direction she has come, desperately endeavouring to escape by moving to port.

In this version of events, the *Titanic* does the correct thing, which happens to be a terrible mistake. It is posited that she followed good seamanship, obeyed the stricture and applied standard procedure to avoid head-on collision. It then becomes unfortunate, in these circumstances, that age-old practice was an active menace because of how the berg presented itself.

In a small minority of all cases, the edict exacerbated danger, yet the rule-makers had to pick one way or the other. In the vast majority of instances, this kept everyone safe. But in the egregious case of the *Titanic* it could be claimed to have cost 1,500 lives. It could well be that one bad manoeuvre at high speed halved her reaction time, making the margin too fine for escape.

The ship did not make one evasion manoeuvre, it is hereby asserted. The Rules meant she in fact made two. These swerves were contradictory and finally hopeless. Royal Mail Steamer *Titanic* slalomed to inevitable impalement.

27

HORROR ON THE HIGH SEAS

AN UNSPEAKABLE TRUTH

The rule is applied, only for gradual discovery in the dark that the *Titanic* is now heading for the centre of a rock of frozen water – perhaps 40 million tons of it – and cannot clear the obstacle to starboard because the ice extends too far in that direction. She now has to apply hard opposite rudder – and here is where 'Hard-a-starboard!' finally comes in, turning back to port in a last desperate attempt to avoid her fate.

Lightoller, in one part of his evidence, sums up the uncertainties presented by an object dead ahead that could be an oncoming vessel with the power to wreck one's own: 'In discerning objects at sea … I will give a case in point. If you were coming up on a schooner, you cannot see her distinctly. She shows no light … They may have a light burning, and it may be invisible, being screened by their sail or something like that. That ship may be standing right across your bows, and you may not be able to distinguish immediately which way she is heading, in the dusk or in the dark … you are fairly close to her, and you have to alter your helm, and give the ship you are in plenty of helm in case you should happen to be crossing her bows.'[1]

A white sail or an iceberg fringe – they must be treated just the same, because frequently none can tell the difference. And an iceberg could be like a ship, confirmed Captain Turner of the *Mauretania* at the liability hearings. A berg 'might be … like a steamship in point of fact. You see a vessel loom up like a dark object much the same.'[2]

In this part of the North Atlantic, in almost any other year, that unidentified object is probably a derelict or sailing ship of invisible light. It is statistically unlikely to be an iceberg. The *Titanic* was in an area frequented by schooners, sealers and sail-bearing 'cod-bankers' fishing the Grand Banks. This may inform Quartermaster Rowe's impression of a windjammer, as a sailing ship was more common than an iceberg.

The question as to whether she applied the rule brings us to another shocking fact about the official investigations. It is staggeringly the case that there was no mention of the Rules of the Road at all in the British or US inquiries. And yet Lord Mersey had no fewer than five fully qualified nautical assessors sitting alongside to assist his deliberations in London. Nobody at all asked *Titanic* witnesses why they had apparently chosen 'Hard-a-starboard!' instead of 'Hard-a-port!', thus appearing to break the rule on collision avoidance.

After all, why would the *Titanic* break the rule? That makes no sense and would certainly be worth querying. When the *Californian* faced ice obstruction ahead that very same night, she turned to starboard and ran to a stop.[3] The answer must be that, in reality, the *Titanic* didn't defy regulation. Instead she *followed* the rule, got into trouble, tried to correct the other way and collided. Her surviving senior officers later disguised the true circumstances because a double, contradictory operation is easily argued before a jury to be incompetence or negligence. This would certainly explain a lot of the garbled, duplicitous and dubious evidence given at the inquiries.

Boxhall said he only arrived on the bridge afterwards, adding: 'I fancied seeing this long-lying growler.'[4] 'Long-lying' is the phrase that appears in the transcript, not 'low-lying'. Long-lying would seem to mean the berg's extended width. While the phrase could possibly have been a stenographer's error, it might equally have been a slip pointing to an issue he was trying not to discuss.[5] It also brings to mind the imagery employed by Fred Fleet, who said the berg 'would be as large as those two tables put together, when I saw it first'.[6] By 'two tables put together' (naturally end-to-end rather than one on top of the other), Fleet is arguably speaking as to the width of the obstruction in front of the *Titanic*. An extended wall of ice.

Width is what frustrates the effectiveness of the initial escape manoeuvre in this scenario. It is what causes eventual collision. And after the accident and sinking, what the *Titanic* surviving high command can never admit to is this right/left slalom. Because, in the eyes of the public, this risks a perception of negligent steering. It might seem like bungling to first do one thing and then the opposite. Negligence, or even the perception of incompetence, could mean massive corporate loss. Even if it were explained that following regulations was what had thrown them into peril, leading to an acquittal of responsibility, the shock among the travelling public would be enormous – resulting in a chastening effect on profits, and not just for White Star. Moreover it would mean admitting the fact that accepted seafaring rules led to the deaths of passengers, which could not be conceded by anyone, including the supposedly investigating establishment.[7]

The easiest course of legal navigation, then, is to claim that there was only one avoidance order given – the last one – because one decent evasion attempt, even if unsuccessful, is more acceptable.

A falsified story also explains at a stroke why the lookouts were so obviously angry at having to lie (and thus risk full blame) when they knew they had spotted the berg in plenty of time for it to be avoided, as will be examined further in Chapter 29. The lookouts did not fail in their duty – they reported the object ahead promptly. Instead time was wasted by turning to starboard and then having to turn back to port, just to get back to the starting position. This is one clear example of how precious time was substantially squandered.

Is there any possible corroboration for the ship initially turning the 'wrong' way?

Actually, yes, there is. If the *Titanic* went to starboard initially, it dramatically supports a claim made in recent years by Lightoller's granddaughter, Lady Louise Patten. She was told as a teenager by her granny Sylvia – the *Titanic* officer's widow – that helmsman Hichens had turned the wheel 'the wrong way'. This was portrayed in Patten's book *Good As Gold* as clumsy confusion as to rudder-direction on Hichens' part (he had been in the Royal Navy, where orders were framed in the opposite manner to the merchant service).[8] But if we allow that the *Titanic* followed the collision-avoidance rule, then Hichens initially turned the wheel the *correct* way, in accordance with regulation, albeit the 'wrong way' for what transpired.

The initial bad luck, and the subsequent omissions, may have been Hichens' long-rumoured 'Big Secret', which he occasionally threatened to tell newspapers, and it chimes to a large extent with the book by Lightoller's granddaughter. This additional turn is also a secret Hichens would definitely have known about, being the helmsman involved. However, he never did publicly disclose his alleged inside information.

It should be noted that Hichens did not adopt a self-effacing attitude in lifeboat 6, as might be expected if he had made a shameful individual blunder. He instead took straight to the boat's tiller, steersman once more, and wouldn't give it up. The evidence of others makes clear he was voluble, not chastened, in that lifeboat. Hichens betrayed no sign of recent calamity on his own part. He exhibited no personal guilt whatever. Likely none had attached. Which is not to say an error was not made.

Canadian Major Arthur Peuchen testified to how Hichens and lookout Fleet, both saved in boat 6, discussed which officer was on watch at the time. This speaks to a desire to attribute blame to that man, and indicates that Hichens (who only followed orders) believed inaction or error had indeed occurred. Hichens further enquired about the officer's identity from another lifeboat nearby: 'They had some conversation – the quartermaster [Hichens] was asking them who was on the bridge and they were calling over, and they did not know which officer was on the bridge, and the quartermaster called out to another boat, to the quartermaster or whoever was in charge ...' When asked what Hichens said, Peuchen replied: 'He said, "You know one officer was on duty on the bridge at the time we struck."'[9]

There is no reason for Hichens to do all this querying in a time of utter horror unless something important hangs on the answer, so these were clearly not idle enquiries on his part. From the wheelhouse he could not have seen the officer of the watch who had been shouting commands.

At the US inquiry, Senator Smith said to Hichens: 'I want you to tell the committee, if you can, why you put the ship to starboard, which I believe you said you did, just before the collision with the iceberg?'[10]

Putting the *ship* to starboard would have meant a hard-a-port command. Hichens' response was at once defensive, even if the senator had completely misunderstood what Hichens had previously said ('I heard the telegraph bell ring; also the order "Hard-a-starboard"')[11] and accidentally put his finger on the reality. Hichens ventured: 'I do not quite understand you, sir.' The subsequent clarification allowed him an escape route, promptly taken. The danger had passed.

However, J. Bruce Ismay might have erred significantly elsewhere in revealing the truth. Senator Smith asked him: 'You remember, I think, the statement of the wheelman, Hichens, that the last thing he did before striking the iceberg was to turn his wheel so as to avoid contact directly?'

Ismay replied: 'I think he said he was told "Hard-a-port", and then "Hard-a-starboard", if I remember rightly.'[12]

He was wrong in recalling what Hichens said, but Ismay might just have let the mask fall for a moment. Was this double manoeuvre what really happened just before the collision?

Turn to 24 May and the concluding stages of Fred Fleet's evidence in London. Is this next extract the point where he seriously considers abandoning all pretence and confessing the actual occurrence?

'Was the vessel still turning to port when she struck the berg, can you tell us?'

Fleet pauses, without answer. After a moment, Lord Mersey interrupts: 'Do not say if you cannot?'

Fleet: 'She went to port all right, and the berg hit her on the starboard bow.'[13]

The lookout says she 'went to port all right', but the pause in answering suggests he might have been mightily tempted to add: 'but she went to starboard too'. Fleet's further bitter comments will be explored later.

* * *

There are other reasons, aside from an initial 'hard-a-port' order and its attached starboard movement, whereby the *Titanic*'s precious evasion time could have been frittered away. But first, let us put a nail in the coffin of the common myth that the *Titanic*'s rudder was unresponsive.

It was claimed in London that tests with the *Olympic* showed it took her thirty-seven seconds to turn two points to port (the posture of her sister on scraping the iceberg) at the *Titanic*'s rate of travel. Fully thirty-seven seconds seems a very long time to turn a ship only two points to port. (There are thirty-two points on a compass, meaning eight in a quadrant. Translated to a clock face, it would mean not even reaching five minutes to midnight in altering the bows from straight ahead in the long lead-in to the moment of mangling.) Yet the wheel was supposedly thrown hard-a-starboard to go to port during this test at 25 land miles per hour, with no other manoeuvre or delay. To move so slowly to port is plainly ridiculous.

Fast and slow are, of course, relative terms. 25mph (22.5 knots) is slow when driving a car. But if there is a small object on the horizon ahead, as Fleet described, it implies a huge amount of time in which to perform evasion.

Charles Lightoller makes clear in his book that White Star vessels were promptly responsive, and at high speed especially. As seen earlier, he recalled how Smith easily handled a particularly bad corner in the approach to New York, with the *Majestic* 'heeling over to the helm with only a matter of feet to spare between each end of the ship and the banks'.[14]

This is the ocean liner as sports car. The *Titanic* would have been highly responsive – as demonstrated by the tight S-bend wake shown in Francis Browne's photograph taken from the stern on the Queenstown leg, which indicates some sharp turns.[15] The Jesuit trainee reinforced his view in writing that April: 'As is usual on ships on the first trip, the compasses were being adjusted, so instead of steering a straight course for a time the great ship steamed in "s" shaped curves, answering the helm perfectly.'[16]

It clearly cannot be a problem with the rudder that was the cause of the collision. Instead, it is inescapably the product of either inexplicable delay or horrendous error, or a combination of both.

Importantly, the *Olympic*'s first westbound passage after the *Titanic* disaster, in May 1912, saw tests on her turning. They were described by an anonymous passenger to the *American Marine Engineer* in June. The correspondent cited tight circles, figure of eights and S-shapes drawn by the *Olympic*. 'We all observed the marvellous rapidity with which this prodigious ship turned from side to side, answering to its steering gear like a yacht answering to the tiller.' He added: 'She went through the manoeuvres before Queenstown – to show that she could turn quickly upon her course if ice were seen ahead.'[17] The magazine is describing exactly what Browne saw, and thankfully recorded, with the *Titanic*.

Moreover in May 1918, during the Great War, the *Olympic* saw a submarine come to the surface at night, about half a mile away, at one and a half points on the starboard bow. Captain Bertram Hayes wrote that he altered course in order to ram. The submarine ordered full speed in the opposite direction to the turning giant, trying to escape her closing arc – whereupon Hayes switched the helm hard-over the opposite way to prevent any such thing. He struck and sank the U-boat.[18] This episode abundantly establishes that elder sister *Olympic* was able to perform two sharp manoeuvres in a window of time in which the *Titanic* could supposedly (by official testimony) manage only one.

28

COMMUNICATION ISSUES

THE INTENTION TO MISLEAD

It is striking in the inquiry evidence how frequently the word 'immediately' is used by wheelsman Robert Hichens in describing how orders were given and carried out. This is also one of the favourite adverbs of Second Officer Charles Lightoller, who employs it no fewer than twenty-four times in his memoirs. Lightoller also uses 'immediately' no fewer than seventeen times in his British evidence, to Hichens' eight.

Other witnesses, in most cases, do not utter the word, and those few who do, use it sparingly, once or twice. Hichens' excessive parroting of it might lead one to suspect he was coached by Lightoller in what to say, particularly in relation to wheel action. It would logically follow, then, that he was also told what to leave out.

Hichens conveyed to official questioners that evasive action was taken as soon as the warning was given. But his over-use of 'immediately', particularly in the London inquiry, where it mattered more, might lead one to wonder if the opposite to promptness was in the fact the case.

The eagerness to convey early and decisive action can be seen in Lightoller's reply to a question about whose decision it would be to act in the event of an imminent collision.

Lightoller: 'Our instructions from the White Star do away with the necessity of notifying the Commander in any *immediate* danger; we *immediately* [author's emphasis] act, as I believe Mr Murdoch did.'[1] William Murdoch was the officer of the watch about whom Hichens had been enquiring from one lifeboat to another. It had fallen to First Officer Murdoch to issue evasion orders after the iceberg was first spotted.

Interestingly, Lightoller, who was in his bed at the material time, is somehow able to say with complete conviction that Murdoch acted instantly in acute danger, with no hesitation. But what if there were vacillation on the bridge that fateful night? Could a painfully slow response have added to catastrophe?

The first reason to consider this question is that it was not the job of the bridge to answer to the lookouts, or to automatically follow their warnings. A lookout's job was simply to report 'anything we see', in Fred Fleet's US phrase.[2] Lookout bells were not necessarily sounded as warnings, either – they were merely guidance notes for the officer class. Under the rigid crew structure, officers alone were charged with navigating the ship and had to reach their own conclusions on information from the crow's nest.

Lightoller was more forthright than Fleet, saying about notice of an obstruction: 'He [the lookout] might be able to identify it, but we do not wish him to identify it. All we want him to do is to strike the bells.'[3]

He was emphatic in America about the lowly status of those located high up.

Senator Jonathan Bourne: 'Principal reliance is placed upon the men in the crow's nest?'

Lightoller: 'We place no reliance on them.'

Bourne: 'What are they there for [then]?'

Lightoller: 'They are there to keep a lookout; to assist you.'

Bourne: 'Then why is no reliance placed upon them?'

Lightoller: 'Because, speaking personally, I never rely on a lookout. I keep a lookout myself, and so does every other officer.'[4]

Fleet himself denied that the bells automatically denoted danger: 'It just tells them on the bridge that there is something about.'[5]

In the event of three bells being sounded, it is the officer's duty (not that of the lookout) to identify the obstacle ahead. This could take time.

It is not known where Murdoch was when trying to spot the object ahead, but if he was on the port wing of the bridge then the angle is an obvious reason why he would fail to see an obstruction extending to starboard. Murdoch could then order 'Hard-a-port!' and never know from his vantage point that the obstruction extended that way. The lookouts need not hear any such helm orders, only see their effect.

It is implicit in what Lightoller says – 'All we want him to do is to strike the bells' – that the officers do not want the lookout to phone the bridge with any opinions. Although there was a telephone in the crow's nest, connected to the bridge, it was primarily there for the lookouts to receive telephone calls, rather than make them. But on this particular night a call was instigated from the crow's nest.

When Senator Smith asked Fleet about his initial impressions of the threat posed by the iceberg, he said: 'I wish you would tell [us] whether you apprehended danger when you sounded these signals and telephoned; whether you thought there was danger?'

Fleet answered: 'No, no, sir. That's all we have to do, up in the nest, to ring the bell – and if there is any danger, ring them up on the telephone.'[6]

So here is another potential truth emerging. While Fred Fleet did not telephone the bridge of the *Titanic* as soon as he finished ringing the bell three times, as depicted in dramatic treatments, he did ring them after some lapse of time, when he saw the ship was in danger as a result of the initial order given for evasion.

Fleet specifically said there was no urgent danger when he struck the three bells. This reflects his depiction of the berg as 'small' or 'very small' at first sight. He only concluded subsequently that there was indeed danger. Thus, it seems fair to assume that he only telephoned later, when serious risk arose.

Another lookout, George Hogg, corroborates this crucial point: 'We struck a bell. We never used the phone. Only ... in the case of anything serious.'[7]

So there was a two-stage process. And Fleet, in fear, only telephoned the bridge after a gap of time from his first notification.

Senator Smith: 'The fact you *did* ring them up on the telephone indicated that you thought there was danger?'

Fleet: 'Yes, sir.' [By then.]

Smith: 'You thought there was danger?'

Fleet: 'Well, it was *so close* to us [author emphasis]. That is why I rang them up.'[8]

Smith: 'How large an object when you first saw it?'

Fleet: 'It was not very large when I first saw it.' [Thus it couldn't have been 'so close'.] Then 'she started to go to port while I was at the telephone'.[9]

Had she been going to starboard first? This is arguably another vitally important clue. If the ship only started to go to port when Fleet was telephoning at a middle point between original notification and impact, this suggests the *Titanic* was being navigated in some other way between the three bells and the telephone – whether that be unheedingly straight ahead or else to starboard.

Dispassionate witness Arthur Peuchen supports a two-stage process, with intervening delay, as a result of what Fleet told him in lifeboat 6 that night: 'I was interested when I found he [Fleet] was in the crow's nest and I said, "What occurred?" He said he rang three bells, and then he signalled to the bridge.'

Senator Smith: 'Did he say how far off the iceberg was when he first sighted it?'

Peuchen: 'No, he did not tell me that.'

Smith: 'Did he say what it looked like when he first saw it?'

Peuchen: 'No, he did not go into that. The only thing he said was that he did not get any reply from the bridge. [Hence why he was forced to later telephone] … I heard afterwards [from Lightoller] that the officers were not required to reply.'[10]

'Not getting a reply' could suggest a lack of visible response, i.e. any evasive manoeuvre by the ship; it could also suggest that the wrong choice for the actual situation was made at some point.

In his evidence, Fleet maintained there was no evasive action prior to his telephoning.

Senator Theodore Burton: 'Did you notice how quickly they turned the course of the boat after you sounded the gongs?'

Fleet: 'No, sir. They did not do it until I went to the telephone.'[11]

But when did he go to the telephone? How long was the gap between a no-danger notification and a 'so close' peril that justified his using the phone?

Now it happens that Fleet and Lee at one point contradicted themselves and testified that both were done together, bells and telephone, instantly ('immediately'?), and resulted in a brisk reply. But this is not what Fleet told Peuchen in the lifeboat, nor what Hichens must have known in the lifeboat, and is certainly not in accordance with usual procedure as defined by a trio of Lightoller, lookout Hogg and Fleet himself.

Fleet is exhibiting a classic trait of lying – telling two different stories at once in an incoherent amalgam. The truth is attempting to bubble to the surface, however. Part of him wants to be found out. (The next chapter looks at his burning sense of injustice in the witness stand.)

To sum up, it was not Fleet's job to ring up and tell the bridge there was an iceberg in front. He did his job by warning of an object dead ahead. His further identification of the obstruction would only interfere with an officer's job and hinder it. Fleet was mandated only to use the phone if there was danger. When he does so, the reported phrase he employs – 'Iceberg dead ahead!' – is actually a challenge we can translate as: 'Why have you not chosen the escape route (or why have you not done anything) in response to my warning?'

It is also worth considering that he may have actually rung to warn: 'The ice extends to starboard!'

Such was never said by anyone in testimony, but then no one at all mentioned the rules on collision avoidance either.

Fleet, in London, said he telephoned from the crow's nest, and the first words that he used were: 'Are you there?'[12]

Are you there? It might as well be, 'Are you awake?'

The implied delay, or absence, in his comment is also inherent in what passenger Carrie Chaffee told the *Chicago American* on 22 April, having claimed to have spoken to 'the lookout who was on duty at the time' while on the *Carpathia*.

'He told me he sighted the iceberg in plenty of time,' she said. '"I signalled the bridge … but I received no response. There was no one on the bridge at the time we struck."'

Another first-class passenger, Catherine Crosby, gave an affidavit to the US inquiry, dated 17 May 1912 at Milwaukee, in which she said something remarkably similar: 'It was reported on the *Carpathia* by passengers, whose names I do not recollect, that the lookout who was on duty at the time the *Titanic* struck the iceberg had said: "I know they will blame me for it, because I was on duty, but it was not my fault; I had warned the officers three or four times before striking the iceberg that we were in the vicinity of icebergs, but the officer on the bridge paid no attention to my signals".'[13]

Fleet was witness number fifty-one of ninety-seven in London. Another lookout, Archie Jewell, was the first witness called, but he wasn't on duty at the crucial time. Fleet, still in America, did not arrive home until 11 May, yet even then didn't testify for nearly another fortnight, only appearing on 24 May. Was Fleet resisting? By the time he turned up in the box in London he was extraordinarily truculent. He introduced that new element – his first asking on the telephone 'Are you there?' before reporting the obstruction as an iceberg.

'Are you there?' uttered upon being answered (when they obviously were there) is a trenchant criticism of what they have been doing, or not doing, up to then. It is a sour complaint, not an identification of what lies ahead.

'Did you say anything to them at once, or did they answer you before you told them?'

Fleet: 'I asked them were they there, and they said, Yes.'

'Yes?'

'Then they said, "What do you see?" I said, "Iceberg right ahead." They said, "Thank you."'[14]

But once again Fleet would prove incapable of giving estimates of height, time elapsed or distance away, as he had likewise been unable to do in America. Yet on another matter (the number of women in his lifeboat) he protests fiercely: 'I know what I am talking about.' Of course he knows what he is talking about when it comes to his job as lookout too, having served in that role in previous ships, but it seems he is deliberately not giving the whole picture with the *Titanic*. That must have been a conscious decision.

Was Fleet induced to lie? There are clear grounds to assume he was asked to muddy his own blameless performance on the *Titanic* for the sake of the White Star Line. And in fact he had earlier admitted to being told to withhold evidence when a reporter managed to get aboard RMS *Celtic*, whereon the crew was held after arrival in Manhattan. This was before Fleet gave evidence to anyone. Hardly an excitable newspaper, *The New York Times* ran a long account of its scribe worming his way onto the ship under the headline 'Sealing the Lips of *Titanic*'s Crew', with a sub-deck 'Detained Sailors are Herded on the *Celtic* Under Close Guard of Detectives,' and a strapline: 'Have Orders Not to Talk'.[15]

In this account, Fleet was highly critical of helmsman Robert Hichens, who had been quoted in the *New York World* the day before, but had not said anything contentious. And the *World* had used the same 'sealed lips' analogy, clearly suggesting it was an imposed policy. It reported: 'Save for the surviving fourth officer, Boxhall, whose lips are sealed, Hickens [*sic*] saw Sunday night's tragedy at closer range than any man now living.'

After a brief and anodyne account, the article finished with Hichens remarking: 'I have only told what I know; what I shall tell any marine court that may examine me.'[16]

Yet it got Fleet's goat. He told *The New York Times*: 'When I get me hands on that guy what gave out the story about me – him as was running the wheel, as he said – why, when I get him he'll be lucky to know if his name's Hitchins [*sic*] or Hawkins. He said he saw me in the crow's nest. Now there was a cabin in between, and he saw nothing of me at all, nothing at all, and what's more, he ain't one of us.'

The New York Times report added: 'The language was a little confusing. Fleet explained that Hitchins, the quartermaster, was making his first trip and hadn't been drilled in the sailor's way of "sittin' tight and waitin' for the boss's word." He went on to add that, as for himself, he had been drilled, so when Mr Ismay said not to talk it meant as far as he was concerned there was nothing to be said. After that Fleet sat very silent.'

This is direct reportage that 'Ismay said not to talk'. We know that Fleet, when giving evidence in America, frequently looked at Lightoller, the senior surviving officer, he of the 'whitewash brush'. *The New York Times* later also reported: 'Before [a Senator] had asked Fleet many questions, that British tar turned to one of his officers who sat beside him and growled: "Wot questions they're arskin' me."'[17]

This alleged aside does not appear in the official transcript, but it shows that Fleet and others were conscious that they were giving answers in the close-watching presence of their superiors.

In the meantime, someone had got to Hichens. The New York *Sun* encountered him at the offices of the Women's Relief Commission as he asked for financial help for his wife and two children in England. Three days after the *Times* article, the *Sun* reported: 'Hichens couldn't talk about the disaster.'[18] He had told them so, and in those terms.

A journalist from the *New York Tribune* had meanwhile encountered two or three of the crew after others had gone to Washington by train to give evidence:

At least one of these men deliberately dodged the United States subpoena servers, and confessed it last night. It was not the confession of a man who thought he had done something clever, but of one who did what he had done with reluctance and was glad that he had someone to whom he could unbosom his soul.

'I dodged the subpoena servers,' said this man, one of the quartermasters of the Titanic, *when asked why he had not gone to Washington.*

'Why did you do that?' he was asked.

He merely shook his head to signify that he did not care to say anything more about the matter. Several times since he had arrived here he has steadfastly refused to say a word about the events that preceded and followed the Titanic's *crash into the iceberg.*

'I was told not to give out any information on the Carpathia,*' he said. 'I was told that if I said nothing I would not have any embarrassing questions to answer later.'*[19]

Someone had plainly issued an edict.

29

THE LONG LEAD-IN
TO LOSS

AND THE FRAMING OF FLEET

The question in the previous chapter of a delay by the officer of the watch in reacting to the object ahead will now be looked at in more detail because it goes to the heart of when the *Titanic* acted on information from the crow's nest.

As we have seen, Fourth Officer Joseph Boxhall maintained that he was off the bridge when the incident occurred, while his fellow junior, Sixth Officer James Paul Moody, was with Robert Hichens in the wheelhouse with no view forward – as Fred Fleet had so clearly pointed out to *The New York Times*. The responsibility for corrective action would therefore rest entirely with First Officer William Murdoch, since Boxhall maintained that he, the captain and others were all absent from the bridge at the crucial time. His answer to a question in London – 'Who, besides Mr Murdoch, was keeping the look-out on the bridge?' – resonates to this day because not having Captain Smith and supporters on watch in a known icefield leaves the *Titanic* exposed. Boxhall replied: 'Nobody. Mr Murdoch was keeping the look-out himself.'[1]

The position created by this testimony is that full responsibility for assessing danger fell to one man alone, with no fail-safe. Therefore, if Murdoch's line of sight was blocked (as it would have been if he was on the port bridge wing), or if he were unwell, asleep, distracted, physically elsewhere or had for any reason momentarily neglected his duty, the whole ship was in jeopardy.

Wealthy and intelligent author Helen Churchill Candee, an American in first class, happened to be saved in boat 6 along with helmsman Hichens, look-out Fleet and Canadian passenger Arthur Peuchen. She declared immediately on landfall that Hichens had told her: 'They could not see it (the berg) from the bridge.'[2] But there supposedly never was a 'they' – just a 'he'.

As we have already seen, Peuchen testified that Hichens yelled from their lifeboat to another: 'You know one officer was on duty on the bridge at the time we struck.'[3]

This created an invidious choice for the White Star Line: if only one officer was on the bridge it was a scandalous risk to have taken – compounded by the absence of the master. But if Captain Smith was present, then the risk to the Line's reputation and its future was even more dire through the perception of his presiding over reckless speed in a minefield.

Mrs Candee spoke of the accident itself: 'She said the coxswain of her boat was the quartermaster [Hichens] who had been at the wheel when the iceberg was struck. She saw the great mass of ice the next day, and it stood high over the water perhaps eighty feet and had two pinnacles. But the quartermaster said they could not see it from the bridge.'[4]

The above all implies inaction, or a wrong decision, or both in a terrible compound. It directly contradicts late-on-the-scene Charles Lightoller's anxiety to convey an instant appraisal by First Officer Murdoch. More importantly, the surrounding circumstances would seem to defeat the oft-repeated contention that evasive action had been taken 'immediately'.

Lightoller was asked: 'At what distance ahead do you think you yourself, in the peculiar conditions which prevailed on this Sunday night, could have picked out an iceberg?'

He replied: 'About a mile and a half to two miles.'[5] And that with the naked eye, he added. But this means a time gap from sighting to potential impact of between four and five-and-a-half minutes at 22.5 knots, the testified speed of travel. That's the math, and it is a lot longer than the thirty-seven seconds needed to turn two points to port as recorded in the *Olympic*'s tests. A period from four to five-and-a-half full minutes would represent an epic waste of evasion time.

Is there anything to support so extraordinary a possibility in the actual circumstance? As it happens, yet again there is.

Supportive of a long delay, whether through inaction or the wrong action, is the evidence of Quartermaster Alfred Olliver. He was entering the bridge, having just performed an errand, when the collision occurred. But he had previously been on the compass platform, located amidships.

'When I was doing this bit of [compass] duty I heard three bells rung up in the crow's nest, which I knew was "Something ahead",' Olliver declared. 'So I looked, but did not see anything. I happened to be looking at the lights in the standing compass at the time. That was my duty, to look at the lights in the standing compass, and I was trimming them so they would burn properly. When I heard the report [three bells from the crow's nest], I looked, but could not see anything, and I left that and came and was entering on the bridge just as the shock came.'[6]

There is thus a substantial gap between Olliver's hearing three bells, returning to his trimming task in the compass platform (between the second and third funnels), climbing down the fifteen steps thereof, turning to walk to a roof ladder and take more steps down to the deck, next walking 200 feet forward and entering the bridge to experience the shuddering blow. His journey is more than twice as long as that of Fourth Officer Boxhall, not counting Olliver's substantial descents. One of these two men must simply be lying about the time lapse involved between bells and impact.

Sailor Joseph Scarrott's memory of events also supports a long gap:

'What did you hear?'

'Three bells.'

'Do you know what time?'

'Not to be exact I do not, but it was round about half-past eleven.'[7]

He later added: 'I judge that she struck about twenty minutes to twelve.'[8] The nominal gap is ten minutes! But he moderated this estimate to from five to eight minutes:

'How soon did you feel this [berg] vibration after you heard three strikes on the gong?'

Scarrott: 'As I did not take much notice of the three strikes on the gong, I could hardly recollect the time; but I should think it was – well, we will say about five or eight minutes; it seemed to me about that time.'[9]

Either way, this is a huge time lapse, and lookout Fleet supported Scarrott in this extraordinary contention. He too said he reported the iceberg shortly after seven bells (which meant 11.30 p.m.):

'Well, I reported an iceberg right ahead, a black mass.'

Senator Smith: 'When did you report that?'

Fleet: 'I couldn't tell you the time.'

Smith: 'About what time?'

Fleet: 'Just after seven bells.'[10]

Examined elsewhere on the point, he repeated this conviction. 'I believe it was just after seven bells … It may have been just after.'

Senator Burton: 'Then it was just after half past 11 o'clock that you saw it?'

Fleet: 'Yes, sir.'

Senator Fletcher: 'What do seven bells indicate?'

Fleet: 'Half past 11.'[11]

Fletcher: 'It was just about that time when you gave the warning of the iceberg ahead?'

Fleet: 'Just a little after that.'[12]

It is true that Fleet also claimed not to know what the bells-to-strike gap was, but we can see here that it seems very large. He thus supports Olliver and Scarrott, all testifying independently from, and seeming to contradict, the central cabal that was attempting to control the narrative.

Mysteries remain, but these shafts of clarity illuminate each other. So, to sum up: it does not follow that hitting the berg means the *Titanic* 'saw it too late'. This is an implausible excuse that defies Lightoller's literal clear-sightedness about icebergs in general, given that the collision occurred on a particular night of no moon but glittering starlight, twinned with atmospheric clarity, good visibility and a smooth sea.

Hitting the berg when they actually saw it early in those perfect conditions means not only that they were going too fast, but also that the ship's command must have reacted either too late or so badly that ability to evade an object ahead was somehow hopelessly compromised. This is the only solution that explains the otherwise inexplicable. It also accounts for the lookouts' extraordinary defiance in giving evidence, when they might have been expected to be subdued, abashed or even ashamed had it really been 'seen too late'.

* * *

At the end of Frederick Fleet's late appearance in the witness box of the British inquiry there is quite a remarkable exchange. It may, in fact, have caused Fleet's testimony to be sped to a conclusion: 'Fleet was obviously unhappy in the hands of counsel. Almost reluctantly he told how he saw the iceberg,' reported the *Derry Journal* of 27 May 1912. He gave his answers 'gruffly' and 'curtly'. Later on, 'the man's resentment revealed itself fully'.

Fleet became angered when asked about testimony given by Second Officer Lightoller on a conversation held between him and Fleet on the *Carpathia*. We have seen Fleet's view, mediated through *The New York Times*, that sailorly matters should remain secret (in the case of Hichens' talking publicly), but now he is to hear for the first time that the officer he trusted and obeyed had woven a tale to the investigators that would seem to implicate him (Fleet) in the demise of the *Titanic*.

Sir Robert Finlay, counsel for the White Star Line, stated: 'There is only one other matter. Do you remember any conversation with Mr Lightoller about the lookout and seeing the berg?'[13]

We can imagine Fleet being startled that the officer should have revealed their discussion (or at least one of them) on the rescue ship on the way back to New York.

'Just let me read you what Mr Lightoller said,' purred Finlay, a mellifluent Scot. '"Did you have any talk with Fleet, the lookout man? – (A) On the *Carpathia*? (Q) Yes. (A) Yes. (Q) He has not been called yet, but you might tell us what he said?[14] (A) I asked him what he knew about the accident, and induced him to explain the circumstances. He went on to say he had seen the iceberg so far ahead. I particularly wanted to know how long after he struck the bell the ship's head moved, and he informed me that practically at the same time that he struck the bell he noticed the ship's head moving under the helm ..."'[15]

Sir Robert looked up at Fleet and asked him if that was right? Lightoller had actually constructed a scenario in which his fellow officer, Murdoch, had already seen the obstruction himself and ordered corrective action just as a tardy Fleet was reaching for his bell in the crow's nest. It was an open invitation to the court to find that the humble lookout had reported the iceberg too late. Fleet was likely aghast at the duplicity and betrayal.

Asked if this was a correct account of their private conversation, Fleet to all intents and purposes retaliated by denying this is what they talked about and calling Lightoller a liar: 'Well, I am not going to tell him my business,' he said. 'It is my place in court to say that, not to him.'[16]

Lightoller had made up the story, Fleet effectively contended (not saying that outright is consistent with his wanting to work again in shipping, not just with the White Star Line). But he must have felt double-crossed by his trusted senior officer.

If Fleet sounded angry, the commissioner, Lord Mersey, is next seen trying to soothe him, saying: 'You really do not understand. That gentleman is not trying to get round you at all,' possibly indicating Mr Finlay.

'But some of them are, though,' retorted Fleet, still furious, probably not meaning lawyers alone.

The commissioner: 'I can see you think most of us are, but we are not. We only want to get from you your own story. We want nothing else.'

Finlay tried again: 'You know Mr Lightoller?'

'Certainly I do,' Fleet responded.

'Did you have any conversation with him?'

'Yes.'

At this point the commissioner declared with a degree of finality: 'That is all we want to know.'[17]

The commissioner did not ask for Fleet's own version of the conversation and nor did Sir Robert. The lookout's bare confirmation of a conversation with Lightoller was taken as practically an endorsement of the officer's evidence.

It must have dawned on the lookout what was afoot, particularly given his own powerless place in the class hierarchy. Now counsel William Dawson Harbinson laboured to his feet, Finlay having promptly sat down. The new lawyer attempted to wander back to other matters: 'Did I understand rightly that when you left [in a lifeboat] there were some women left behind on the boat deck?' he asked.[18]

The transcript shows this: '[No Answer.]'

Fleet is likely quietly boiling with justifiable rage. This is how the record next reads: 'The Witness: (After a pause) "Is there any more likes to have a go at me?"'

He knows he is being fitted up as a patsy. Passenger Catherine Crosby had quoted the lookout on *Carpathia*: 'I know they will blame me for it ... but it was not my fault.' 'They' are now mounting an attack, those predicted powers and forces, even though he did his full duty throughout, and furthermore had played his part in dovetailing his own story to cover failures elsewhere that were not of his making.

There was a 'double cross' – the ship's movement towards, and then diametrically away from, the iceberg. Fleet has loyally helped to disguise the fact. But now he himself is being double-crossed.

Fleet was twenty-four years old at the time and illegitimate by the standards of the day, abandoned by a mother who went to America. Having grown up in orphanages in Liverpool, he was ill-educated but making a hard and honest living at sea. He would leave the White Star Line in August 1912 (the same month as the White Star Line's marine superintendent at Queenstown) and never again work for it as long as he lived.

After Fleet's outburst, Lord Mersey glanced around the courtroom and attempted to restore equilibrium: 'Well, I rather sympathise with him. Do you want to ask him anything more?'

The Attorney General of the United Kingdom, Sir Rufus Isaacs, replies: 'Oh, no.' The witness then declares tartly: 'A good job, too.' Presumably the corpulent William Harbinson just looks stranded and helpless, because the stenographer records nothing from his mouth.

The commissioner turns pleasantly to Fleet, 'smoothing his ruffled feelings', and encourages him to step down (and shut up).[19] He says: 'I am much obliged to you. I think you have given your evidence very well, although you seem to distrust us all.'

No wonder.

30

INDIVIDUAL EFFECTS

TRIMMERS AND FIREMEN FIRST!

White Star Line managing director J. Bruce Ismay controversially escaped the sinking ship in collapsible C, one of the last lifeboats to leave, abandoning not only ship but trusted employees like the captain and chief engineer, and many of his company's customers – women and children among them.

Ismay did his best to help prior to his escape; in fact, he had rushed onto the bridge straight after the accident, though whether this was any place for an 'ordinary passenger' is highly doubtful. But then we already know that he was the one responsible for the ship's needless speed. His time on the bridge, post-collision, equipped Ismay with information as to the seriousness of the event that was not available to some officers who leapt from their bunks and were instantly delegated lifeboat duty. But those officers naturally had their own inklings regarding Ismay's insidious influence on the ship's speed throughout. There is testimony that the White Star Line managing director was still urging haste even after the crash – but now with regard to loading the lifeboats. 'There is no time to lose!' he yelled at Third Officer Bert Pitman, who 'did not take any notice'.[1] Ismay repeated such frantic injunctions ('Lower away, lower away!') with Fifth Officer Harold Lowe, and later demanded to know why Fourth Officer Joseph Boxhall had not begun to fill lifeboat 2.[2]

There might have been more than meets the eye behind these officers not taking 'any notice' of Ismay that night, if they felt convinced the owner's obsession with swiftness had helped bring about this horrid situation in the first place. Lowe even snapped at Ismay as he urged quicker lowering: 'You will have me drown the whole lot of them!'[3] And Boxhall responded to him with acid restraint: 'I await the Commander's orders.'[4]

Second Officer Charles Lightoller claimed in evidence that one of those in authority, Chief Officer Henry Wilde, had shown the imperious owner kindness that night by putting Ismay into a lifeboat after telling him there were no more women on board.[5] Wilde lost his life and was not in a position to confirm this story, but Quartermaster George Rowe, also saved in C, gave evidence of Ismay and another male passenger climbing aboard at the last moment, and declared that he had not heard any instruction for them to do so.[6] If Wilde had spoken, he would have known it, he insisted. Lightoller, of course, was not there; and when asked, proved unable to recall the original source of his information.

Some were grateful to the company chief for his conduct, however. Fashion buyer Edith Russell credited Ismay with saving her by demanding she get into a boat. 'I was wearing a sheath dress, a very narrow skirt, long fur coat, woollen cap, some furs, evening slippers and one thing and another,' she told the BBC in 1956, adding she 'looked at that very high rail, with the lifeboat swinging way out in its davits, and knew I could never make it, not in that skirt.' Ismay had two sailors eventually pick her up and pitch her in. She lamented the diamond buckle that fell off one of her slippers and which may lie muddied in the debris field today.[7]

One thing is clear, however: once Ismay was at an oar, his escape craft inching from the *Titanic* in her throes, he did not look back.

* * *

Elsewhere, amid the chaos, Sailor Joseph Scarrott single-handedly fought off a rush of men at lifeboat 14, using 'a bit of persuasion' – a tiller – before armed Fifth Officer Lowe arrived and soon after began firing.[8] They put off with a full complement of women and children.

Lightoller did not leave the ship, but, as he told the US inquiry, the ship left him. Immersed in the finish after behaving with exemplary coolness and bravery, he managed to swim to an overturned and awash collapsible lifeboat, effectively a raft. The others that he found there he largely kept alive until daylight, when another boat (No. 12) finally took them off.

Science teacher Lawrence Beesley was fortunate indeed to leave early in proceedings, especially as his fellow second-class males died in large numbers. The highly observant gentleman wrote that his lifeboat (No. 13) entered the water that Monday morning at 12.45 a.m. Also in his boat was leading hand fireman Fred Barrett, who had been in charge of fighting the nasty bunker fire. Other stokers were there too, indicating they knew the ship would sink, unlike the passengers. Beesley wrote: 'It has been said frequently that the officers and crew felt assured she would remain afloat, even after they knew the extent of the damage. Some of them may have done so, and perhaps, from their scientific knowledge of her construction, with more reason than those who said she would sink, but at any rate the stokers in our boat had no such illusion.'[9]

He referred to Barrett (not by name, but identifiably) and his stokehold mates: 'It seems this particular knot of stokers must have known almost as soon as anyone of the extent of injury.'[10]

Indeed, while Beesley was writing of passenger unconcern and curiosity in the early stages, many firemen were getting topside as soon as possible, some with visible injuries. 'That the stokers of the *Titanic* were the first to realise the seriousness of the accident and came rushing pellmell to the upper decks for safety was the story related by one of the survivors to John R. Joyce, a passenger aboard the *Carpathia*,' reported the New York *Evening World* on 19 April. '"Soon after the crash," said Mr Joyce, "I was told that about a dozen stokers came scrambling to the upper decks. They were whispering excitedly and edging their way cautiously toward one of the lifeboats."'

Wealthy passenger Helen Churchill Candee wrote of the firemen: 'That black crew huddled together, awaiting the order to man the lifeboats. They knew, these hard-faced toilers, that only little boats could save from death at sea.'[11]

Henry Sleeper Harper told his family-owned imprint: 'Four or five stokers … jumped' into his early lifeboat. 'The sailor in charge said: "I suppose I ought to go get my gun and stop this." But he did not go and get any gun, and neither did he order the stokers out … I stepped in and sat down among the stokers. There was no one in sight on the decks.'[12]

Matters developed quickly. Arthur Peuchen gave eyewitness evidence to the Senate inquiry: 'When I came on deck first, there were about 100 stokers came up with their dunnage bags. They seemed to crowd this whole deck in front of the boats.

'One of the officers, I don't know which, but a very powerful one, came along and drove these men right off that deck … he drove them, every man, like a lot of sheep. I don't know where they went, but it was a splendid act.'[13]

Fireman John Thompson admitted that he and coal passer William McIntyre tried to get to the boats 'but were driven back by First Officer Murdoch', who 'had the whole crowd under his thumb all the time'.[14]

The stokers undoubtedly knew more than the passengers at this point. Joyce said officers assured all aboard the *Titanic* that there was no immediate danger. 'There was a feeling among the passengers that they were being misled,' he recorded.

While William Taylor said his fellow firemen 'never see a boat in Southampton', and their studied refusal to drill has been examined, now, in the early part of the crisis, this category of worker was eagerly on the boat deck, unlike passengers or cooks, stewards, plate-washers or pantrymen.[15] Taylor said another fireman (Frank Dymond) commanded his lifeboat, commenting: 'I know of seventy-three firemen saved.' In his lifeboat, No. 15, there were 'about six firemen'.[16]

He was asked: 'How do you account for the fact that so many [firemen] were saved?'

Taylor responded: 'I could not tell you, sir.' But he added: 'We were all going up, what there was of us.'[17]

He acknowledged that dining room stewards, bedroom stewards, 'engine men' and carpenters, indeed every man among the crew (including stewardesses and other women) had their own assignments. Among the other crew, Taylor said, 'a majority of them did not realise she would sink'. The feeling among seamen, he agreed, was still that she was an unsinkable ship.

A group of firemen effectively commandeered lifeboat 3, one of the earliest away. A bunch of stokers jumped in before she launched, without official approval. Second-class pantryman Wilfred Seward testified there were 'about ten firemen' in this boat, along with four sailors and the remainder passengers.[18]

Sailor George Moore confessed the officer present had not permitted firemen to get in: 'No, sir; he never told them. He got all the women and children in, and the men started to jump in; and when we thought we had a boat full there, we lowered away.'[19]

Mrs Frederick Spedden told author Archibald Gracie that No. 3 included 'ten or twelve stokers in the bow with us who exercised complete control over our coxswain (boat commander)'.[20] Passenger Phillip Mock agreed: 'Some stokers ... had pushed their way into boat No. 3 or No. 5.'[21]

Elsewhere, the firemen faced opposition. Irish steerage passenger Daniel Buckley was at another lifeboat when 'a big crowd of men', who were 'passengers and sailors and firemen, mixed', suddenly 'all jumped in'.[22] In response, 'officers drew their revolvers, and fired shots over our heads, and then the men got out,' but someone threw a shawl over him and he was overlooked.

Buckley later heard an interesting opinion on the sinking. 'One of the firemen that was working on the *Titanic* told me when I got on board the *Carpathia* he did not think it was any iceberg; that it was only they wanted to make a record, and they ran too much steam and the boilers bursted. That is what he said,' testified Buckley.[23]

That fireman's complete exoneration of the iceberg is ridiculous, of course, but there is a germ of truth to his tale, which goes to show two kinds of anxiety prior to the sinking: eagerness from the higher-ups to strive for output, and concern on the part of the lower orders as to whether this was wise. Was there an early burst or blast that was occasioned by the grievous impact with the iceberg?

There are stray reports of wounded, injured firemen. Off-duty Alfred Shiers told of helping a fellow fireman whose foot had been cut open to the medical room, but the doctor was not there.[24] Third-class Swedish passenger Olaus Abelseth said fireman Thompson had 'burned one of his hands', which he hardly did on an iceberg.[25] Some passengers saw a face-bloodied stoker, and newspapers gave lurid accounts of crew injuries, which they reported were caused by the collision.

Second-class survivor Charlotte Collyer wrote: 'Suddenly there was a commotion near one of the gangways, and we saw a stoker come climbing up from below. He stopped a few feet away from us. All the fingers of one hand had been cut off. Blood was running from the stumps, and blood was spattered over his face and over his clothes. The red marks showed very clearly against the coal dust with which he was covered.'[26]

Her account may have been 'improved' by the paper wherein it was recorded, however. The fireman was quoted as saying that it was 'Hell down below', the magazine putting a cockney-accented 'dynger' in his mouth when Collyer asked about danger.

The account continues: 'He staggered away, and lay down, fainting, his head on a coil of rope. And at that moment I got my first grip of fear – awful, sickening fear. That poor man with his bleeding hand and his speckled face brought up a picture of smashed engines and mangled human bodies.'

And there was also the aforementioned clearance of the firemen from the deck: 'I saw First Officer Murdoch place guards by the gangways, to prevent others like the wounded stoker from coming on deck. How many unhappy men were shut off in that way from their one chance of safety I do not know.'

The altogether sober *Times* of London on 20 April meanwhile offered some support for Daniel Buckley's second-hand tale, from second-class passenger Emilio Portaluppi, who said that 'He was first awakened by the explosion of one of the ship's boilers.'[27] Although there was never any sworn evidence to support this claim (and leading stoker Fred Barrett denied any such explosion in his area forward), an internal explosion in the wake of sudden trauma is widely canvassed in the case of the *Lusitania*, just three years later, since there were two distinct blasts, yet only one torpedo fired (although contraband munitions are commonly blamed, even if they were likely to be inert in actual fact).

Could something similar to a boiler blast (albeit on a lower scale such as a steam pipe rupture) have happened with the *Titanic*? How otherwise did some firemen apparently suffer blood and burn injuries?

Trimmer George Cavell was working in a coal bunker (unaffected by the fire) in boiler room 4, further aft than 6 and 5. He said in London: 'I felt a shock, sir, and with that all the coal round me fell around me. I had a job to get out … The coal surrounded me before I knew where I was.'[28] He was carried down with the coal, showing the hefty effect of metal meeting mountain, even as far back as his location.

Arthur Peuchen recalled that 'The ship shoved past this ice' and fireman George Beauchamp said the shock was like 'the roar of thunder'.[29] Such agitation might possibly have caused an explosion if there was still a spontaneous coal fire in one of the bunkers, as would later be claimed during firemen interviews in New York. Even coal gas elsewhere could have violently changed its state. And the compressive, concussive jangle might also have affected other features – watertight doors, for example.

* * *

Ismay spoke of the duties of the guarantee group: 'A door might jam, or a pipe might burst, or anything like that,' while Captain Turner, later of the *Lusitania*, accepted that even watertight doors could jam.[30]

Steward Henry Etches, who found it hard to rouse some passengers even without such complications, spoke of hearing a 'loud shout' about seven minutes post-collision. He looked out into the E deck corridor. 'Close watertight bulkhead doors' was the demand of the bosun, forty-seven-year-old Sydneysider Alfred 'Big Nick' Nichols.[31] Etches said: 'A seaman was running with him … they were going along to close those doors.' These were manual doors, not the reportedly automatic ones dropped from the bridge. They had to be cranked down from the floor of E deck to the bottom of F deck below. Norman Chambers, occupying E8, commented: 'I remember being somewhat surprised these doors were not nowadays operated by electricity.'

George Harder and his wife, Dorothy, came out of E50 with lifebelts and 'noticed about four or five men … one had one of those T-handled wrenches, and two or three others had wrenches … I did notice this one man trying to turn this thing in the floor. There was a brass plate. It was marked, W. T. and I do not know whether D after that … naturally, seeing the initials I thought it meant watertight doors.

'We heard one of these men say: "Well, it's no use. This one won't work. Let's try another."' Not stopping to watch, the Harders hurried higher.[32]

Michigan passenger Dickinson Bishop reported that 'some people', including Mr Harder, had told of this effort by members of the crew. 'They failed to turn the one on that side, and they immediately went to the other side, and could not close that.'[33]

Meanwhile there is separate evidence of jammed doors in passenger areas of the ship after the collision.

Sixty-year-old first-class passenger Anna Warren told her hometown newspaper: 'Continuing up to the boat deck we tried to get out the port side, but we were unable to open the door. Noticing the starboard door standing open, we went out that way.'[34]

Fireman Thomas Knowles' daughter Dorothy wrote in a 1973 letter of his recollections: 'Many cabin doors were jammed and many passengers were unable to get out.'[35] This must be an exaggeration. But author Walter Lord also heard such a tale and included it in his seminal 1955 book: 'A locked (stateroom) door raised a different problem. It was jammed, and some passengers broke it down to release a man inside. At this point a steward arrived, threatening to have everybody arrested for damaging company property when the *Titanic* reached New York.'[36]

31

DILLEY AND 'AN OFFICER' DESCRIBE

CONTINUED CRISIS

John Dilley died of 'burns and shock.' But that was ten years later, in a spontaneous coal fire explosion aboard the White Star liner *Adriatic*. The *Titanic* survivor was buried at sea in 1922, just eighty-eight nautical miles southwest of where his crew comrades went down a decade before.

Dilley was a twenty-nine-year-old fireman when he escaped the maiden disaster in mid-April 1912. The Londoner was an experienced stoker and had been on the *Olympic* before joining her new sister. He was one of the team tasked with dousing the coal bunker fire that continued to combust ominously during the voyage. His story was splashed on the front page of the New York *Evening World* on Saturday 20 April, alongside an article titled '*Titanic*'s Seamen Closely Guarded – White Star Officials Place Watch to Keep Interviewers Away From Survivors.'

The Dilley tale was headlined: 'Fire in *Titanic*'s Coal Hold Raged – Stokers in Relays Unable to Halt Blaze, Ready to Give Up.' It read:

The White Star liner Titanic *was on fire from the day she sailed from Southampton. Her officers and crew knew it, for they had fought the fire for days.*

This story, told for the first time today by the survivors of the crew, who were sent back to England on board the Red Star liner Lapland, *was only one of many thrilling tales of the first – and last – voyage of the* Titanic.

'The Titanic *sailed from Southampton on Wednesday April 10 at noon,' said J. Dilley, fireman on the* Titanic, *who lives at No. 21 Milton Road, Newington, London North, and who sailed with 150 other members of the* Titanic's *crew today on the* Lapland.

'I was assigned to the Titanic *from the* Oceanic [sic], *where I had served as a fireman.*

From the day we sailed, the Titanic *was on fire, and my sole duty, together with eleven other men, had been to fight that fire. We had made no headway against it.*

'Of course, sir,' he went on, 'the passengers knew nothing of the fire. Do you think, sir, we'd have let them know about it? No, sir.

'The fire started in bunker No. 6. There were hundreds of tons of coal stored there. The coal on top of the bunker was wet, as all of the coal should have been, but down at the bottom of the bunker the coal had been permitted to get dry.

'The dry coal at the bottom of the bunker took fire, sir, and smouldered for days. The wet coal on top kept the flames from coming through, but down in the bottom of the bunker, sir, the flames was a-raging.

'Two men from each watch of stokers were tolled off, sir, to fight that fire. The stokers, you know, sir, work four hours at a time, so twelve of us was fighting the flames from the day we put out of Southampton until we hit the damned iceberg.

'No, sir, we didn't get that fire out, and among the stokers there was talk, sir, that we would have to empty the big coal bunkers after we put our passengers off in New York, and then call on the fireboats there to help us put out the fire.

'But we didn't need such help. It was right under bunker No. 6 that the iceberg tore the biggest hole in the Titanic, *and the flood of water that came through, sir, put out the fire that our tons and tons of water hadn't been able to get rid of.*

'The stokers were beginning to get alarmed over it, but the officers told us to keep our mouths shut – they didn't want to alarm the passengers.'

Here ended the account – which, incredibly, seemed to prompt but one question at the US inquiry. Presiding Senator William Alden Smith asked Major Peuchen three days later whether there was any fire aboard the ship between Southampton and the place of catastrophe. The Canadian passenger replied: 'Everything seemed to be running very smoothly on the steamer, and there was nothing that occurred. There was no mention of fire in any way.'[1]

But it wasn't just the *Evening World*. The same day's *New York Tribune* ran with 'Steamer On Fire Below'. This time it did not quote Dilley, but said the fire had been extinguished at 2 p.m. on Saturday afternoon, meaning more than a full day before contact with the berg, even if that left brittle steel behind. The *Tribune* was emphatic, however: 'Every stoker who was interviewed declared that the *Titanic* was afire from the time she left Southampton until Saturday afternoon at 2 o'clock. This story was first told by an officer of the ship, who requested that his name be withheld, saying that all the men had been warned not to talk about the disaster.'[2]

(*The New York Times* reported: 'The men were told they would be dismissed from the White Star Line's service for good and all if it were ascertained any of them had disobeyed the instructions against talking.'[3])

The source for the *Tribune* added:

The fire was in the coal bunkers, forward, in stokeholds 9 and 10, on the forward end, in what is known as the second and third sections. The fire must have been raging long before she pulled out of her pier in Southampton, for the bunker was a raging hell when, one hour out past the Needles, the fire was discovered [by the new arrivals]. *Immediately we began to work on the fire, and it took us until Saturday afternoon to extinguish it. We were compelled to dig out all the coal from these sections.*

In my opinion this fire played no small part in the disaster, for when the bow was stove in, the waters readily tore open the watertight bulkheads, behind which had been this coal. If the coal had been still in the second and third sections when the vessel struck the iceberg it would have probably helped the bulkhead to resist the strain.

The quoted senior figure was indeed an authority, for he gave precise and detailed locations that would have been unknown even to many of the ship's own crew. He cited stokeholds 9 and 10. Number 9 was in boiler room 5, and number 10 was in boiler room 6, the furthest forward. Coal bunkers W and Y were either side of a separating bulkhead. Sections 2 and 3 are transverse working areas in each boiler room where these two stokeholds are located. Section 3 is the forward area of boiler room 5, representing the stokers' space between hungry boilers and the bunkered coal against the bulkhead. On the far side, past the equivalent bunkering, is section 2 in boiler room 6. (The boiler rooms counted backwards from the bow: 6, 5, 4, etc.; but the sections confusingly ascended in number from the bow: 1, 2, 3 and so on).

The grasp shown by the informant must help convince us that coal bunkers W and Y were both evacuated, leaving only a brittle bulkhead averaging only half an inch thick to resist the impending inrush of water.

'This fire played no small part in the disaster,' said the officer. Yet White Star officials emphasised the word 'small' and the fire's importance was never dignified by the British inquiry.

For Dilley to be correct about continuing bunker combustion right up to the iceberg's arrival, there would have to have been another, third bunker fire. It is unknowable whether his lone assertion is correct, but it should be noted that there were horizontal roof bunkers, not just vertical ones, in boiler room 6. Bunker Z, over the firemen's heads, located to starboard and hard against the hull, contained 143 tons of coal. The port version of the same had a capacity of 142 tons. Is it conceivable that the fire could have spread to Z?

Dilley was in the second watch of firemen, meaning he worked from 4 to 8 o'clock, both morning and evening. If bunkers W and Y were finally cleared and extinguished, he ought to have known about it. Uncertainty extends to how Dilley was saved, but he was photographed with fellow survivors at the Seamen's Friend Institute on West Jane Street in New York City. He was not named in the course of either inquiry.

* * *

Duly repatriated, Dilley gave a deposition about his experiences on arrival in Plymouth, but this has never come to light. A peculiar feature of the firemen's return is that none other than Harold Sanderson, the whiskery White Star chief and ally of Ismay, was present to oversee the men's homecoming on the *Lapland*. The Plymouth *Daily News* reported:

The official programme was made doubly plain late last night when Mr Harold Sanderson, managing director [sic] of the White Star Company, arrived in Plymouth, accompanied by Mr E. C. Grenfell, another director, and Mr [John] Furniss of Hill, Dickinson and Co., the company's solicitors [in Liverpool].

Mr Sanderson received a body of Press representatives at his hotel and explained the position. The White Star Company, he said, realised the public were anxious for details of the wreck of the Titanic *from the lips of those who have arrived on this side of the Atlantic, but – this was hinted rather than stated – the company were in the hands of the Board of Trade. The Receiver of Wreck was responsible for taking the statements of possible witnesses at the forthcoming British inquiry … it was inadvisable in the circumstances, Mr Sanderson added, that the Press should be allowed access to the crew, and measures would be taken accordingly.*[4]

A total of 167 men arrived the next day to be taken off the *Lapland* and brought to a fenced area. White Star Line officials announced that even the men's relations would be refused admission, the *Daily News* revealed. 'So remarkable was the hedging-in of the men that Mr [Tommy] Lewis, one of their leaders, wired the Board of Trade asking if the men were prisoners.'

These 'extraordinary conditions' of 'strict isolation' were enforced until Whitehall at length thought better of quasi-internment, with the result that the 'detention ended by official telegram'. Here was a murky and unedifying episode indeed, and the role of White Star officials and their lawyers in purporting to act in support of the civil power seems highly improper.

The crew depositions given at Plymouth to different teams of interrogators and notaries are now missing. Whether they still exist in some dusty file must be doubtful; it seems more likely they were destroyed, either deliberately or through the depredations of time. Because so few ordinary crew members were called to give evidence in Britain it would seem inescapable that these dozens upon dozens of unseen depositions represent a different *Titanic* history, one that was lost on dry land in contrast to the untaken accounts of the dead who went down at sea.

It is likely, meanwhile, that Dilley and many of his fellow survivors suffered from what is now called post-traumatic stress disorder. They were haunted men, as this article entitled '*Titanic* Survivor Fined' would attest:

John Dilley, 30, ship's fireman, of Park Place, Hackney, was charged at North London Court with wilfully breaking the glass of a fire alarm post in Mare Street, Hackney, doing damage to the extent of 3d.

The prisoner said that he was on the Titanic *at the time of the disaster, and his nerve had been shaken.*

A constable said that the prisoner had been drinking, but was not drunk.

Mr Hedderwick said he thought that if the prisoner had been aboard the Titanic *it would have been enough to sober him for the rest of his life. Fined 5s., with 3d. the damage, or five days* [jail in default].[5]

The above could have been a psychological breakdown for troubled Dilley. Perhaps he was still trying to raise the fire alarm; the weight that hung on his conscience as a result of the ship's blaze brought to physical pressure in breaking the glass. He did it with drink taken, after all, yet retained his wits and was not inebriated. Arrested by responding police, whatever reasons he might have offered for his act are not aired in court. All that is encompassed in a brief news report is that his 'nerve' was shaken by events on the *Titanic*.

Dilley was again in court just after the outbreak of the Great War, leading to a report headlined 'A *Titanic* Survivor's Plea':

At Scarborough, John Dilley (32), ship's fireman, London, a survivor of the Titanic *disaster, was charged with stealing an overcoat.*

Dilley, who has joined the 10th Hussars, asked: 'Cannot I be liberated and go to the front?' He was told the magistrates had no power to deal with the case.

The prisoner said the shock received in the wreck had so affected his mind that when he took drink he did things which otherwise he would not have done.[6]

Dilley served three months. Freed just before Christmas, he was soon in uniform and next with the field guns in France. In October 1917 he received a shrapnel wound to the left shoulder. He recovered, only to develop scabies. Surmounting hostilities and horror, he returned home and was demobilised.

Dilley went back to his old calling as a ship's fireman, returning to White Star despite his *Titanic* experience. And it was on the *Adriatic* that he died in a devastating detonation. The Line issued a statement describing the calamity:

At 1.30 am on the 11th (August 1922) an explosion took place in the No. 3 hold, a reserve bunker, opened from the adjoining bunker hold with the object of working out the coal.

Chief Engineer F. W. Ruddle said seven men were at work. Others were asleep on the upper hatch over No. 3 hold. One of these, Stephen McGuinness, 49, a fireman of Liverpool, was not found afterwards and it is supposed he was blown overboard. Two of the men in the hold were killed outright. One was a J. Dilley, fireman, forty, of Liverpool.

The *New York Tribune* reported:

About fifteen passengers were up and about when the blast occurred. These men and women dashed forward to where the shaft of flame lifted its terrifying head and kindled the rope rigging of the mast.

Instantly Captain [Charles] David was on deck. 'Are the wires all right?' he asked calmly, but sharply, of a junior officer. The reference was to radio equipment ... a moment later he rushed a message broadcasting notice over the seas that his ship was in danger.

Ten answers flashed back through the night. The steamship Reliance *reported herself sixty miles away; the* Lafayette, *thirty.*

Engines were stopped, lifeboats made ready. Deckhands went about their accustomed tasks to allay fears. A porter continued his rounds, gathering shoes to be shined.[7]

Dilley had been killed instantly, along with a coal trimmer named John Redmond from Liverpool. An electrician and two other trimmers were so badly injured they succumbed days later. McGuinness had been blown overboard, making six dead in all.

The explosion was found to have arisen from 'spontaneous combustion' of Welsh coal, the same problem Dilley grappled with on the *Titanic*.

32

WHAT HAPPENED BELOW?

SNAPSHOTS OF A SINKING

Passengers and many crew rushed for the top of the *Titanic* in barely suppressed terror after the impact, their first instinct to reach the outside – even if cloaked in a spoken anxiety to 'find out what's going on', or to assist in preparing boats. The herd mentality was simply to ascend, and the lifeboat evacuation then became the story for these people. It was far tougher to *descend*, where witness could be had to the ship's internal agony.

Thomas Threlfall, leading stoker, told how 'he was off duty at the time of the collision and in his bunk. When he got on deck about midnight, Second Engineer [Harry] Hesketh told him to get all the men below.'[1]

There was understandable reluctance among the firemen to head to their caverns below the waterline. The solicitor general, Sir John Simon, said of leading hand Fred Barrett: 'Orders were given him to get some firemen back in order to draw the fires in No. 5, and he did get fifteen or twenty men to come back.'[2]

Fireman Walter Hurst reflected: 'My mates received orders to remain below and rake out the fires to prevent explosions. They obeyed at the sacrifice of their lives.'[3]

Threlfall went to No. 4. 'I had ten firemen and four trimmers under me and we had to look after five double boilers with thirty fires; that is, fifteen fires in each stokehold. I don't mind telling you it did not feel nice going down below, because we knew that a bad accident had happened, but every man jack of my gang went on with his work and never murmured. The engineers were running about a lot, and this made things look black, but my men went on with the stoking until about 1.20 a.m. Then we were warned that the end was close at hand, and ordered on deck. All fires had been drawn, and what trouble there was with the boilers must have been caused when steam had been largely reduced.'[4]

Even before they left, however, it was clear that the area had descended into chaos. There was some trouble when steam from drawing the fires was at its height, hampering visibility. The tragic death of engineer Jonathan Shepherd was ascribed in evidence to his falling into an unseen manhole, opened in the stokehold floor of No. 5 'to get to the valves to turn on the pumps or something'.[5] Shepherd screamed in agony, having broken his leg. Found in the murk, he was carried to the pump station (in the very same boiler room). Lying there helplessly, Shepherd would drown when the boiler room was suddenly blasted by incoming water.

Shepherd was not the only casualty at the time. On homecoming, steward Percy Keen told about a member of the engineering staff who was jammed in one of the watertight doors: 'There was no hope the engineer could live. He was dreadfully crushed, and begged piteously to be put out of his misery. At his own request he was shot dead.'[6]

This story appears to be corroborated by first-class steward Alfred Theissinger, who declared one day after landfall: 'In the engine room one unfortunate, an engineer, had his leg caught as a door swung to. It was crushed and he was held as in a vice. Before leaving the *Titanic* I was told how he had begged to be shot to end his agony. His wish was complied with, but this is the only shot I know of.'[7]

His last phrase shows that Theissinger, a stolid German, was not being overly excitable, but his story is nonetheless hearsay. Many wild claims were made in the press, especially before the actual arrival of survivors in New York, but a minority of later-told tales may be freighted with truth.

What happened below was largely overlooked in the press and in the inquiries since it was an area forbidden to passengers and there was heavy loss of life among those situated under the waterline. A fireman who gave a false surname to the *New York Tribune* (possibly Edward Self) said: 'Just before the crash came the signal was given to stop. The chief stoker ordered the dampers closed. This we did. We were standing around for fully a minute, wondering what was wrong, when the crash came. Almost a minute later came a message from the engine room over the telephone. Engineer [Herbert] Harvey, after hanging up the receiver, shouted: "All the men on deck!" The men responded by scrambling up the steel escape ladders.'

There are indications that firemen in at least the two forward boiler rooms were ordered up the escapes in the minutes after the collision – making the recall of some of them difficult thereafter. Whether the initial order was precautionary or reflected knowledge of pre-existing vulnerability must be a moot point.

* * *

The nervous passengers who mounted the stairs to A deck and the boat deck wanted answers, particularly as they had been brusquely woken, ordered to don life preservers and then to ascend. Was the ship going to sink? The officers were dispensing commands and their set faces brooked no conversation, but Thomas Andrews, the Harland & Wolff chief, was in civilian clothes – a passenger like themselves.

William Sloper saw the 'designer of the ship' come 'bouncing up the stairs three at a time'. Actress Dorothy Gibson, who sat at Andrews' dining table, 'rushed over to him, put her hands on his arm and demanded to know what had happened. Without answering and with a worried look on his face, he brushed Dorothy aside and continued up the next flight of steps, presumably on his way to the Captain's bridge.'[8]

Mrs Anna Warren saw him, too. 'One of the designers of the vessel rushed by, going up the stairs. He was asked if there was any danger, but made no reply. But a passenger who was afterwards saved told me his face had on it a look of terror. Immediately after this the report became general that water was in the squash court … and that the baggage had already been submerged.'[9]

It had been different before Andrews went below for a personal inspection. Mrs Eleanor Cassebeer ascended so quickly on deck after the shock that she claimed to have seen the iceberg astern. 'In answer to many questions he [Andrews] assured everybody we were absolutely safe and that the *Titanic* was absolutely unsinkable,' she told her local newspaper. 'He said she could break in three separate and distinct parts and each part would stay afloat indefinitely.'[10]

Now Andrews was back, his confidence severely shaken, as evidenced by the look on his face. The change was recorded by the New York correspondent of the *Daily Mail* 'from the lips of Mr A. A. Dick, one of the survivors': 'Mr Andrews announced his intention of going below to investigate. We begged him not to go, but he insisted, saying he knew the ship as no one else did and might be able to allay the fears of the passengers. When he came back we hung on his words. They were these: "There is no cause for any excitement. All of you get what you can in the way of clothes and come on deck as soon as you can. She is torn to bits below, but will not sink if the after bulkheads hold. She has been ripped by an underlying peak of ice, and it has torn away many of the forward plates and bolts." It seemed impossible to us that this could be true, and many in the crowd smiled, thinking that this was merely a little extra knowledge which Mr Andrews thought fit to impart.'[11]

Those smiling may have heard 'will not sink' without registering the qualifying 'if' that came afterwards. Dick importantly rendered it fully: 'if the *after* bulkheads hold'. The corollary of what Andrews imparted after his investigations is that he was not at all sure of the *forward* bulkheads.

A prime worry must have been bulkhead E, the fire-damaged thin steel wall between boiler rooms 6 and 5, which had not only been rendered brittle, but was now without shoring room-deep banks of coal. The starboard bunkers on either side of E were empty. All that was left was half an inch of steel that sworn testimony would later say was damaged, dented, dinged and warped.

'If The Bulkheads Hold' said the cross-head over the column reporting Andrews' eerie fears. He had almost certainly previously been down to inspect this very bulkhead with members of his guarantee group. While there is no direct evidence for this, the likelihood is established by Joe Mulholland's account of Andrews visiting the boiler rooms on the delivery trip, by Chief Engineer Joseph Bell's remark that 'Builders' men wanted to inspect that bulkhead' and by leading hand fireman Fred Barrett's recognition of one of those men when he finally went on deck, not to mention by what Andrews' own steward would testify.

Henry Etches was two years older than the Harland & Wolff chief and had 'met him several times at Belfast'. Besides attending to his stateroom ('He had charts rolled up by the side of his bed, and he had papers of all descriptions on his table during the day'), Etches encountered Andrews about the ship: 'at different parts of deck E more often than anywhere else'.[12]

He was asked by Senator Smith: 'Did you see him in the boiler room?'

To this key question, Etches replied: 'He had a [boiler] suit, and I have seen that suit thrown on the bed when he had taken it off. I have seen him in the chief engineer's room.'

The senator pressed: 'You mean by that that he had a special suit which he wore when he went into the boiler room?'

Etches confirmed: 'It was there for the purpose. I knew exactly what it was. It was a suit the surveyors put on. He had an engineering suit on then – an ordinary blue suit, sir.'[13]

Blue dungarees are a common feature in the detailed lists of the clothing on crew bodies recovered after sinking, since all thirty-six engineers died. Andrews had a boiler suit. Therefore, it is clear that he regularly visited the boiler rooms, and he certainly inspected the fire-affected bulkhead after the collision. Now he feared it would not hold – realising that his earlier optimism had been grossly misplaced.

* * *

Like Andrews, before going below, the captain had also been reassuring passengers. Honeymooner Eloise Hughes Smith, daughter of a congressman, who would lose her new life partner, was one of those given a guarantee. She told on arrival: 'Captain Smith assured us there was no danger. The *Titanic* could not sink for at least twelve hours, he said, and by that time several steamers would reach us.'[14]

But within a short time her husband, Lucien, insisted that she get into a lifeboat. 'He said that in my marriage vow I had promised to obey him and that this would be the only occasion that he was ever going to exact [her compliance].' And so it proved.

Captain Smith was disabused of his 'Edwardian confidence' by Andrews, and possibly the carpenter, some period after the collision – but in the meantime the ship had, remarkably, resumed her course.

This is a staggering truth, cited by greaser Fred Scott, who witnessed it all in the engine room and who only survived because he climbed out on a davit, a lifeboat lowering arm, long after all boats were gone, performing an Indian rope trick until he fell into the water. Miraculously, he was pulled into lifeboat 4. Scott, who would be killed aboard ship in a boiler explosion three years later, declared in London: 'they rang down [after the collision], "Slow ahead!"' (the eloquent exclamation mark is in the transcript).[15]

He later confirmed this order again: 'then they rang down "Slow ahead." For ten minutes after the collision she was going ahead. Then they rang down "Stop," and she went astern for five minutes.'[16] He repeatedly confirmed these instructions, pointing out they had appeared on the telegraph.

Captain Smith, for whatever reason, was now further pushing water ingress against a weakened bulkhead. Quartermaster Alfred Olliver confirmed: 'whilst on the bridge she went ahead, after she struck. She went half speed ahead.'[17]

He repeated: 'Half speed ahead, after she hit the ice.' Asked who gave the order, he carefully responded: 'The captain telegraphed half speed ahead.'

Proper inspections had not yet been completed, nor the extent of damage gauged. But J. Bruce Ismay had already appeared on the bridge.

Senator Theodore Burton asked: 'You know he went ahead, half speed?'

Olliver reiterated: 'Yes, sir; I know he went ahead half speed.'

Scott and Olliver's account of events was backed up by steward William Ward: 'The ship moved for ten minutes after the collision.'[18]

Second Officer Charles Lightoller was asked whether she was already stopped or slowing down when he emerged from his cabin, answering: 'She was proceeding slowly, a matter of perhaps six knots or something like that.'[19]

Passenger Arthur Peuchen and others spoke of her tentatively resuming travel – but science master Lawrence Beesley, as ever, gave the best description: 'I stayed on deck some minutes, walking about vigorously to keep warm … The ship had now resumed her course, moving very slowly through the water with a little white line of foam on each side. I think we were all glad to see this: it seemed better than standing still.'[20]

It was folly, however.

Sylvia, Lightoller's widow, wrote to *Titanic* author Walter Lord in 1958: 'Naturally my husband discussed the disaster freely with me so I know all the details.' She also claimed in writing to have a *Titanic* secret.[21] Lightoller's granddaughter, businesswoman Lady Louise Patten, recalled what she was told by her granny. She says of the Slow Ahead order: 'For my grandfather, it was a decision so foolish as to border on the criminal … He shared with my grandmother his suspicion that despite the risk, Ismay planned to salvage his company's massive investment in *Titanic* by crawling the rest of the way to America.'

Lady Patten continued: 'Whatever the motivation, it was a fatal decision. The forward thrust through the sea added enormously to the pressure of the water already coming into the damaged ship.' She wrote: 'Granny was clear that … the decision to get *Titanic* underway so soon after the collision was criminal, as my grandfather had often told her.'[22]

Like 'immediately', the word 'criminal' was a Lightoller familiar, used three times in his memoirs, which also referred to an incident during the First World War where Lightoller himself made the decision to steam in reverse over fears for a forward bulkhead.[23] Lightoller was commander of the destroyer *Garry* when, on 19 July 1918, two days after the sinking of the *Titanic*'s saviour *Carpathia*, he encountered UB 110. The destroyer rammed and sank the submarine, but the action so damaged the stem of the *Garry* that he decided to steam 100 miles in reverse to relieve the strain as he headed for safe harbour. He did this because reversing did not push water against the damaged forward bulkhead.

Lightoller's concern must have been informed by his *Titanic* experience six years' earlier. It may even have been influenced by the *Titanic*'s astern order given after the Slow Ahead, as if this was an alternative means of progress contemplated, however briefly and ludicrously, by Captain Smith. Certainly there was early wireless traffic suggesting the crippled maiden voyager was making for Halifax, Nova Scotia, and would even be 'beached' there.

Scott's account 'that she went astern for five minutes' after going forward is supported by Major Peuchen: 'After the collision it seemed to me not immediately, but after a short space of time, it sounded as though we were reversing. She still was going, even if they were reversing for a certain period.'[24]

Greaser Thomas Dillon, on duty in the engine room, also recounted an astern order. But he testified this came two minutes after impact: 'They went slow astern.'[25] The retreat went on for two minutes, he said (which could also suggest a fear about grounding on a shelf). After that manoeuvre, the engines 'went ahead again, for about two minutes'. But soon thereafter a stricken Andrews bounded up the staircase – and it is commonly agreed that the vessel next became stationary, imperceptibly drifting.

Beesley had gone down to his cabin while she was moving gingerly forward. When he returned to the boat deck 'even the breeze caused by the ship's motion had died entirely away, for the engines had stopped again and the *Titanic* lay peacefully on the surface ... motionless, quiet, not even rocking to the roll of the sea.'[26]

33

ENABLING THE FLOOD

THE PIERCING OF LEGEND

They reopened many of the watertight doors along the boiler room belly of the *Titanic* after she came to rest. These were electrically unclutched from the bridge, allowing firemen to crank them up to allow a full working avenue to operate from aft as far forward as bulkhead F, between boiler rooms 4 and 5.

Frederick Scott, an experienced greaser and prime witness from the ship's vitals, testified to why this was done. According to him the engineer of the watch in the engine room 'told us to heave all the watertight doors up … as we went through we opened them up'. They were opened 'right up. Just over 6 feet [high], I think. I could walk through them easy without bending down.'[1]

All the watertight doors aft of the main engine room were opened first, he explained. 'Why they opened them was they had to … get a big suction pipe out, which they used for drawing the water up out of the bilges … it takes four men to carry it. I think I saw four men coming through with it. They took it to the stokehold.' They passed through with the heavy hose about an hour after the jolt, he said. 'What they did with it I do not know.'[2]

Commissioner Lord Mersey grasped the importance of what he was hearing: 'If this evidence is right, there were no watertight bulkheads at all serving after a quarter to one (12.45 a.m.) from the bulkhead between (boiler rooms) 4 and 5, right away aft.'

Attorney General Sir Rufus Isaacs, agreed: 'That's right, my Lord. That is as I understand the evidence … so far as we know at present, there is no question after that of closing the watertight doors.'[3]

Another miraculous survivor, Thomas Dillon (he was hauled unconscious into a lifeboat), was on duty in the engine room with Scott. He told of getting an order 'to get out of the engine room and into the stokehold and open the doors … I assisted to open them as far as we could forward'.[4] He went successively through boiler rooms 1, 2, 3 and 4, stopping at the forward bulkhead separating it from No. 5. They were never closed again, he confirmed.[5]

Barrister Frederick Laing, representing Harland & Wolff, pointed out that the watertight doors were fitted with a float, 'so that if any material quantity of water comes, the float automatically releases the door and it comes down again by itself'.[6] The court promised to adduce further evidence on this point, optimistic the watertight doors might have 'floated' back down as flooding progressed – but never heard any at all.

Lord Mersey nonetheless pronounced grandly on the matter in his final report: 'Though it is probable the engineers who remained below would have closed those doors as the water rose in the compartments, yet it was not necessary … as each door had an automatic closing arrangement which would have come into operation.'[7]

Despite the use of 'probable' and 'would', Mersey had precisely no concrete evidence on which to ground his assumption. He even mused that opened doors might have been a positive point: 'It is probable, however, that the life of the ship would have been lengthened somewhat if these doors had been left open, for water would have flowed through them to the after part of the ship, and the rate of flow into the ship would have been for a time reduced as the bow might have been kept up a little by the water which flowed aft.'

This was arrant gibberish.

Mersey also reported an astounding piece of double-think: 'It is thus seen that the efficiency of the automatic arrangements for the closing of the watertight doors, which was questioned during the inquiry, had no important bearing on the question of hastening the sinking of the ship – except that, in the case of the doors not having been closed by the engineers, it might have retarded the sinking of the ship if they had not acted.'

'The engineers would not have prevented the doors from closing unless they had been convinced that the ship was doomed. There is no evidence that they did prevent the doors from closing.'

The reader may have to reread these quotes to fully appreciate the logical somersault and re-somersault involved as Lord Mersey sought to defeat in his own mind the very purpose of those watertight doors.

In his recommendations Mersey left it to the Board of Trade to convene a Bulkhead Committee to consider in detail where watertight doors might be located and what type they should be. He also managed to declare: 'In other ships constructed like the *Titanic*, it is probable the efficiency of the closing arrangements of the watertight doors may exert a vital influence on the safety of the ship.'

Yet this probably 'vital' factor was only for other ships constructed like the *Titanic*. In the case of that ship herself, he opined: 'There does not appear to have been any appreciable effect upon the sinking of the ship caused by either shutting or not shutting the doors. There does not appear to have been any difficulty in working the watertight doors. They appear to have been shut in good time after the collision.'[8] Lord Mersey omitted here that they had been opened again, which could be construed as a deliberate obscuring of the evidence.

Forward of where the doors were opened lay a boiler room with a fire-damaged bulkhead. Mersey did not refer to the forward movement of the ship after the collision, and if he had no idea what had happened down below – which seemingly he did not – he ought to have reported as much, without seeking to sugarcoat what would soon become a rapid sinking.

Scott destroyed the idea of the engineers sedately assessing whether they should or should not close the watertight doors as matters progressed. There was a dramatic instant, by his evidence – while doors were still open – when everyone was abruptly ordered out. One of the senior engineers rushed from boiler rooms forward 'and told everybody to go out of the engine room'. It was twenty minutes past one. Scott climbed the first available escape ladder, followed by scores of firemen and engineers. 'They came up the ladder just behind me.'[9]

He ascended to E deck, and walked aft along the main alleyway known to crew as Scotland Road. Scott was asked by the attorney general about 'these watertight doors in the alleyway'. He replied: 'They were open.' Pressed, he repeated: 'They were open, and they were open at the time I left the alleyway.'[10]

He went aft to obtain a lifebelt from a locker, fourth to do so in a queue of about forty fretting firemen, before climbing to the boat deck. Scott's ability to pass through what must have been a series of open watertight doors was amply demonstrated by his presence in court. The transcript lurched onto which lifeboat he entered, and within fifteen questions of his alleyway revelation he had left the witness box. But he had earlier revealed that when finally on the boat deck, near him had been 'all the engineers and firemen'.

'All the engineers?' the attorney general immediately queried, those same gentlemen having been exultantly hailed in the press for 'remaining at their posts'.

Scott confirmed his simple, bubble-pricking statement: 'Yes.'[11]

Sir Rufus then asked: 'Do you mean the officers?' and Scott spelled it out again: 'Yes, the engineers that were on watch.'

'Then, if I understand it aright, all the engineers had come up too?'

'They were all at the top.'

'Did they come up when you came up?'

'Just afterwards, but some of them went up on the boat deck with me. They came up the ladder just behind me ... that is the last I saw of them.'[12]

So the engineers did not remain below to die at their posts, as has been widely believed. A number of blue boiler-suited men were among the unidentified bodies later recovered. This account also wrecks Mersey's final report contention that it was 'probable that the engineers *who remained below* [author emphasis] would have closed those doors'.[13]

The alternative idea, possibly hatched by his assessors, that they had strategically chosen to leave the doors open to allow for an even-keel sinking (as if mathematically and mentally computing how it would come about) does not bear a moment's scrutiny. Both alternatives are shredded, leaving only a flimsy notion that mechanical floats would have allowed the boiler room doors to drop in sequence, for which zero supporting testimony was adduced. After all, the floats worked by electricity, insisted Scott, yet the electric lighting had shorted out in different sections of the ship as the flooding advanced.[14]

The British inquiry averted its attention from the mayhem and mistakes below deck, lifting its eyes to the lifeboats instead, their filling and lowering, and allocating five-minute departure intervals between them, as if they were a scheduled service from St Pancras station. Meanwhile trimmer Thomas Dillon confirmed that the final evacuation order below had come at 1.20 p.m., fully an hour before the sinking. He gave it as: 'All hands on deck; put your life-preservers on.'[15]

Up to then Dillon had been in boiler room 4, where the water was rising from the floor-plates, themselves six feet above the tanktop, above the reservoirs over the keel. He did not know why no effort was made to close the watertight doors again, but no such order was given and the engineers evacuated 'in a bunch'.[16]

He had an idea, he said, why they had stopped opening these doors by boiler room 4 – it was because there was 'too much water' in No. 5, directly ahead.[17]

George Cavell, a trimmer working in No. 4, corroborated Dillon about water gradually coming up over the stokehold plates. The men were soon working up to their knees. 'We stopped as long as we could. And then I thought to myself it was time I went for the escape ladder.'[18]

He may have lost his nerve. But after gaining an internal deck, which was deserted, he eventually thought he should return. Bravely, he forced himself to do so. Cavell climbed down the escape ladder again, but No. 4 was now deserted. He could not see anybody. He could not say how high the water had risen – 'I never went right to the bottom' – but scrambled back up.[19]

This evidence all points to the central importance of boiler room 5, even if water was leaking into boiler room 4 and possibly further aft.

Leading hand Fred Barrett had earlier quit boiler room 6 after the crash, when a large volume of 'pretty heavy' water 'came pouring in' through a gash in the ship's side. It was a significant tear, extending all along. 'I jumped from that section when she struck' back to No. 5 'and the watertight compartment closed up'.[20]

There were stokers left behind, he said, and only one of them – George Beauchamp – was saved. Any others? 'I could not tell you.' He had seen only Beauchamp since.[21] But there had been fourteen on duty in his stokehold.

When next observed (via an escape ladder from the deck above) boiler room 6 held floodwater much higher than a man's head, at eight feet above the plates. The dampers had been closed, said Beauchamp, and the fires hastily drawn until an order 'That will do!' sparked emergency evacuation – yet his evidence is unclear and he might properly have been talking about No. 5.[22]

On Barrett's looking down from above into No. 6, the water was far above the height of the furnaces with their closed lids. But there was 'no explosion' of a boiler at any time, he said.[23] Neither did he mention any floating corpses.

Barrett next got at least fifteen men down into No. 5 to draw the fires that were there as No. 6 steadily filled.[24] Some time passed as they did so, and the leading hand received a telephone order from the engine room 'to send all the stokers up, and me to remain there'. Only he and three engineers stayed.[25] They were Herbert Harvey, Bertie Wilson and Jonathan Shepherd – the last about to break his leg in a stokehold 'thick with steam'.

Water had already been pouring 'rapidly' into the empty coal bunker W because the iceberg-inflicted tear in the ship's side extended a couple of feet there. The rest of No. 5 had not been penetrated, but bunker W was hard against bulkhead E, which formed the warped and dented wall to No. 6, the very bulkhead that had been metallurgically weakened by the prolonged coal fire and made 'somewhat brittle' in the words of Edward Wilding of Harland & Wolff.[26]

After a quarter of an hour, 'all at once I saw a wave of green foam come tearing through between the boilers and I jumped for the escape ladder', Barrett recalled. 'A rush of water came through the pass – the forward end.'[27] The pass was the space between boilers, themselves twenty-four feet in diameter, and was wide enough to admit a trimmer with a wheelbarrow of coal. The pass instantly 'filled up' with charging water, as if the bulkhead had given way.[28] He did not stop to look.

Based on Barrett's previous estimate of a rate of filling in No. 6, which rose eight feet in ten minutes, that same boiler room would have been full by this time, which he estimated at ten minutes past one 'as near as I can recollect'.[29] Something had given way, he twice insisted, adding he had no idea whether it was the bulkhead itself or instead the interior wall of a coal bunker. This bunker had been steadily filling in No. 5 as a result of the rent to the ship's side, water pouring into it 'just the very same as an ordinary fire hose would come in', and whose door he had previously slammed down shut.[30]

Whatever its cause, Harvey, Wilson and Shepherd all died in the deluge that flooded No. 5, with Barrett himself barely outpacing the water as he monkeyed up a slippery ladder. Shocked and panting in the alleyway above, which was now wet with more water sliding down from forward, Barrett paused to collect himself, then sprang again, this time for the boat deck.

34

GÖTTERDÄMMERUNG

TERMINATION FOR *TITANIC*

Just ten minutes separates the time Barrett fled boiler room 5 and the general order to evacuate all firemen and engineers from below at 1.20 a.m. Yet Lawrence Beesley says his lifeboat – with Barrett in it – was launched at 12.45 a.m. These impossible times are reconcilable, however. If Beesley had changed his wristwatch before going to bed (by the forty-three minutes it was planned to put back the ship's clocks that night), his boat would depart at 1.28 a.m. by run-on time.[1]

Barrett and the other firemen, under no illusion about the ship's chances, eagerly clambered into the lifeboat. The question of whether there had by then been a collapse of merely a water-filled coal bunker or instead the whole fatigued bulkhead wall of No. 5, remains an open one.

Yet a crewman called Alfred White now offers some end-time insights, mediated through a newspaper because he was never called to give evidence. The New York *Sun* called him an 'oiler', the equivalent of the British term 'greaser', just as US papers preferred 'stoker' to 'fireman'. In its first issue after the *Carpathia* docked, the *Sun* reported White's assertion that although meeting the berg had opened seams below the waterline, it 'did not even scratch the paint' above.

'I know, because I was one of those who helped make an examination over the side with a lantern,' said White. This inspection is nowhere confirmed in evidence, yet a work cradle could easily have been rigged (one was photographed in that exact location while the vessel was at Southampton). Hauled inboard from his investigations by lamplight, White went down to his duty in what he called the 'light engine room', meaning the turbine room. It was located in the bowels of the ship, behind the main engine room near the stern. 'I never dreamed it was serious … we even made coffee, showing there wasn't much thought of danger,' he recounted.[2]

'I went down ... at 12.40 o'clock,' White said, giving an important time marker. 'An hour later I was still working around the light engines.' It was thus 1.40 a.m. The sands of time were rapidly running out.

White said that it was in this desperate ebbing of the *Titanic*'s life that: 'I heard the Chief Engineer tell one of his subordinates that No. 6 bulkhead had given way.'

It was this that sealed the ship's fate.

The *New York Tribune* disclosed the same day that an anonymous fireman had separately made a direct report to the same effect to Joseph Bell, the overlord of those infernal regions: 'A fireman said that he had reported to Chief Engineer Bell that the forward bulkhead had given away, and the engineer had replied: "My God, we are lost!"'[3]

These two distinct and late accounts, from the same short time frame, neatly cross-reference each other. A fireman told an appalled Bell that a bulkhead had failed, and White next heard the chief engineer inform someone else.

It is all too terribly credible. The *Tribune* had a reputation as a sober and influential paper. It was not given to Hearstian outbursts of the 'J. Brute Ismay' variety. Choosing to remain above the fray of yellow journalism then raging between the *World* and the *Journal* at the cheaper end of the market, the *Tribune* – like the *Times* – would not remotely consider concocting a phrase like 'My God, we are lost!' In fact, it tucked away the whole tale on page two, though mention was briefly made on the front, beneath the headline '*Titanic*'s Speed 21 to 23 knots, Evidence Shows; Stories of Heroism.' The conclusion must be that Bell's tormented exclamation was used by the newspaper because it had been faithfully relayed by a fireman survivor.

The *Tribune* added: 'When the water came rushing in after the collision with the ice the bulkheads would not hold because they did not have the supporting weight of the coal.' The paper had also heard from crew about the fire that 'had broken out in the coal bunkers of the *Titanic*'.

The *Sun*'s coverage was equally restrained. It did not have the 'My God' quote, only White's almost nonchalant remark about Chief Bell telling one of his lieutenants about the failure. 'At that time things began to look bad,' commented White with decided underplay. The *Titanic* was far down by the bow, he added, intelligence that must have earlier come down from on high. 'I was told to go up and see how things were going and made my way up through the dummy funnel to the bridge deck.' By that time all the lifeboats had left the ship, White said.

A reporter from the Richmond *Times-Dispatch* was evidently listening to this account, because that paper printed further details from White in a 'special' transmission from New York that led off: 'A great many of the sailors rescued from the *Titanic*, who are waiting in port to be taken back to England tomorrow by the steamer *Lapland*, agreed today that Captain Smith gave the general order "Every man for himself" before *Titanic* made her final plunge.'

The article continued: 'Captain Smith did not resort to this measure until all the *Titanic*'s boats had cleared the ship and until the bridge itself was awash. One man who told of this fact was Alfred White, a greaser for the pumps in the engine room.'

The tale evolved, with specific mention of 1.40 a.m., 'which was when the first apprehension was felt by those below'.

1.40 a.m. This is the very latest time for any story from the stokehold by a named and verified member of the *Titanic*'s crew. The stern sank at 2.20 a.m., yet she may have commenced to break up at 2 a.m.

Captain Smith was 'knee-deep in water' when he released his lads. White then 'slid down some loose boat falls, dropped into the water and was picked up by a boat'.

The *Times-Dispatch* added that the same order – every man for himself – had been sent to the engine room where a last handful may have remained. If so, it was too late for Bell and the diehards.

On 21 June 1912 Alfred White wrote a letter to the family of William Marsh Parr, an electrician from Harland & Wolff lost in the sinking. He gave the same end time: 'I am truly sorry I could not answer your letter before as I have been very ill and unable to do anything at all. I knew Mr Parr very well for the short time we were together. I was with him nearly till the last. That was at twenty to two on the 15th April in the main light room of the *Titanic*.'

White's next reference might reveal when the bulkhead gave way: 'Work was going on as if nothing had happened, when, at twenty to two, the ship seemed as if she had started again, and flung us off our feet.'

Was this, then, the crucial collapse?

White continued: 'Mr (Peter) Sloan and Mr Parr said to me, "Go up and see how things are going and come and tell us." Telling you the truth, I had a job to get up the engine room ladder ... I could not get back as the boat was sinking fast.'[4]

The lurch that threw them off their feet was a 'start' indeed, the terrifying beginning of the end. It was also felt on deck. Barber Gus Weikman told the *Tribune*: 'While I was still helping at the boats there came an explosion from below decks and the ship took an awful lunge, throwing everybody into a heap.'[5] Baker Charles Joughin was on E deck when he 'heard a kind of a crash as if something had buckled, as if part of the ship had buckled'.[6] It was some time 'after half past one' (agrees with White), but 'like as if the iron was parting', rather than an explosion.[7] He was much closer to its source than Weikman, but agreed the *Titanic* then 'gave a great list over to port and threw everybody in a bunch'.[8]

The effect may have been less pronounced for some, depending on where they were. Stewardess Annie Caton said: 'As we stood waiting for our boat, we felt the ship shiver under our feet.'[9]

In any case, there was now nothing at all to prevent the invading North Atlantic from feasting on the vessel's entrails and the drag of millions of gorging gallons instigated the break-up. It would be the start, too, of a torrent of vain-glory that drenched the ship anew in a metaphorical sense, turning needless loss into redemptive nobility. Thus every engineer stayed evermore at his post, the Anglo-Saxon morally conquered other races through self-sacrifice, and Captain Smith's last words were 'Be British'.

But he had been brittle himself, and perhaps not such a bulwark of stoicism. Instead of the clear eye, lifted chin and resolute jaw, he was seen by some to be weeping. First-class lady's maid Roberta Maioni was quoted saying, 'An elderly officer with tears streaming down his cheeks, helped us into one of the lifeboats. He was Captain Smith, the Master of that ill-fated vessel.'[10]

Third-class passenger Edward Dorking declared: 'As I passed the engine room, I saw Captain Smith, standing in the doorway, giving orders to the crew. The perspiration was pouring down his face in streams, but he was calm and collected, and as I recollect him now, he appeared like a marble statue after rain.'[11] But Dorking later gave personal appearances in theatres saying Smith had wept, not perspired.

The emotion is understandable, no matter what its wellspring. Smith had been told by Andrews after the latter's inspection that the ship would sink in an hour and a half. But with her compartments, bulkheads and watertight doors, the *Titanic* might have done much better than she managed. It is arguable she should have lasted into daylight with her damage, the White Star liner *Republic* having taken thirty-six hours to sink in 1909 with equally fearsome, if dissimilar, wounds.

'Captain Smith appeared nervous; he came down on deck chewing a toothpick,' French aviator Pierre Maréchal told *Le Matin* in an account soon reprinted in translation.[12] The wireless operator on the *Olympic*, Alec Bagot, confirmed in his memoirs: 'The old man [Captain Smith] played with a toothpick – a peculiar little habit, like holding a pencil or an unlighted cigarette between the lips.'[13]

In a letter to her sister composed on *Lapland* going home, *Titanic* stewardess Mary Sloan of Belfast wrote: 'I saw Captain Smith getting excited. Passengers would not have noticed, but I did.' She wrote of an earlier encounter: 'Poor Mr Andrews came along. I read in his face all I wanted to know.'[14] In another letter, Sloan noted that Andrews' visage 'had a look as though he was heartbroken'.[15]

Stewardess Annie Robinson, who saw both Captain Smith and Andrews visit the engine room in the early stages of the tragedy, also described the carpenter John Maxwell during this time. He was on E deck, peering down into the mailroom, the two storeys of which were within six feet of being full. Maxwell had the sounding lead-line in his hand and was the principal assessor of the flooding. Two mailbags and a Gladstone bag had been fished out and lay soggily on deck. 'The man looked absolutely bewildered, distracted. He did not speak.' Maxwell died in the disaster.

Night watchman James Johnson told the British inquiry that after feeling *Titanic*'s shock he first looked around, and then encountered a fellow crewman who came up for some hot water. Johnson asked him: 'Do you mind going down to the engine room and have a look?' The man did go down. He came back and said: 'I think it is a bit hot.' Johnson explained: 'That is a racing phrase. He meant it was a bit serious.'[16]

The man was a greaser, he said. 'I think he might have been a man they called White.'[17]

White's son, Alfred Jr, claimed to his local newspaper in 1998: 'My father saw it all. The picture of hell stayed with him until his dying day. The order came down from the bridge to shut the watertight doors … my father saw a man caught in the massive doors and cut in half. Everything was panic and confusion. He got out … up the false funnel.'[18]

Later his father was 'keeping a pub in Southampton and willing to talk about his experiences on the *Titanic*, although what he had seen obviously festered. Once, me and my sisters were in bed and he came in and tipped the bed up, shouting "Get those watertight doors shut!" There was a blanked-off recess at the top of our stairs and one night he tried to run through it, obviously thinking back all those years to when he had to make an escape from the engine room.'

The toll was not just the 1,500 lives exacted that night. Some survivors ended their own lives. For example, on 9 October 1914, in a thick North Atlantic fog, the stewardess Annie Robinson jumped overboard from the Leyland liner *Devonian* and was lost forever. The parents and siblings of some victims also took their own lives. At least two *Titanic* crewmen, John Anderson and George Pelham, ended up in mental institutions, while another, William Lucas, shot himself in a moving train.

Robert Hichens, the man at the wheel when the grisly spectre was struck, declared in 1935: 'Today there are few of my shipmates alive. Of those who survived the disaster, some have died through shock, some have committed suicide because of the hell they went through, and there are some who were killed – mercifully, perhaps, for them – in the Great War.'[19]

He added in the same interview: 'Every night I see again the shocking chaos I saw 23 years ago.' But he had not mentioned any of this at the inquiries.

There was much anger and resentment felt by the survivors and their relatives in 1912. 'The women were bitter against the officials of the White Star Line,' reported first-class passenger Carrie Chaffee, who declared she would devote her life and fortune to bring punishment to those she considered responsible for the wreck.[20]

'"Don't ask me what I think of him [Ismay]," Mrs Chaffee cried through clenched teeth. "I would not care to put my real thoughts into words. I can tell you this, however, that the utmost of criminal negligence was responsible for the disaster.

"'Mr Ismay and all of the ship's officers were aware that we were passing through the ice field. All of them talked about it, even at the tables. When several of us passengers begged that the ship's terrible speed be reduced, all we received in answer were smiles.'"

Little did they realise how thoroughly those smirks were soon to be wiped from their faces.

35

CRISIS MANAGEMENT

PLANNING FOR CREW EXTRACTION

'When I got on board the ship I stood up with my back against the bulkhead.' The speaker is J. Bruce Ismay, and the solid bulkhead to which he refers belongs to the Cunard liner *Carpathia*, rescuer of all who lived in the *Titanic*'s lifeboats. 'Somebody came up to me and said, "Will you not go into the saloon and get some soup, or something to drink?" "No," I said, "I really do not want anything at all." He said, "Do go and get something." I said, "No. If you will leave me alone I will be very much happier here." I said, "If you will get me in some room where I can be quiet, I wish you would." ... Then he took me and put me into a room. I did not know whose it was. This man proved to be the doctor of the *Carpathia*.'[1]

Dr Francis Edward McGee escorted Ismay away, even as bedraggled *Titanic* escapees filled the saloon, clutching mugs and shuddering in blankets after a night of exposure. Somehow Captain Arthur Henry Rostron learned the head of the rival White Star shipping concern was aboard his vessel, one of 712 plucked from saltwater after a horrifying sinking.

'Very shortly after I got on board,' said Ismay, 'the captain came down to me and said, "Don't you think, sir, you had better send a message to New York, telling them about this accident?"'

Rostron, later knighted and made an aide-de-camp to King George V, soon to be awarded a gold Congressional medal and festooned with honours and decorations, was showing deference in attending on Ismay. Manners maketh the man.

It was about 8 a.m., some two hours after Ismay had ascended the saviour's side. He wrote for transmission to White Star on Broadway: *Deeply regret advise you* Titanic *sank this morning after collision iceberg, resulting serious loss life. Full particulars later. Bruce Ismay.'*

'He turned to Rostron. "Captain, do you think that is all I can tell them?" He said, "Yes." Then he took it away.'[2]

Ismay, who had maintained great composure, was soon to dissolve into nervous exhaustion and remorse. Dr McGee's granddaughter says: 'My grandfather gave up his cabin to him. Ismay never left it and was so shattered he had to be kept under some drug. He took Ismay to stay in his cabin actually to protect him from passengers – or from a possible suicide. They were worried about him. He gave a tranquilliser to Ismay.'[3]

This is the first time a feared Ismay suicide from the *Carpathia* has been raised, but McGee's granddaughter insists it was mentioned in a letter written by the doctor to his wife, since lost. The chemical calming of Ismay is confirmed by a *Carpathia* telegram sent that afternoon by Rostron to Captain Herbert Haddock on the *Olympic*, steaming eastbound. 'Ismay is under opiate', it declared.[4]

Ismay was clearly agitated, and fear of self-harm may also appear obliquely in Charles Lightoller's evidence: 'I tried my utmost to rouse Mr Ismay, for he was obsessed with the idea, and kept repeating, that he ought to have gone down with the ship because he found women had gone down. ... I tried to get that idea out of his head, but he was taken with it; and I know the doctor tried too.'[5] Lightoller invited senators to call the surgeon, but McGee did not give evidence to either inquiry.

Interestingly, perhaps, within a few days of the disaster, a rumour swept Liverpool, his home town, that Ismay had taken his own life.

The precise nature of Ismay's survivor guilt may only be guessed at, yet he was soon restored to his former ebullience. White Star's chief in New York, Philip Franklin, must have been astonished to receive a brisk new wireless message from the boss of the Line: '*Very important you should hold* Cedric *daylight Friday for* Titanic's *crew. Answer. Yamsi.*'[6] Ismay was now using a company cipher, his name spelt backwards. There was no mention of any provision for surviving passengers, the vast majority of whom possessed only the clothes they stood up in – if they could stand at all.

Franklin complied with the peremptory instruction to respond, but he did not address Ismay's demand that he delay sailing another White Star liner for England so that the remnant of the *Titanic*'s complement could be rushed aboard at landfall. The reply was guarded, and included reference to an American millionaire (lost) with whom Ismay dined on the fatal Sunday night: *'Accept my deepest sympathy horrible catastrophe. Will meet you aboard* Carpathia *after docking. Is Widener aboard?'*

It appears Ismay did not appreciate his desires being turned aside in this way. He returned to what he wanted, cabling: *'Most desirable* Titanic *crew aboard* Carpathia *should be returned home earliest moment possible. Suggest you hold* Cedric, *sailing her daylight Friday, unless you see any reason contrary. Propose returning in her myself. Please send outfit of clothes, including shoes for me, to* Cedric. *Have nothing of my own. Please reply. Yamsi.'*

The effect upon Franklin must be what it is on the reader. The managing director has specified a need for shoes to put on his feet. Also a full set of clothes. And he would like his wishes complied with in relation to the *Cedric*. His concern at this point appears to be to get the *Titanic's* surviving crew members (and himself) home at the 'earliest moment possible'. It is interesting to note, however, that he still has not mentioned 500 of his paying passengers, similarly afloat, who are now destitute.

Franklin replied on Wednesday 17 April: *'Have arranged* [to] *forward crew* [in the] Lapland *sailing Saturday, calling Plymouth. We all consider most unwise delay* Cedric *considering all circumstances.'*

He signed it Franklin, but he had prudently secured the support of 'we all', his entire office, in begging to differ from the figurehead. Delaying the *Cedric* and her passengers in order to spirit away the *Titanic* crew to Britain may have been considered 'unwise' in terms of perception and public relations.

Ismay sent another message, received by Franklin early on the morning that the *Carpathia* was due to dock in New York: *'Send responsible ship officer and 14 White Star sailors in two tugboats to take charge of 13* Titanic *boats at quarantine. Yamsi.'*

He later explained: 'That message I sent at the request of the captain of the *Carpathia*, who told me it would be impossible to dock the ship with these lifeboats on deck. He was all hampered up, and would not be able to handle his ropes and what not. I drew up that message and showed it to the captain and asked if that would answer the purpose, and he said "Yes," and I gave it to him, and he sent it, I presume.'[7]

And soon Ismay became even more insistent regarding the *Cedric*: *'Very important you should hold* Cedric *daylight Friday for* Titanic *crew. Reply. Yamsi.'*

Followed by: *'Think most unwise keep* Titanic *crew until Saturday. Strongly urge detain* Cedric, *sailing her midnight, if desirable.'*

And then: *'Unless you have good and sufficient reason for not holding* Cedric, *please arrange do so. Most undesirable have crew New York so long.'*

Let's pause here for one moment. 'So long'? It would have been a day and a half at most. Franklin was suggesting sending the crew home at midday on Saturday at the latest. What was 'most undesirable' about their being in New York for that short span of time?

Lightoller's phrase about Ismay being 'obsessed' is here seen in another light. The dead women passengers no longer seem to concern the managing director, and the living ones – men, women and children – never seize his attention at all in these Marconigrams. This was despite their being imminently due to arrive at the Statue of Liberty – tired, poor, huddled masses yearning for dry land. They were in such a state that even normal immigrant screening and bureaucracy was suspended for their benefit.

But Ismay was not yet done with introspection. He had apparently brooded over Franklin's replies, sending him: *'Widener not aboard. Hope see you quarantine. Please cable wife am returning* Cedric. *Yamsi.'*

Senator Smith later probed at the US hearings: 'Judging from the messages, it was your intention to return the night you landed, if possible?'

'Yes, sir,' Ismay replied. 'At that time, you understand, I had not the slightest idea there was going to be any investigation of this sort.'

If the owner was a touch obtuse in not expecting an investigation, having courted the press in the past he must surely have anticipated a swarm of reporters meeting the rescue ship. The officers could be relied upon to preserve silence, but the uncontrollable crew was a different proposition.

Lightoller attempted to relieve Ismay's predicament, as revealed by his private wishes in wireless cables. 'I think I am principally responsible for the telegrams being sent,' he said of the *Cedric* affair, when it was a matter of restraining a ship rather than goading her onwards. 'Our whole and sole idea was to keep the crew together for the inquiry, presumably at home. We naturally did not want any witnesses to get astray,' he declared.[8]

Senator Smith asked why Lightoller had suddenly volunteered such a tale in Washington. 'Why did you not make that statement in New York?'

Lightoller soothed: 'Because the controversy in regard to the telegram[s] had not been brought up then ... I mean all this paper talk.' News management had not remotely entered their minds on the *Carpathia*, and yet the New York press had done its job, uncovering the wireless exchanges between Ismay and Franklin. Ismay even admitted composition.

The senior surviving officer took full responsibility, however. 'I think I even suggested, if they would not hold her [*Cedric*] at the dock, to exchange at Quarantine.' This would mean sailors, pantrymen, stewards and firemen switching from ship to ship, hardly setting a shoe on shore.

Lightoller had the crew's well-being uppermost in mind, he claimed. 'Their income stops, you know, from the time the wreck occurs, legally,' he said, the charity of getting them home obviously not matched by financial compassion. It was customary, he said, 'in anything like that, to choose your own company's ships [for repatriation], because everything is more comfortable for them. They are your own fellows,' he added.

But his efforts to assist had the result of disclosing conferences, planning and anticipation by the ex-*Titanic* command on the way to New York. What else did they plan and anticipate?

Lightoller: 'Previous to having the conversation with Mr Ismay in regard to any telegrams that were sent to our office in New York with reference to holding the *Cedric*, the other three officers and myself had spoken about it casually, saying we knew the *Cedric* and thought it a jolly good idea if we could get home with her, if we were in time to catch her. ... We were very much disappointed at the delay [to the *Carpathia*] through fog. We were saying all the time, "It is a great pity if we miss the *Cedric*. If we could only get everybody on board the *Cedric*, we shall probably be able to keep the men together as much as possible."'

He explained: 'Otherwise, you understand, once the men get in New York, naturally these men are not going to hang around ... They want to get to sea to earn money to keep their wives and families, and they would ship off ... They simply would stand this off as a loss or bad debt ... In a case like this, where the men are brought into prominence, they are very frequently offered berths immediately.'[9]

The phrase 'brought into prominence' is most revealing, potentially suggesting full knowledge of the power of the New York press, but Lightoller claimed he was merely discussing the potential loss to an inquiry of 'probably some very important witnesses'. The whole sorry *Cedric* saga was thus, according to Lightoller, the very opposite of what any cynical senator might suspect – they simply believed that a loss of testimony (at home in England) was earnestly to be avoided. If they were not immediately corralled, the crew would only disperse. 'They would perhaps ship on some yacht, which very often they do … on gentlemen's yachts in New York, because they know they are thoroughly capable men. They are just as good men as they can obtain in the world, and there is great demand for them; much to our regret, because we lose them.'

Unfortunately, from Lightoller's perspective, the man he sought to protect was saying the very opposite.

Ismay's train from New York to further hearings in Congress was awaited by reporters: 'He declared the reason he was anxious to get the survivors of *Titanic*'s crew back to England was that they were likely to get into mischief on land. "Sailors are prone to get into trouble when loafing, and this was why I did not want them to stay here," said Ismay.'[10]

Lightoller's granddaughter wrote in her 2010 book: 'While they were still on *Carpathia*, the Chairman of the White Star Line had shown my grandfather where his duty lay. Rightly or wrongly, my grandfather decided that his first duty was to protect his employer and his fellow employees, and in his autobiography he made it clear this was exactly what he had done.'[11]

Meanwhile the grubby *Cedric* affair was not even mentioned at the British inquiry.

36

INQUIRY AND NON-ENQUIRY

SMOTHERING THE FIRE

In June 1913 the Hamburg-American giantess *Imperator*, at 50,000 tons the largest vessel afloat, glided into Manhattan to complete her maiden voyage. She was the new 'colossus of liners', 919 feet long, said the New York *Sun*, 'double-hulled and called unsinkable'.

But there was disappointment: 'The slowness of the latter part of *Imperator*'s trip caused many persons with friends aboard to call up the papers and the office of the Hamburg-American Line and ask why the ship was delayed.

'In response to a wireless message sent by *The Sun*, Commodore [Hans] Ruser flashed this reply of assurance while the liner was between Nantucket and Fire Island: "Delay was due to bad weather and persistent fog."'

Two months later, Second Officer Otto Gobracht died fighting a fire that broke out in a starboard storeroom while the vessel was at Hoboken packed with passengers.

'Fireboats belonging to the harbour authorities got the fire under control after a struggle lasting four hours. The steamer has a list of 15 degrees and the damage sustained is believed to be considerable.'

The list was because 'nearly 2,000,000 gallons of water were pumped into the hold of the vessel,' continued the *Evening World*. It was only then that 'the fire had finally been drowned out'.[1]

John Dilley's claim the year before that the *Titanic* firemen feared she might have to avail of New York fireboats is thus not so fanciful. And his claim that 'the officers told us to keep our mouths shut' on the voyage chimes with remarks on landfall by Robert Hichens, Fred Fleet and others that they 'couldn't talk' or had been told to 'keep quiet'. There appears to have been a suggestion that stopped *Titanic* pay from the moment of the sinking could be reviewed by the company in light of suitable behaviour, and the printed wages slip of fireman William Major, for instance, shows a later 'bonus' payment for days not worked on the voyage.[2]

Alfred White, who told of the end-time in the engine room, was to the fore in wage complaints. Unfortunately in its report of this the *Washington Herald* referred to him as 'Ralph' White, being unfamiliar with the English abbreviation of 'Alf' for Alfred. 'We asked for some advance money on the wages due us,' stated White, 'and although we were all without a cent and uncertain where we would get the next meal or a bed, were told we would receive no money on our wages until our return to England.

'We signed up for the entire voyage, but White Star officials claim our wages ceased when the *Titanic* went under. In the face of these circumstances, it would have been better had we all gone down with the ship, as in that case our families would have been provided for by the workingmen's compensation law, and we would not have faced actual starvation, as now seems to be our lot.'[3]

The newspaper added: 'White stated that White Star officials refused to cable relatives of members of the crew that they were safe, giving excuse that it would be too great an expense.'

The firemen and other crew interviewed by the press were by no means wholly negative, although the first-named uniformly spoke of the fire. Nonetheless they praised Captain Smith and his officers for their conduct during the sinking, some even hailing Ismay's efforts to assist.

But they told more negative aspects too. 'A fireman who feared to give his name told a story of horror that brought tears to his eyes,' said the *New York Tribune* of 20 April. '"I jumped," he said, "as the boat was sinking. I came up near a raft [Collapsible A]. Someone helped me aboard. There was just barely room for another. A man in the uniform of an army officer [probably Major Archibald Butt, aide-de-camp to US President William Howard Taft] crawled onto the raft, but he stiffened out at once and died. We threw him overboard to make room for a living man.

'"There were many men swimming around our raft, and they tried to get a hold on it. But some of us had to be prepared for this, and we beat them off with oars. We struck some on the hands to make them let go their hold, for they might have overturned the raft, and others we had to beat on the head."'

Fireman Harry Senior had been happy to give his name to *The New York Times* the previous day: 'I swam around for about half an hour ... I tried to get aboard a boat, but some chap hit me over the head with an oar.'

Braining swimmers was bad publicity, especially any hint that the crew, *in extremis*, would give priority to saving themselves – as had happened in the sinking of *La Bourgogne* fourteen years before. A total of 549 died, and press sensation arose from the fact that half the crew survived – compared with one in eight of the passengers.

The Plymouth *Daily Herald* quoted *Titanic* fireman Charles Judd: 'With my own eyes I saw an officer (whose name he mentioned) shoot two or three first-class passengers.' The officer may have come safe to shore, as the newspaper did not identify him.[4]

But Judd – who was never called to any inquiry – said worse when interviewed fifty years later for a gloomy anniversary. He told the *Belfast Weekly Telegraph* in 1962: 'I learned from other members of the crew why more third-class passengers were not saved. It is because somebody among the officers started the cry "British First!" This, of course, did not discriminate against Americans, but it encouraged forcing back into the water Portuguese, even the women, Italians, and other foreigners, to save people who cried for help in English.

'"A British life above all others," was the word passed round, said a seaman to me. There was no command so far as I know to get the steerage people up onto the decks ready for the boats.

'There were lots of babies on deck during the last moments. One Portuguese woman had three. God knows where they all went to, but we're pledged to tell all we know, no matter who suffers.'

Judd was by then eighty-two, yet his claims drew precisely no letters nor any interest from the authorities. He and unspecified mates may have been pledged to tell all (the article innocuously quoted a fellow Belfast survivor), but there would be no opportunity. Three years later Judd was dead.

The *Western Daily Mercury*, whose reporters met crew members after their release from detention in Plymouth, commented: 'Almost without exception they declined to consent to publication of their names, fearing unpleasant consequences.'

An extract from the British inquiry will illustrate. Lord Mersey asked lawyer William Harbinson: 'Now who are the two people you want to have represented here?' to be told: 'One is Thomas McCormack, who alleges in a statement–'

Mersey: 'Never mind what he alleges. What is the other name?'

'The other name is Bernard McCoy.'

'And where are they living?'

'At the present moment in America.'

'Are they coming over here?'

'Subject to what your Lordship may say, it was my wish, were I allowed to appear, to apply to your Lordship to have their evidence taken on commission.'

Lord Mersey: 'I think I am very unlikely to do that.'[5]

James Farrell, MP for Longford, home county of the steerage pair, then stood, mentioning he and his Lordship were former colleagues in the House of Commons. He availed: 'Thomas McCormack alleges that when swimming in the sea [after leaving the *Titanic*] he endeavoured to board two boats, and was struck in the head and the hands and shoved back into the sea and endeavoured to be drowned.'

Lord Mersey said he could not try any question of attempted manslaughter.

Farrell then asked, 'Is it not a matter for investigation by this Court?', going on to say that McCoy was making a similar charge.

Mersey: 'That I do not think comes within my jurisdiction at all.'

Farrell objects: 'But, my Lord, we also appear for others. We have gone to a great deal of expense.'

In response, Lord Mersey told him to confine himself to a 'legitimate position'.

Neither the fire nor this alleged attempted drowning was ever going to qualify as a legitimate issue to be considered by the man brought out of retirement to preside over the *Titanic* tribunal, whose very name, taken on ennoblement, was that of the greatest shipping river of the world. His Lordship joked he was 'leaving the Atlantic to F. E. Smith', another barrister who acted for the great maritime concerns.

Mersey must have known fellow Liverpudlian J. Bruce Ismay, and once ruled in favour of his sister-in-law in a road traffic matter. On Valentine's Day 1908 Mersey raised a toast at the annual dinner of the Chamber of Shipping, proposing 'the Shipping Interest' to murmurs of approval, adding in a speech following the clinking of glasses that 'those connected with the industry had to see nothing was done by legislation, or in other ways, which would decrease the carrying power of this great country'. *The Times* reported the pledge of fealty three days later. It seems fair to suggest, then, that Mersey was not interested in finding fault with anyone or anything within the industry, whether to do with boats, drills, the ship's speed, the fire or collision-avoidance rules.

Four years after hoisting his drink in homage to British maritime power, Mersey was spouting combatively: 'What are these questions directed to? Spontaneous combustion in a coal bunker is by no means an unusual thing ...'

Clement Edwards responded: 'No, My Lord, with respect, that is not the point.'

'What is the point?'

'The point, with very great respect, is this – that the part of the particular bulkhead which showed damage, according to the evidence, was a bulkhead which stood in the bunker where there was evidence that a fire had existed continuously on the journey from Belfast to Southampton, and even subsequently; and that the coal had to be taken out ... and black paint put on so as to hide whatever marks there might be, or the damage caused by the fire. It would be a matter, of course, for your Lordship's consideration as to whether–'

Mersey: 'Do let us confine ourselves to the real serious issues of this Inquiry. That fire in the bunker has nothing to do with it.'

Edwards managed: 'With very great respect, My Lord, I should have thought it was.'

The bench condescended: 'I differ from you there entirely.'

The lawyer and MP persisted: 'With very great respect, I would suggest that it was a little premature for your Lordship to say this until after you had heard the expert builders, and perhaps other experts as to what is calculated to be the damage done by a continuous fire.'[6]

Several examples, at least, could be adduced of similar browbeating by Mersey – or strategic interruption and invitation of legal argument when events in testimony were taking a turn he did not like. But Clement Edwards persisted, drawing evidence to suggest the bulkheads had not been rigorously inspected. He told the court 'that if there had been the right tests to the strength of the bulkheads – I am going to suggest that the bulkhead between 5 and 6, on the evidence, did give way – [then] possibly that bulkhead might not have given way. I am further going to suggest to your Lordship that in this case the ship was not constructed according to the rules laid down by the Board of Trade. What I am going to call attention to is this, that either Messrs. Harland &

Wolff, the builders, defied the Board of Trade, or that there was extraordinary laxity on the part of the officials of the Marine Department of the Board of Trade to allow, in the construction of this ship, a departure from those rules which they have already laid down.'

He continued a little later: 'I have not abandoned, and I do not abandon, the suggestion that this bulkhead was seriously damaged by fire on the evidence exactly as it stands before the Court.'[7]

Mersey was unimpressed, although Ismay readily conceded that bulkheads might in future be carried higher up (a prolonged point of contention in the *Titanic*'s construction between Harland & Wolff and the Board of Trade). Mersey would deflect that whole issue to a Bulkheads Committee in his recommendations at the end of the inquiry. He sneered at one point to Leonard Holmes, representing the Officers and Masters Association: 'I have had very little evidence about fire. I do not know what your suggestions amount to, or why we should do anything. There was that fire, for instance, that Mr Edwards took so much interest in.'

Holmes suggested His Lordship should recommend 'further and more stringent provision' be made for the supply of fire extinguishing appliances to ships.

Mersey again interrupted: 'I cannot do that; I have not heard sufficient evidence.' The attorney general promptly agreed with him.[8]

A handful of firemen entered into evidence – but some only because they happened to be in the same lifeboat as Sir Cosmo Duff Gordon (an aristocratic British fencer and pistol-shot who had competed at the Olympics), who was alleged in tittle-tattle to have bribed the men to row away from the sinking ship and not return to the aid of anyone in the water. It had caused a high society *frisson*, but Sir Cosmo would be resoundingly vindicated of such nonsense when the report came out.

Mr Edwards tried again: 'My Lord; what is perfectly clear is this, that in spite of the existence of bulkheads, this ship went down.'

The commissioner: 'Yes, that is because she had holes knocked along her side. It has nothing to do with bulkheads.'

Edwards: 'It may not have anything to do with bulkheads as bulkheads, but it may have a very great deal to do with bulkheads as part of the strength of the ship relied upon for resisting a shock of this kind. I will be very short.'

Mersey: 'I am not sure about that.'

'Your Lordship has rather a suspicious mind.' Edwards nonetheless established that the bulkheads had never been tested with water, although the ship's double bottom had been.[9]

Mersey: 'You are not helping me much.'

Edwards: 'I am very sorry.'

Mersey: 'You are trying very hard, no doubt.'[10]

When a frustrated Edwards asked surveyor Francis Carruthers, a highly defensive Board of Trade official, whether he had 'any views [of his own] apart from the regulations' on the height of bulkheads, the bench interrupted to address the witness: 'I hope you will say no.'

Exasperated, Clement Edwards complained, 'This is very great incitement, My Lord.'[11]

But there would come another day. Two years later, Edwards would have cold revenge on the Mersey verdict, one that had been clandestinely celebrated by the White Star Line.

37

THOMAS WHITELEY

THE MAN WHO KNEW TOO MUCH

The White Star Line managed to extricate itself well from the inquiries. Mersey had done his best for the company in his findings – by blaming the passengers. There was some reasoning in his final report: 'The event [*Titanic*'s sinking and horrific loss of life] has proved the practice [of going full speed in clear conditions] to be bad. Its root is probably to be found in competition and in the desire of the public for quick passages, rather than in the judgement of navigators.

'Unfortunately experience appeared to justify it. In these circumstances I am not able to blame Captain Smith. He had not the experience which his own misfortune has afforded those left behind, and was doing only that which other skilled men would have done in the same position.'[1]

This is a scandalous claim – what about Captain Turner's evidence and the prudent stopping of other ships?

Mersey continued: 'It was suggested he [Smith] was yielding to influences which ought not to have affected him – that the presence of Mr Ismay on board, and the knowledge he perhaps had of a conversation between Mr Ismay and the Chief Engineer at Queenstown about the speed of the ship and consumption of coal, probably induced him to neglect precautions he would otherwise have taken. But I do not believe this.

'The evidence shows he was not trying to make any record or indeed any exceptionally quick passage. He was not trying to please anybody, but exercising his own discretion in the way he thought best. He made a mistake, a very grievous mistake, but one which, in face of practice and past experience, negligence cannot be said to have had any part.'

The best Mersey could conclude, while dismissing all evidence of a fully intended 'exceptionally quick passage', was that 'what was a mistake in the case of the *Titanic* would without doubt be negligence in any similar case in the future'.[2]

But that inquiry was only Round One. Legal battles followed on both sides of the Atlantic, focused on the alleged negligence of speeding in a known ice area. An English jury in a case taken by the father of an Irish steerage emigrant held that the ship's navigation that night had indeed constituted negligence. After the proceedings in October 1913 it awarded £100 for the life lost. White Star appealed this ruling all the way to the House of Lords, which upheld the verdict.[3]

Thomas Whiteley, a waiter, thereafter sued the White Star Line, citing 'steering error' and 'negligent steering'. He further claimed the fundamental unseaworthiness of the *Titanic*. He was represented by Clement Edwards MP. Whiteley's step was momentous for one of modest means, indicating he was convinced of his own rectitude. The Londoner was making a set of allegations tantamount to meaning she should not have sailed in the first place and endangered passengers by doing so.

The Associated Press reported on 16 January 1914:

The plea that the Titanic *was unseaworthy when she left England in April 1912 ... is to be advanced in a suit for damages brought by Thomas Whiteley, one of the surviving stewards. The plaintiff sustained a fracture of the right leg in the wreck.*

Whiteley's counsel, Clement Edwards, a Member of Parliament, will also argue on behalf of his client that there was negligence in the steering of the ill-fated vessel.

This will be the first time that a suggestion in regard to the unseaworthiness of the Titanic *has been raised in the courts.*[4]

Whiteley had not yet turned twenty, having been only eighteen during the fateful voyage. He had previously served as a steward on the *Olympic*, but was transferred to the *Titanic* for the inaugural crossing. He might have thought himself ideally placed to receive a few nice tips, since maiden voyages always attracted high rollers. But all went awry, especially from the moment when, as he told the *North Berks Herald*, the venerable ship's surgeon, William O'Loughlin, rose from his seat at the Wideners' dinner party that Sunday night to propose a toast to the mighty *Titanic*. A few hours afterwards Whiteley found himself in a maelstrom of life and death. Somehow he reached the sanctuary of a boat in the darkness. He recalled someone hit him with an oar as he tried to board, but he persevered. Dawn saw him lifted, exhausted, aboard the *Carpathia*.

While other crew went home to England, Whiteley remained in hospital, and ten days after the disaster was one of only three still detained. But a bedridden Whiteley had already hit the headlines. On 20 April he was interviewed and photographed in his ward. Whiteley claimed the bridge had been warned in advance by the lookouts of a deadly obstacle-course of ice, although he did not mention any steering error at this point. The resulting story received most prominence in the *New York Herald*, which splashed his tale on the front page. It was sensational indeed:

That three warnings were given to the officer on the bridge that icebergs were ahead, less than half an hour before the fatal crash, was the declaration made last night by Thomas Whiteley, a first saloon steward who now lies in St Vincent's Hospital with frozen and lacerated feet.

Mr Whitney [sic] also says he understands that the first officer of the Titanic, *Mr Murdock [sic], did shoot himself after the crash. This has been rumoured, but never verified.*

Mr Whiteley does not attempt to explain why warnings were ignored, the speed of the vessel never reduced or the course changed, but he is positive, he asserts, that the first officer was warned distinctly three times. The warnings came from the two men in the crow's nest, Mr Whiteley said, and the fact that their warning was unheeded caused the lookouts much indignation and astonishment.

After being thrown from the Titanic *while helping to lift women and children into the boats, Mr Whiteley finally swam to a small boat and was helped in. It was while there that he heard a conversation between the two lookouts, neither of whom he recalled having seen before, but who, he is confident, were on board the steamship.*

The two men talked freely in his hearing and expressed wonderment that their attempts to get the officer to slow up or take other precautionary methods to avoid the bergs had failed. Mr Whiteley says he carefully marked every word they uttered.

'I don't recall the exact words of the men, but I am certain of the sentiment they expressed. They were very indignant. I was particularly astonished when I heard one of them say: "No wonder Mr Murdock shot himself."'

Asked if he knew how the reports from the crow's nest to the first officer were made, whether in person or by telephone, the steward said he did not know, but his idea was it was done by bells – three bells meaning danger straight ahead, two bells starboard and one bell port.

'My only information is that I heard one of the two men say that he had reported to the first officer that he saw an iceberg.

'I heard one of them say,' he said last night in hospital, 'that at a quarter after eleven o'clock on Sunday night, about twenty-five minutes before the great ship struck the berg, he had told first officer Murdock that he believed he had seen an iceberg. He said he was not certain, but that he saw the outline of something he thought must be a berg. A short time later, the lookout said, he noticed what he thought was another mountain of ice. Again, he called the attention of the first officer to it.

'A third time he saw something in the moonlight [sic; there was no moon] he felt certain was an iceberg. A third time he reported to the first officer he had seen an iceberg. This time, as I recall it, he did not say merely that he fancied he saw one, but that he had actually seen one.

'His words as I remember them, were – "I saw the iceberg. It was very large, and to me it looked black, or rather a dark grey instead of white."'

Mr Whiteley is not in a serious condition and will be out soon. He is a man above average intelligence and seems very certain of what he says.[5]

There are some obvious problems with Whiteley's allegations, one being that lookouts Fred Fleet and Reg Lee were saved in separate lifeboats so could not have had such a discussion. Of course, there's also the fact that neither made admissions in evidence about having previously warned the bridge of bergs or any prior ice at all, though Whiteley's account has obvious echoes with passenger Arthur Peuchen's sworn evidence and the account of Helen Churchill Candee in boat 6.

Senator Smith asked Fred Fleet: 'Did you see any other icebergs; field ice, or growlers while you were in the crow's nest Sunday night?'

'Only the one I reported right ahead.'

'Only that one?'

'That's all.'[6]

Lee affirmed at the British inquiry: 'Before half-past eleven on that watch … had you reported anything at all, do you remember?'

'There was nothing to be reported.'[7]

But Whiteley's story has accurate detail too – about the number of bell-strikes for objects in different directions, for instance, while some minor errors may be journalistic.

The following day, the *Herald* confidently reported that Whiteley's 'new and startling' tale would be 'followed up immediately' by the Senate investigation.[8] Instead of setting the agenda, however, the allegations rapidly withered. At the end of Fleet's evidence, Senator Smith made oblique criticisms of the press and declared the course of his inquiry would not be diverted in any particular direction.[9] The British stayed away from the story altogether, it likely not being conducive to the prestige of their mercantile marine, while suspiciously sensational in nature.

Whiteley subsequently returned home quietly and never claimed the balance of wages owed to him by White Star, unlike those who returned on the *Lapland*. There is no indication he gave a deposition on the disaster to the Receiver of Wreck or any solicitor for White Star. He was never called to give evidence, nor paid standby witness expenses.

But he did do something momentous. He sued.

'Another *Titanic* case,' the headline read. 'In Mr Justice Darling's court yesterday Mr Raeburn on behalf of the defendants in Whiteley v. Oceanic Steam Navigation Company (Limited), asked that a date should be fixed for the hearing.

'He said the plaintiff ... alleged negligent steering and unseaworthiness of the vessel, and it would be necessary for a number of nautical witnesses to attend ... Monday March 2nd was provisionally fixed.'[10]

Nothing transpired in early March. Nor did the case appear in the advance warning lists in late February. The explanation seems obvious – it was struck out because the Oceanic Steam Navigation Company, trading as the White Star Line, settled with the waiter. And the proof that he was paid off lies in another newspaper clipping:

At the West London County Court yesterday Thomas Whiteley, a music hall artist, made application to his Honour Sir W. Lucius Selfe, for a payment into court from a sum which had been paid into his credit, in connection with the Titanic *disaster.*

In replying to his Honour, applicant said he jumped from the ship, and had a leg broken among the wreckage ... he had been in hospital till two months ago, and had now succeeded in obtaining an engagement as baritone ...

His Honour: What do you want now?

Applicant: My mother has had to keep me for two years, and I want £25 for her.

His Honour: And the balance?

Applicant: I leave it to your Honour.

His Honour: Well, I'll take care of it for you. There will be an order for payment of £25 to Mrs Whiteley.[11]

So Whiteley took money in return for dropping his lawsuit. This seems to be further proof of the severity of the fire and of the fact that the *Titanic* was 'unseaworthy' when she left England, long before she entered an icefield or collided with a berg. She should not have sailed in the first place.

And there is yet further proof of this – because the *Daily Mirror* carried a photograph of Whiteley within days of the disaster, headlined 'Steward's Premonition'. (Whiteley himself was then incommunicado on the *Carpathia*.) It said he 'appears to have had a foreboding that misfortune would overtake the vessel. Bidding goodbye to some friends at Southampton, he said: "I don't think I shall ever see you again. We are going to have a wreck."'[12]

The friends told the story as soon as the ship went down. It seems likely then that Whiteley must have known about the fire in the coal bunker burning since Belfast, that which had caused the original firemen to leave en masse. Its 'volcano' potential was why he feared a wreck – and feared it prior to leaving port, just as others did. This knowledge of the fire was why he was able to claim 'unseaworthiness' before she left, and why Clement Edwards MP was ready to take the case.

White Star had no need to have such lurid claims ventilated. No doubt they took the view that the case could conceivably affect bookings more substantially than the relatively small outlay needed to mollify an injured steward. And so a deal was arrived at. They bought him off – and yet they continued to tenaciously fight the passenger cases.

Clearly, alleged 'unseaworthiness' and 'steering error' were viewed as far more threatening than claims of reckless speed amounting to negligence.

38

IT HAPPENED BEFORE
(AND AGAIN)

ATLANTIC AND VOLTURNO

It was a crisp day in April when the White Star Line suffered the worst recorded loss of life on the North Atlantic. The date was the foolish first of the month – in 1873 – and gruesomely shows that the operators of RMS *Titanic* had a corpse-strewn history of sending ships to sea with not enough coal.

The SS *Atlantic* was but two years old, one of the largest and most luxurious steamships in the world. She sailed from Liverpool with a mixed cargo, including copper ingots and beer. The ship called at Queenstown on 21 March and took on four saloon passengers, 143 adult steerage and no fewer than twenty children and eight babies. There were now 952 on board, including 141 crew and 200 minors.

The outward passage soon became an ordeal. Within two days a gale pounded the ship, worsening to a storm the following day. A wheelhouse window was smashed and a lifeboat torn away. Stores on deck were ripped off by malevolent waves and headway bought at huge expense of coal. The battering would last five days in all.

After eight days at sea Captain James Agnew Williams became worried at how much coal had been consumed. Sails were raised to augment their energies, but howling winds would rise further and tear them to shreds. By now the barometer was indicating another tempest on the way.

Ten days into the crossing saw the *Atlantic* 460 miles east of Sandy Hook with just 128 tons of coal remaining. The seriousness of the situation can be gauged by the fact the boilers were eating 70–75 tons a day for results that averaged 200–240 miles. In short, they needed two full days' coal to make New York and had the equivalent of one and three-quarters.

Captain Williams figured the coal could run out 80 miles from his destination. Feeling he had no alternative, he altered course for Halifax, Nova Scotia, ironically the port to which the *Titanic* was being towed by erroneous early wireless reports in 1912. That night the weather turned from the merely demonic to the screamingly satanic as the ship inched towards Nova Scotia's treacherous coast. Captain Williams left word that he was to be roused at 3 a.m. as they drew near to landfall.

Second Officer Henry Metcalf left the bridge unattended – contrary to all regulations – as he went to rouse the skipper at 3.12 a.m. As he shook the master conscious, a voice rang out: 'Breakers ahead!' Metcalf dashed back to his post and pulled the telegraph handle to full speed astern. The quartermaster flung the wheel over as far as it would go. But the *Atlantic* threw herself bodily onto a rock at Marr's Head.

Hundreds of steerage passengers struggled in the darkness as perishingly cold water poured into their accommodation. Within eight minutes of collision the *Atlantic* had heeled over onto her starboard side, entombing hundreds. Dozens climbed the masts and rigging. A quartermaster managed to get a rope to a jagged peak ashore and a perilous evacuation began ... 40 agonising yards in the midst of fury to the doubtful sanctuary of a wave-lashed outcrop. Nonetheless some 250 people achieved the feat.

By now, word had got to shore and desperate rescue attempts were organised. Still the anguish dragged on – until, at 5 a.m., the sea broke the back of the *Atlantic*'s resistance. Her stern broke off and immediately sank.

Passenger Patrick Leahy said: 'A large mass of something drifted past the ship – as it passed by, a moan seemed to surge up. It was the women. The sea swept them out of the steerage, and with their children, to the number of 200 or 300, they drifted thus to eternity.' Not a single woman lived.

By daylight, fishing boats came alongside the hulk to pluck off what survivors they could. Captain Williams' hair had reportedly begun to turn white from the harrowing scenes. He was persuaded to embark – and left some eighty people clawed into the rigging. Twelve-year-old steerage passenger John Hindley still clung to the mizzen mast at 8.45 a.m., his parents and brothers having drowned. Local reverend William Ancient took a boat close to the wreck and hauled him aboard, the single child survivor of 200 aboard.

A total of 562 people died in what was the world's worst merchantman wreck. 400 males survived. The White Star Line's supreme head, Thomas Henry Ismay (father to J. Bruce Ismay), was said to 'tremble under the calamity'.

There was an inquiry, of course. The final report declared: 'It would have been more judicious to have had at least 100 tons more fuel on board ... the *Atlantic*, though in other respects well found and equipped, was not supplied with sufficient coal of a quality suitable for a passenger ship of her class for a voyage to New York on the 20th of March last.

'We therefore share the opinion ... that Captain Williams was justified in bearing up for Halifax to obtain fuel.

'In arriving at the conclusion that the *Atlantic* was insufficiently coaled for this voyage, considering the character of the coal, we are compelled to differ with several gentlemen of well-known position and experience ... it appears to us that not enough margin was allowed for waste, bad stoking and the swift-burning character of the coal.

'No passenger ship of her class should be short of coal on the 11th day of her voyage to New York, as the *Atlantic*, in our opinion, undoubtedly was.'[1]

The finding in relation to coal was damning, so much so that the White Star Line protested and appealed, seeking to quash the findings. Instead they would be upheld, raising age-old transport questions (applicable today, for example, in aviation) over fuel loads and margins of safety.

Titanic second-class passenger Lawrence Beesley recognised that coal had to pay for its own weight with more coal to power its propulsion. He wrote: 'The considerations that inspired the builders to design the *Titanic* on the lines on which she was constructed were those of speed, weight of displacement, passenger and cargo accommodation.

'High speed is very expensive, because the initial cost of the necessary powerful machinery is enormous, the running expenses entailed very heavy, and passenger and cargo accommodation have to be fined down to make the resistance through the water as little as possible and to keep the weight down.'[2] Bulkheads could not have much bulk.

* * *

Catastrophe happened again, the year after the *Titanic* went down. The Uranium Steamship Company vessel *Volturno* caught fire in mid-Atlantic. Christopher Pennington, her wireless operator, had a 'vivid and horrifying' dream prior to leaving port that his ship was ablaze in mid-ocean and that panic reigned aboard. 'I could see myself at the apparatus, sending frantic calls for help.' The vision so impressed him he wrote a letter seeking a transfer, but was refused.[3]

A few weeks later, on 2 October 1913, *Volturno* left Rotterdam for New York carrying 561 passengers. Her captain was Francis Inch, a thirty-six-year-old Londoner. The weather was fine until Bishop Rock, when it changed and began blowing a gale. It worsened the next day, 6 October. At midnight two days later 'it was blowing very hard and the ship was rolling heavily', far out into the Atlantic.

Inch was woken early next morning by the chief officer, who reported smoke billowing out of No. 1 hatch. He ordered all hands turned out and gave strict instructions not to tell the passengers, but they already knew. Before the captain finished dressing, the fore part of the ship was in flames. When he got on deck he was met by a quartermaster 'with his face all burnt'. Inch asked how and was told 'the forecastle – there are men in there burning'. Next came two small explosions and a very violent detonation, 'which seemed to shake everything'.[4] The chief officer reported the compasses had been wrecked, and both the steering gear and the engine room telegraph were jammed. They were now completely helpless.

How did it start? A German named Frederick Badke said the steerage knew anyone caught smoking below would be fined five dollars, 'but of course it is impossible to stop Russians smoking unless you muzzle them.

'When a steward appeared suddenly, one of the Russians, afraid of being caught in the act, probably dropped a lighted cigarette through a hole in the floor. There were holes everywhere.' But he had not witnessed any such thing and this was supposition.[5]

It was also believed the fire could have been caused by friction in the cargo as it shifted in heavy seas. It consisted of saltpetre, barium chloride, paint, oil liquor and barium superoxide. A later inquiry heard of the loss through fire of the *Rialto* in 1897 and the *Cygnet* in 1903, both carrying unstable barium superoxide. This was ruled 'probable cause', although no one knew for sure.

A major body of opinion believed a spontaneous coal fire in a forward bunker had been to blame in *Volturno*'s case. The British magazine *John Bull* had no doubt that this was the cause, denouncing a 'tragedy of incompetence' at the Board of Trade and calling for its chief to be hung:

The country was amazed by the accuracy with which our prediction of the Titanic catastrophe [over lifeboats] came true. It is now being staggered by the fulfilment of our forebodings regarding the recent holocaust at sea.

Just over a year ago [7 September 1912] we published an article exposing the lamentable shortcomings of the Board of Trade, in the course of which we said –

'A very serious source of danger to those on board, and one from which some day will come a huge disaster, is the risk of fire breaking out in the coal bunkers.

'Nevertheless, the fire appliances are usually absurdly deficient, and crews are ignorant of fire drill ...'

From reports to hand, as we go to press, of the awful catastrophe, it is clear that our forebodings have come true in every particular, for we are told that 'the flame burst through amidships from the engine room and bunkers'.[6]

Captain Inch found huge orange tongues were reaching back to the bridge just five or six minutes after he first came on deck. He gave orders to take to the lifeboats. Number 2 was lowered, but the block on the after fall tumbled off, tipping her immediately and causing everyone to spill out. All were lost.

Other lifeboats met a similarly ghastly fate before Inch received word from Pennington that the *Carmania* was coming to their assistance. Launches were suspended and the choking passengers crowded aft. Inch and the chief engineer gravely discussed the possibility of flooding two forward holds, but the risk was too great since the bow was already dipping. Third Officer Dusselmann declared the only trouble was when some stokers became excited and tried to rush the boats, whereupon the captain drove them back with a pistol.

A fleet of ships, summoned by wireless, was soon on the scene but found it impossible to get near the burning ship because of the churning seas. All the brasswork in the *Volturno*'s forecastle melted and disappeared, along with the glass in portholes half an inch thick. Steel girders became white hot. Captain Inch told how he pushed a hose as far as it would go into a burning hatch, only to see flames rise and melt the nozzle. Darkness fell.

One woman with a babe in her arms, overcome with fatigue, fell asleep against the rail. When she awoke the baby was gone. It had rolled into the sea. But the winds abated in daylight and the swells dropped, with the tanker *Narragansett* spreading calming oil, allowing lifeboats from the vessels standing by to eventually ferry all remaining to safety.

Captain Inch suffered intense agony on the *Kroonland*. The film over his eyeballs had dried and he was blind for four days. A total of 136 people died.

The abandoned *Volturno* became a derelict. She was seen adrift a day or two later by *Titanic* rescuer Captain Arthur Rostron, now commanding the *Campania*. He warily circled the smoking hulk, saw no signs of life, and steamed on.

39

SUMMARY DECISIONS

OIL AND TROUBLED WATERS

Six months after the *Titanic* disaster, in October 1912, the White Star Line and Harland & Wolff discussed making the *Olympic* and *Britannic* oil burning. They were clearly no longer enamoured of coal.

It happened when the *Olympic* was brought into Belfast to be made even more unsinkable through a new interior double skin, and higher and better bulkheads. The third sister, *Britannic*, was in the early building stages. She had originally been earmarked for the name *Gigantic*. However, after the *Titanic* and the pulpit fulminations against a 'blasphemous' pride in unsinkability, this intended name had to be speedily dropped. It was not to be the sole response.

The *Liverpool Daily Post* stated: 'Our Belfast correspondent learns that as a sequel to the *Titanic* disaster practically all work on what is intended to be a considerably larger ship, the *Gigantic*, has been temporarily stopped until Mr Bruce Ismay returns, when doubtless the plans for the new vessel, especially with reference to the question of longitudinal bulkheads, in addition to transverse compartments, and other matters relating to its stability and the extension of the double-bottom, will be fully discussed.'[1]

Many considerations awaited the outcome of the British inquiry (which proved gratifyingly positive for the Line), but by September the possible switch to a new fuel had seeped thoroughly into senior thinking. The Harland & Wolff board minutes say: 'Lord Pirrie referred to the question of the adoption of oil fuel in the *Olympic* and *Britannic*, and it was arranged that subject to confirmation after his meeting with Mr Ismay on the seventeenth instant, the double skin and double bottom of the *Olympic*, while the vessel is here, is to be made suitable for carrying oil in case it is required for fuel, one of the double bottom tanks to be filled with oil with the object of testing its tightness.'[2]

For one reason or another the conversion to oil was long-fingered, the Great

War intervening. The *Britannic* would become the largest merchantman loss of that conflict in terms of tonnage when she went down to a mine in the Aegean.

Nonetheless, the immediate post-conflict period would see postcards issued of the *Olympic* with a legend proudly declaring her: 'The First Great Liner to be Fitted With Oil-Fired Engines.'[3]

The coal bunker fire on the *Titanic*'s one and only voyage had to form part of the rationale that propelled White Star in this pioneering direction – just as the fire impelled the maiden voyager to ever-increased endeavour across the Atlantic.

The man who became the salvor in possession of the *Titanic* wreck (after its discovery on the seabed by Robert Ballard in September 1985) believed that the uncontrolled fire aboard the ship offered multiple reasons for attempting to reach New York quickly. George Tulloch of RMST Inc. was convinced that the initial iceberg bump triggered a massive explosion, suggesting after his own deep submersible investigations that such a blast blew an *outward* hole in the hull. The *Daily Express*, citing Tulloch, considered that this claimed detonation had been 'fuelled by gas from a fire that had been raging in the bunker'.

The report quoted the explorer, whose company recovered a wealth of artefacts from the debris field: 'Though it was quite common for coal fires to occur on board ships in those days, there is no doubt they had the potential to create more serious problems.

'I know I wouldn't have wanted to travel for ten days on top of an uncontrolled fire,' said Tulloch. He found it incredible the ship could have set sail with one of her 30-feet-high coal bunkers ablaze.[4]

Walter Lord, the doyen of *Titanic* authors, who breathed new life into the story of the great ship after the Second World War, saw a degree of merit in one of these arguments. He wrote: 'Perhaps George Tulloch's theory about the fire in the coal bunker dictating a need to arrive a night early in New York, under cover of darkness, bears some credibility.'[5] Tulloch's idea was that a Tuesday-night arrival might cloak the fireboat operations to drown the outbreak – while morning would dawn bright and clear for untrammelled boasting about the speed of the crossing and the vessel's imperviousness to obstacles that wrecked the plans of other ships.

The search for a credible explanation for a swift sinking is fuelled by the absence of the 300-foot continuous gash, which the public was told in 1912 was responsible for the *Titanic*'s demise, and which Lord Mersey used to render irrelevant all other arguments towards possible bulkhead frailty.[6] Only tiny openings on the starboard side of the hull can be attributed to the berg's effect (there are far larger openings on the port side, where she did not strike while on the surface, caused instead by the plunging bow hitting the seabed), but these are not enough to meet the minimum calculations for water ingress and flooding.

Sonar probing of the extensive part of the bow that is buried in mud has not offered any evidence of long lateral tears. The alternatives seem to be that the vessel suffered rents in her keel through grounding on a spur (which might explain bottom-up flooding in boiler room 4 and other oral accounts), or that her relatively swift sinking arose from internal failures – since it was not caused by bulkheads being bypassed by an extended laceration.

Bulkhead fitness is an issue, since their bestowed integrity was the sole reason the *Titanic* carried so few lifeboats, in agreement with the Board of Trade. The ship was supposedly 'her own lifeboat'.[7] If that internal strength had held, she might have stayed afloat long enough for everyone to be ferried to a flotilla of rescue vessels, as with *Volturno* – which may have been on fire, but did not have the twin effect of piercing, pounding seawater flooding into her.

The double-skin and improved bulkheads that were subsequently installed on the *Olympic*, coupled with early consideration of conversion to oil, seem to indicate that White Star and Harland & Wolff knew the public had been misled as to the whole cause. Long before the wreck was ever found, men like Joseph Mulholland and James McGiffin were justified in believing the outcome was the result of speed, even if they might also have sensed they did not have all parts to the jigsaw.

Professor Robert H. Essenhigh of the Department of Mechanical Engineering at Ohio State University took a different route – approaching the question from the perspective of scientific observation in modern times, with no contemporary word-of-mouth to assist him. In a paper in 2004, Essenhigh addressed why the *Titanic* proceeded at full speed into an icefield she had been warned about – and came upon the coal fire. 'The most effective containment solution involved sailing at full speed to draw down the coal in the bunker,' he noted.[8]

He next used bunker data supplied to him by Harland & Wolff, along with the results of experiments at Sheffield University in the 1950s, to conclude that 'a fire that originated in the top half of the bunker would still have been in the bunker at the time of collision'. This contradicts some stokehold witnesses but would support *Titanic* fireman John Dilley, who insisted all uncontrolled fire had not been extinguished prior to the ship meeting her nemesis.

Essenhigh said computer models for the initiation of fires in coal piles 'show a possible behaviour pattern relevant to the *Titanic* bunker fire'. He was working long before Imperial University in London found through simulations that there would be sustained high temperatures sufficient to warp the forward bulkhead – and in exactly the pattern testified by eyewitness Fred Barrett in 1912.

The most powerful evidence was given soon after the disaster by trimmer George Cavell. It was proof of the most power output all voyage, and was witnessed just minutes before calamity. Cavell was a twenty-two-year-old Southampton man, son of a former ship's fireman. He told the British inquiry he saw 225 pounds of steam pressure on his gauge that deadly night. Asked by Solicitor General Sir John Simon if this level had been demanded, he answered without guile: 'That was not the order. That is what steam there was.' '225lbs?' 'Yes.' He knew it by reading the gauge 'just before I went into the bunker' – in which he would become entombed by a thunderous fall of carbon occasioned by collision.[9]

Cavell remembered the steam pressure clearly, but sour interruption came from the commissioner. Lord Mersey asked Sir John: 'Have you no better evidence on this point than this?'

Attorney General Sir Rufus Isaacs volunteered: 'All the engineers are drowned. We are getting the best evidence we can.'

It was a subtle invitation to the court to write off Cavell's testimony because it did not come from the lips of an engineer.

Thomas Scanlan, counsel for the National Sailors' and Firemen's Union, was not so easily turned aside: 'Are you quite sure that you noticed on the gauge an indication of 225lbs steam?'

Cavell: 'Yes.'[10]

'Do you know that those engines are only designed for a working pressure of 215lbs?'

'No.'[11]

This is indeed the case, confirmed by an appendix tucked into the back of the British inquiry report and evidence. There it is certified by Harland & Wolff, by main boiler constructors Cockburn & Co., and by the Liverpool Engineering and Condenser Company. The maximum pressure of steam, pounds per square inch, is to be 215 and no more. The *Titanic* was punching an extra ten pounds of pressure beyond that design ceiling, thrashing her engines and prodigiously working all shafts to turn her propellers.

So said Cavell – although he was met by those who did not want to hear what he was saying.

Fireman George William Beauchamp told the same inquiry of the boilers: 'Sometimes they carry 210 [pounds of pressure] and sometimes 200. I think we were carrying thereabout 210 then.'[12]

Yet when Beauchamp was asked: 'Can you say what pressure of steam was being carried at that time [on Sunday 14 April, when the ship struck]?', he replied: 'I could not say.'[13]

Cavell very much could, and did, repeatedly. But his evidence was ignored and no others were asked about the pressure of steam in the stokehold that night – although such information might still lie in the lost depositions given at Plymouth by firemen never called.

There is, however, the New York *Sun* interview with hospitalised fireman John Thompson, who said: 'They carried 215 pounds of steam all the time. The boilers could not stand any more.'[14]

Storekeeper Frank Prentice pronounced 'with feeling' many years later: 'If ever a ship was thrown away, it was the *Titanic*. The whole tragedy of the sinking was speed. That was the only thing they thought about.' They were 'going flat out' from Queenstown, 'and on the morning of the fourteenth we knew there was ice all over the place'.[15]

Second Officer Charles Lightoller admitted: 'In those days ... everything was devoted to making a passage. The ship was driven smashing through everything and anything in the way of weather.' Fifty pages further on, concerning conditions in the stokehold: 'The instructions were to keep up that "arrow", indicating steam pressure, at all costs, regardless of body or bones.'[16]

Indeed. And there is one peculiar admission made by J. Bruce Ismay while on the stand in America, the significance of which has been overlooked. Early afternoon questioning of the White Star chief on 30 April turned to his visit to the bridge in the wake of the accident. Wearily, Ismay replied: 'When I went up to ask him [Captain Smith] what had happened, he told me we had struck an iceberg, and I asked whether he thought the matter serious, and he said he thought it was. That was the first intimation I had.'

He was soon asked: 'Did the chief engineer of the *Titanic* state to you the extent of the damage?'[17]

Ismay answered the question without realising its importance. He told of Bell's reply: 'He said that he thought the damage was serious; that he hoped the pumps would be able to control the water.' The significance, however, was in the meeting itself, not in its detail.

Senator William Alden Smith, presiding, asked how long after the accident this meeting had been. Ismay replied: 'I should think perhaps half an hour afterwards; 35 or 40 minutes.'

Ismay also declared that he visited the bridge twice.[18] The first occasion may have been 'ten minutes after' impact, and 'when I went up the second time to the bridge' thirty-five minutes had elapsed. Yet his only conversation with Captain Smith was on the first occasion. There was none at all, apparently, on the second.

Leaving aside a double visit by an 'ordinary passenger' to the command centre at the height of the crisis, Ismay insisted he never once went below to the engine room, or paid any visit to the working spaces. Within a minute or two of beginning to give evidence in America, however, on his very first morning, Ismay declared that after receiving Smith's pessimistic reply, 'I'm afraid she is', to his query on whether she was seriously damaged, 'I then went down below.'[19] The phrase 'down below' has connotations of the engine room or boiler rooms, but Ismay corrected himself as he realised the import of what he had started to tell the senators: 'I then went down below, *I think it was*, where I met Mr Bell, the chief engineer, who was in the main companionway.'

Consider this statement. Ismay's cabin was on B deck. He belatedly mentions the 'main companionway' or crew passage on E deck (the chief engineer was never on the bridge after collision; Quartermaster Olliver carried messages down to him). There Ismay fortuitously met Bell ... but given that he had descended so far in the vessel, we must conclude that Ismay was actively *seeking him out*, and would have continued into the engine room if necessary (and may in fact have done so). He had no other motivation to 'go below' to that degree, other than to seek a second opinion to that of his captain from his own close confidant.

Here is Ismay as 'Super Captain', distrustful of Smith: 'I asked if he [Bell] thought the ship was seriously damaged, and he said he thought she was, but was quite satisfied the pumps would keep her afloat.'[20]

Ismay had usurped Captain Smith's role every step of the way. He issued orders to everyone: officers, chief engineer and captain alike. And so he bears full responsibility. It was his order alone for the highest possible speed, despite Ismay himself having zero navigational experience – and despite an ice warning being physically thrust into his hand. It must also have been his order, when he first went on the bridge, to get the ship underway again, as alleged by Lightoller's granddaughter. And it was only when he returned there after meeting Bell below, thirty-five minutes after the accident, that he reluctantly consented – despite his claim of no conversation with Smith on this occasion – to the cessation of Slow Ahead.

EPILOGUE

EMBERS

Charles Lightoller's memoirs of 1935, *Titanic and Other Ships*, can be interpreted as a thinly disguised confessional or a treasure map towards the truth. It begins with his rounding the Horn as an apprentice in the sailing ship *Primrose Hill*. Close to Antarctica, the region is infested with icebergs.[1] Suddenly a frozen wall is sighted 'right ahead', as will be the plight with the *Titanic*. Lightoller writes: 'The vital question was, in what direction did the ice extend?

'If to windward, as well as leeward, then we should undoubtedly strike and sink,' meaning both evasive options would be fatal. With the ice one-eighth of a mile away, 'we must take the chance'. And on this occasion, a move is executed and their luck holds.

A similar situation, this time involving an island, crops up twenty-three pages later, with Lightoller now aboard the *Holt Hill* in the South Pacific. Officer Robert Mowatt is confronted at night by an obstruction ahead in a heavy squall. 'In his excitement, he [gives] the wrong order, though he wasn't to know that.' The ship collided with the lonely outcrop of St Paul's Island. Land extended to windward, to which Mowatt turned, but far less to leeward.[2]

Most notably the Mowatt order was countermanded by the skipper, George 'Old Jock' Sutherland. 'She had just gone off so far that she was back on her original course [after the initial avoidance manoeuvre had been reversed], heading straight for the land.'

The author sympathised. It was the 'hardest possible choice the Captain of a ship is ever called on to make ...'

The *Holt Hill* struck, but Lightoller called the captain's decision correct. 'By doing it he saved the lives of pretty well everyone on board.' The crew managed to scramble ashore and just days afterwards signalled a passing ship to secure rescue.

With the advent of steam, Lightoller tells in his chapter 'Greyhounds of the Atlantic' of speedy services between Europe and the New World, bringing huge improvements for all aboard, though weather problems remained. One physical hazard was fishing boats and sailing vessels, typically from Newfoundland and France, which could be encountered off the Grand Banks. Visibility at night was at a premium, he emphasised, when 'every possible precaution and care is taken to avoid a collision. Two lookout men are always on their stations. In fog, these are always doubled, as also is the lookout on the bridge; the ship is slowed down ...'[3]

The *Titanic* was not in fog, but there was anticipated danger. Nevertheless, she was not slowed down and her lookouts were not doubled.

Lightoller relates one near miss: 'A slight loom ahead, helm hard over, and gliding by within biscuit-throw goes a big topsail schooner. A quiet exchange of glances on the bridge, a sort of general sigh at the escape, and everyone again freezes into immobility and intense concentration – watching and listening.'[4]

Such a 'narrow shave' is similar to the iceberg account of lookout Reg Lee and to Quartermaster George Rowe's windjammer impression.[5] But on the *Titanic*'s bridge there was no one for First Officer William Murdoch to exchange meaningful glances with, because we are told he was alone. Why wasn't 'everyone' maintaining vigilance?

Lightoller's key chapter on the 'Loss of the *Titanic*' is puzzling, even maddening, unless it is grasped that there is a method to his meandering. From the first mention of the vessel, Lightoller becomes obsessed with fire – which Lord Mersey pronounced had 'nothing at all' to do with the tragedy. Lightoller firmly denied in evidence the bunker blaze had ever been mentioned to him on the maiden voyage. However, it may be he was operating under some kind of psychological need in 1935 to confess the scale of the on-board fire, and that he had known about it all along:

From the Oceanic *as First* [Officer], *I was appointed to the* Titanic *of tragic memory ... it is difficult to convey any idea of the size ... it took me fourteen days before I could with confidence find my way from one part of that ship to another by the shortest route.*

A sailor does not walk round with a plan in his pocket, he must carry his ship in his head, and in an emergency such as fire must be able to get where he wants by sheer instinct – certainly without a chance of getting lost on the way.

Touching on fire, the modern ship's equipment is such that it is almost impossible, with fair play, for a fire to get a serious hold. I say this, despite the fact that quite recently no less than three modern liners have been burned out.

Generally speaking, the fire-fighting equipment is based on something like these lines. Close adjacent to the bridge is the Master Fire Station, where a fireman in full regalia is on duty night and day ... in close touch with secondary Fire Stations situated in commanding positions throughout the ship.[6]

Lightoller goes on to refer to shipboard fire and attendant precautions eight more times in the course of a two-and-a-half-page treatment, ending abruptly: 'But to return to the *Titanic* ...'[7]

The reader might note that the crisis he automatically associates with the *Titanic* is not one of collision but 'an emergency such as fire'. This certainly establishes doubt regarding his outright denial of any awareness of an outbreak during his time on the ship, especially when some of the most humble crew and passengers clearly knew. If his sworn evidence is to be taken as truth (despite his own reference to the 'whitewash brush'), then that long digression about fire when beginning to write about the *Titanic* is puzzling indeed.

And Lightoller has demonstrable form in coding his memoirs. The *Olympic* was nearly wrecked within weeks of the *Titanic* (see endnote 3, Ch. 10, p. 278), but White Star covered it up. It emerged in 1987 that Lightoller wrote sly references. From page 115 of the first edition (dropped from the paperback): 'One of our crack Atlantic Liners (I won't mention names) coming home from New York; instead of being well south of the Scillies, found herself north of these islands', heading for a reef that has claimed over 200 vessels. He disguised details, making it sound as if this befell a rival operator. But the ex-*Titanic* officer (who spied for the British government along the German coast before the Second World War) referred to it as 'a narrow shave', the phrase of Fred Fleet in the crow's nest.

Lightoller's granddaughter, Lady Louise Patten, meanwhile draws attention to his four-time denial to the US inquiry that he ever talked with William Murdoch after the accident. Yet in his book Lightoller admitted attending Murdoch's cabin, where senior figures obtained firearms.[8] 'He did, of course, talk to his fellow senior officers and he did, of course, learn what had gone wrong,' says Patten.[9] 'He knew of Hichens' steering error, the blunder which had cost Murdoch the critical minutes he needed,' she claims.

Patten goes on: 'He knew, too, that Bruce Ismay had gone up to the bridge and persuaded Captain Smith that it would be safe to move *Titanic* slowly forward, despite her damaged hull – a decision which almost certainly led to the ship sinking many hours earlier than she might otherwise have done.

'All this my grandfather learned not only from conversation in Murdoch's cabin, but also during snatched briefings while the lifeboats were being loaded.'

She adds: 'By stating that he hadn't spoken to Murdoch, he [Lightoller] could claim ignorance of what might have gone wrong up on the bridge.

'So to avoid awkward questions, my grandfather said that not once during the hours between collision and sinking had he bothered to ask why, in calm seas and on a clear night, the iceberg had not been avoided.'[10]

* * *

There is, meanwhile, another piece of 'grey evidence' about Ismay's influence on the bridge that was not offered in any official setting. It comes from a high-society woman who travelled from Manhattan to far-off Nova Scotia, where the *Titanic* corpses were landed in 1912. The *Halifax Chronicle* reported:

Among the many persons to come to the city last week to await the arrival of the MacKay-Bennett *with the bodies … was Mrs* [John R.] *Beam, the widow of a wealthy New Yorker.*

She came not to identify and claim the body of any of her kind, but that of one of the ill-fated ship's stewards, one who had faithfully served her late husband and herself when passengers on the Oceanic *and which ship the late Captain Smith commanded.*

Mrs Beam interested herself in the steward [Thomas Clark] *and his family, and when she heard he had perished with his ship and that there was possibility of his body being brought to Halifax started for this city with the hope of securing and giving it burial.*[11]

What really matters is what the fifty-eight-year-old railroad heiress said next:

Mrs Beam has travelled with Captain Smith and also Mr Ismay. In conversation with a well-known citizen she related a circumstance, which has an important bearing on the in-vestigation now being conducted at Washington.

The Oceanic *was making very heavy weather. The seas were pouring over the ship. It was the time when the big ventilators were carried away. Captain Smith sent word to Mr Ismay – sent word by the very steward whose body Mrs Beam is in search of – that the water was pouring down the funnel opening, and suggested slackening speed. Mr Ismay's reply was not one of fear. 'That is nothing,' he said. 'That is what the ship was built for. Tell the Captain to keep her at it.'*

Carrie Beam got the captain wrong – John G. Cameron commanded in February 1904 when *The New York Times* reported the *Oceanic* was almost submerged in a hurricane on being struck by one 'great mass of water'. It tore away twenty feet of the forward starboard railing, other solid fixtures, and 'seemed as though it would carry away the deckhouse'.

The *Times* trumpeted: '*Oceanic* did not reduce her speed, but continued to plough through the great head seas which rolled at her and piled over her from time to time.' It added: 'J. Bruce Ismay, Chairman and Managing Director, was a passenger on the vessel.'[12]

Despite her captaincy error, Mrs Beam's account is corroborated in its salient points. The ship did not slacken speed in dangerous conditions and Ismay was responsible. The lady fully knew that the magnate had displayed both prior hubris and a readiness to play supreme navigator, overruling the inclinations of the master.

Aware of his role in the tragedy, Ismay was broken by the disaster. In November 1912 he purchased Costelloe Lodge in Ireland, lapped by the unforgiving Atlantic. Leaving White Star the following year, he increasingly retreated there, availing of one of the finest salmon rivers in the British Isles. But while temporarily unoccupied in September 1922, the house was burned to the ground by insurgents of the Irish Republican Army. Within two months Ismay was seeking compensation. Two and a half years later came a court award of £7,215 for loss of the house, outbuildings, trees and shrubs, a boathouse and precious rowing-boats – worked by a ghillie when fishing. It was much more handsome redress than the £100 received by a pioneering Irish plaintiff from a farm 100 miles away for the loss of his son on Mr Ismay's steamer.

The ship owner died in 1937, *The Times* noting that the *Titanic* 'affair' had cast a shadow over the remainder of his life. Fire had a last say in his personal history in the form of cremation, and his ashes were then interred in an ornate family tomb at Putney Vale, London.

The *Titanic*'s fire story dwindled to an ember in the years following the disaster, but a whisper may have emboldened self-proclaimed survivor Johann Bergmann to tell the *Münchner Merkur* (Munich Mercury) on the fiftieth anniversary the sensational story that firemen had shut off colleagues in the flames to prevent its spread. He was a liar, however, never having been on board.

Fire folklore persisted nonetheless. It formed a major component of Beryl Bainbridge's novel *Every Man for Himself*, winner of the Whitbread award (and shortlisted for the Booker prize) in 1996.

In 2012, months after the centenary drew worldwide attention, an elderly woman called into a British provincial auction house and enquired whether what she carried was 'worth anything'. She presented the Kempster album, an unparalleled series of pin-sharp images of the *Titanic* at Belfast, taken by the managing director of the electrical plant at Harland & Wolff. Some of the images show a diagonal mark on the hull in the starboard area where the ship would later strike the iceberg, and they rekindled controversy, leading to scientific consideration of the 1912 fire in a television documentary. Two experienced marine professionals who saw the programme came to identical conclusions. Naval architect David Hutchings suggested the shape and angle of that smudge on the *Titanic*'s exterior could have come about because 'high temperatures sprung rivets along a strake and released some sooty smoke down the ship's side – the downward angle being caused by the draught along the ship's side'. Former Royal Navy officer Mark Mitchell, who taught damage control and firefighting, opined that the straight edge of the topmost part of the mark 'is a split seam where rivets have popped. Smoke would escape here but be dragged downward by wetting and the salt-laden atmosphere.'

Popped rivets could be repaired in port, or at least given a temporary patch. The mark, however, is above the waterline – whereas it is down below that the berg wreaked havoc. In the final analysis these photographs are inconclusive, yet have allowed a draught of oxygen onto the buried bunker fire story that seared and scarred firemen told on landfall in New York.

Those who got there, that is. One of their number was just another corpse, floating on the waves for the *MacKay-Bennett* to find and to bring to the port where Mrs Beam and scores of others stood vigil. Newly married stoker Joseph Dawson was ultimately identified by his National Sailors' and Firemen's Union card. He was twenty-three and wore dungarees and a grey shirt. Body 227 was buried in Halifax under a stone later marked 'J. Dawson'. Decades of neglect abruptly ended when flocks of teenage girls began to mourn the young 'Jack Dawson', as they thought he was the character played by Leonardo DiCaprio in the 1997 movie *Titanic*. They left flowers, soft toys, cinema stubs, even love notes. Truth can be stranger and more surreal than fiction. This tragic trimmer lies in cold, often frozen, Canadian soil, though he had been accustomed when animated in life to sweated labour in the roaring 120-degree heat of a transatlantic stokehold.

It was coal, combustion and compulsion that ultimately impelled the *Titanic* to icy disaster. Along with his fellow Josephs, J. Bruce Ismay and chief engineer Bell, lowly Joseph Dawson may indeed serve as emblem and embodiment of a fire-fuelled fiasco.

APPENDIX 1

THEY COULDN'T
STAND THE HEAT

DELIVERY TRIP FIREMEN WHO
QUIT AT SOUTHAMPTON

(95.6 per cent)

LEADING HAND STOKERS
John Cullen, William Barnes, William Emnes, Samuel McGaw, Michael Nolan, Thomas Brennan, Barney McKenna, Hugh Whinnery, Thomas Murphy, Stokes Barker, Hugh Woods. (11)

FIREMEN
David Gorman, Samuel Strange, Charles Kinstry, Andrew Shaw, Samuel McGee, Patrick McGee, Robert Bittle, Thomas Tinsley, Robert Pierce, John Boal, James Black, John Cardwell, William Bridan, Nicholas Ferrant, Adam Boyd, Robert Fletcher, David McCarron, Joseph Dunlop, James Phillips, Charles McEntee, Barry McIlroy, John Keenan, George Hall, William Keenan, Daniel Mulholland, Patrick Cullen, David Kernaghan, Thomas McMillen, John Hale, William Ward, George Hutton, David Lowery, William McMillan, Thomas Croskery, John Hadley, James Stevenson, Robert Cochrane, William Chevers, John Stevenson, Frank McGough, William Jameson, John McGill, Archibald Andrews, Hugh McAllister, John Quinn, Michael Flinn, John Craig, Patrick Welsh, George McDonald, William Hanley, James Massey, David Craig, Thomas McBarty, William Miller, John Denver, James Cleland, William Swarbrick, John Farley, John Martin, Thomas O'Flannagan, Daniel McAllister, Joseph Halpin, Charles Decker, Nicholas Holme, Michael Croughane, James Walls, George Ferris, Robert Woodmy, Thomas Neill,

Frank Burness, David Glass, William Philips, William Hepburn, James Reid, John Smyth, David Bain, James Holland, James Armstrong, William Pidgeon, James McArthur, Robert Cairnes, Thomas McGivern, William Maxwell, Joseph Mulholland, Thomas Holland, William McIlroy, Robert Barkley, Patrick Morgan, James Lewis, James Little, Samuel Harkin, John Baker, William Mayes, Barry McGown, William Gregg, James Henry, Samuel McMillen, Patrick McMullen. (98)

TRIMMERS
William Simms, Robert Malken, James Carson, William Benson, Joseph Swarbrick, David Shannon, Hugh Herd, Thomas James, Robert Bradley, James Barry, Robert Wallace, William Cassidy, James Auld, William Flemming, Robert McIlroy, Matthew Stewart, John Crossley, James McIlwaine, John Harvey, James Waugh, Thomas Morrison, John Bryan, Alex Horner, Joseph Kirkpatrick, Richard McMullan, Thomas McGill, Joseph Ellison, Thomas Holman, William Bailey, William Kerney, John Stewart, Matthew Patton, Thomas Lyttle, John Flack, William Cosgrove, John Cosgrove, William Taggart, Joseph Loughran, Francis Beattie, Andrew Stevenson, Thomas Gibson, Henry McGivern, Joseph Smith, William Meehan, Arthur Valler, Patrick Keenan, William Hamilton, Thomas Robinson, Samuel Munn, Richard McGreevy, Daniel McDonald, John Mathers. (52)

GREASERS
Thomas Curran, William Gibson, William McMullan, Thomas Palles, William Burns, Patrick Rogan, John McErline, John McTeer, James McIlroy, William Gambell, James Connor, John McGrogan. (12)

DESERTED AT QUEENSTOWN
John Coffey

TOTAL: 11 + 98 + 52 + 12 + 1 = 174

THE FOLLOWING STAYED WITH THE *TITANIC*
(8; of whom 5 lost, 3 saved)
Leading hand: Joseph Beattie – drowned.

Firemen: William McQuillan – drowned; Richard Turley – drowned; William Murdock – survived; Thomas Connor – drowned; Hugh Calderwood – drowned; John Haggan – survived; Thomas Graham – survived.

APPENDIX 2

A SILENT MAJORITY

STOKEHOLD SURVIVORS NEVER CALLED TO GIVE EVIDENCE

Ernest Allen – trimmer; James Avery – trimmer; Walter Binstead – trimmer; Patrick Blake – trimmer; William Clark – fireman; George Combes – fireman; Robert Couper – fireman; John Diaper – fireman; John Dilley – fireman; Frederick Doel – fireman; Albert Dore – trimmer; Frank Dymond – fireman; Edward Flaherty – fireman; Walter Fredericks – trimmer; Albert Fryer – trimmer; George Godley – fireman; Thomas Graham – fireman; John Haggan – fireman; William Hebb – trimmer; Albert Hunt – trimmer; Wally Hurst – fireman; Charles Judd – fireman; Franz Kaspar – fireman; George Kemish – fireman; George Knight – fireman; Thomas Knowles – fireman; William Lindsay – fireman; William Major – fireman; Frank Mason – fireman; Thomas Mayzes – fireman; James McGann – trimmer; William McIntyre – trimmer; John Moore – fireman; William Murdock – fireman; Henry Noss – fireman; William Nutbeam – fireman; John O'Connor – fireman; Harry Oliver – fireman; Charles Othen – fireman; John Pearce – fireman; George Pelham – trimmer; Edgar Perry – trimmer; John Podesta – fireman; George Prangnell – greaser; John Priest – fireman; Charles Rice – fireman; Edward Self – fireman; Harry Senior – fireman; Eustace Snow – trimmer; Henry Sparkman – fireman; Albert Street – fireman; John Thompson – trimmer; Thomas Threlfall – fireman; George Thresher – fireman; Robert Triggs – fireman; Arthur White – greaser; William White – trimmer. (57 in total)

ENDNOTES

Prologue

1. Harris, Irene, 'Her Husband Went Down with the *Titanic*', *Liberty Magazine*, 23 April 1932, p. 26.
2. The three members of the 'guarantee group' in first class with Mrs Harris were chief designer Thomas Andrews, draughtsman Roderick Chisholm and electrician William H. M. Parr. All drowned. Andrews later offered advice to a stewardess, telling her to wear a life jacket 'if you value your life'.

1 Outward Bound in April

1. So said the accident report that was issued afterwards, penned in part by the marine assessor Fitzhugh Charles Annesley Lyon, who would later sit in judgment on the *Titanic*. Report 5 August 1910. https://plimsoll.southampton.gov.uk/SOTON_Documents/Plimsoll/19751.pdf.
2. 'Fire in an Emigrant Ship', *The Times*, 8 April 1910, p. 8.
3. 'The Fire in an Emigrant Ship', *The Times*, 9 April 1910, p. 6.
4. *The Times*, 8 April 1910, p. 8.
5. *Ibid.*
6. Official inquiry report, No. 7374, 5 August 1910. https://plimsoll.southampton.gov.uk/SOTON_Documents/Plimsoll/19751.pdf.

2 The Price of Unrest

1. *Daily Sketch*, 24 January 1912.
2. The guard's van was a part of the train that was not usually open to the public.
3. Editorial, *The Times*, Monday 26 February 1912, p. 9.
4. John Bull is the embodiment of England, and usually is portrayed with top hat and Union Jack waistcoat.
5. The cartoon ran in several daily newspapers, such as the *Leeds Mercury*.
6. Titanic International Society historian Jack Eaton in *Voyage*, No. 42, Winter 2003, pp. 72–3.

7. A White Star Line notice distributed to freight forwarders in March 1912, and featuring an illustration of the new steamer, declared proudly that the *Titanic* 'will be dispatched from Southampton to New York on her maiden voyage on Wednesday, April 10th, 1912, at noon', with that 'will' brooking no resistance. In smaller print it added: 'Shipment is at shippers' risk of loss or damage by fire and/ or flood.'

3 Crossing the Line

1. The US Bureau of Mines was formed in 1910. Its first bulletin, issued in 1912 by the government printing office in Washington DC, was a booklet by Horace C. Porter and F. K. Ovitz explicitly titled 'The Volatile Matter of Coal'.
2. *The Fort Wayne Sentinel*, 1 March 1912, p. 7.
3. *Cincinnati Enquirer*, 2 March 1912.
4. Author interview with Dr Guillermo Rein, screened in the Blink Films programme for Channel 4, *Titanic: The New Evidence*, broadcast on 1 January 2017.
5. Question 5240, posed at the British Wreck Commissioners' Inquiry into the sinking of the *Titanic* (henceforth Br.) on Thursday 9 May 1912. The transcripts of evidence for both the British and American inquiries into the *Titanic* disaster are online at www.titanicinquiry.org and fully searchable. American questions were not numbered, but a quotation may be found in the evidence of an individual witness or by keyword/quote search. However, this book references the original volumes, which are more accurate.
6. Br. 5239.
7. Br. 5233–7.
8. *A Voyage Closed and Done* (Michael Russell, Norwich, 2005), by his granddaughter, Pauline Matarasso, p. 16.
9. Original Sanderson reply Marconigram now in the National Maritime Museum, Greenwich (henceforth Nat. Mar. Mus.) TRNISM/3/1.
10. Br. 19111.
11. International Mercantile Marine Company: *Ships' Rules and Uniform Regulations*, consolidated 1908, p. 45.
12. Br. 19630–1.
13. Br. 19631–2.
14. Br. 19633.

15. Br. 19634.
16. Br. 19635.
17. Br. 19702.

4 An Old Man's Memory

1. The Blue Riband is an accolade given to the passenger liner in regular Atlantic service with the record highest speed. Traditionally, the record is based on average speed, as opposed to passage time, as ships often followed different routes.
2. *Sunday Independent,* 15 April 1962, p. 20.
3. In 1998 the *Irish News* quoted ninety-two-year-old journalist Paddy Scott, who had once interviewed Mulholland, claiming the encounter had occurred in Valparaiso, Chile.
4. Jessop, Violet (edited by John Maxtone-Graham), *Titanic Survivor: The Memoirs of Violet Jessop, Stewardess* (History Press, Stroud, 2007).
5. *A Night to Remember* information folder written and compiled by Robert Herrington, *c.* 1955 (The Rank Organisation), p. 59. Originally sent to newspapers and distributors, a copy is held by both the author and the Titanic Historical Society.
6. Liverpool, as opposed to Belfast, was considered the ship's home port because White Star's company headquarters were located there.
7. *Titanic* crew agreement Belfast–Southampton. Public Record Office of Northern Ireland (henceforth PRONI), Belfast. Ref: Trans 2A/45/381 C.

5 The Last Word

1. 'Impressions of the *Titanic*', *Omaha Sunday Bee,* 19 May 1912, p. 1.
2. Beesley, Lawrence, *The Loss of the Titanic* (Houghton Mifflin, Boston, 1912), p. 9.
3. Beaumont, J. C. H., *Ships – And People* (Frederick Stokes & Co, New York, 1926), p. 99.
4. '*Titanic*'s Tragic Voyage', *Irish Independent,* 18 April 1912, p. 3. This was published anonymously but was written by Browne.
5. Private collection, Richard Edkins. Viewable at www.williammurdoch.net/articles_05_williams_letters.html.
6. Wilde letter sold at auction for £29,000, March 2012 at Henry Aldridge & Son, Devizes, Wiltshire. Lot 340.

7. *Southampton Pictorial*, first issue, 6 April 1912.

8. *Chart and Compass* magazine, republished in Hyslop, Donald, Forsyth, Alastair and Jemima, Sheila (eds), *Titanic Voices: Memories from the Fateful Voyage* (Southampton City Archives, Southampton, 1994).

9. *Maclean's* magazine, Vol. 91, No. 2, 23 January 1978, pp. 38–9.

10. Private letter, quoted in Hyslop, Forsyth and Jemima (1994), p. 86. Beedem discovered the *Olympic* stowaway Edward Rich, mentioned in the next chapter.

11. *Belfast Weekly Telegraph*, 6 April 1912, p. 10.

12. The Jeffery letter is in the possession of *Titanic* collector Steve Raffield.

13. United States Senate *Titanic* inquiry transcript (hereafter US), p. 374.

14. US, p. 51.

15. Lightoller, Charles, *Titanic and Other Ships* (Bay Tree, London, 1939), p. 144.

16. New York *Sun*, 21 April 1912, p. 3.

17. Br. 14534. 'I may say I saw the watertight doors myself tested in Belfast; they were all in perfect working order.' But Lightoller subsequently admitted he had no direct knowledge of their operation on the night of the emergency.

18. Jewell's letter, with another written by him aboard HMHS *Britannic*, was sold for £17,500 at Sotheby's on 17 December 2008. Lot 9.

19. Privately published under the clumsy title *Jigsaw Picture Puzzle of People Whom I Have Known*. Cited in 'A *Titanic* experience recollected' by Robert Bracken and Michael Findlay, *Voyage*, No. 42, Winter 2003, p. 63. Titanic International Society.

20. The *New York Herald* reported Williams' desperate cry in its edition of Sunday 21 April 1912.

21. First-class passenger Catherine Crosby gave Elmer Taylor's name in an affidavit to the US inquiry. Taylor had remarked to her that on the evening of the sinking 'he noticed the boat was going at full speed'. Mrs Crosby, who talked again with Taylor on the rescue ship *Carpathia*, declared: 'I don't know anything about workmen being on the boat, and that the boat was not finished, and that the watertight compartments refused to work; I have read it in the papers, but personally I know nothing about it.' She had heard rumours, however, some of which originated from Taylor. For example: 'Elmer Taylor informed me after we got on the *Carpathia* that a dinner was in progress at the time the boat struck, this banquet was given for the captain and the wine flowed freely; personally I know nothing or did not recollect anything of importance.' US, pp. 1,446–7, dated Wednesday 15 May 1912.

22. US, pp. 1,446–7, dated Wednesday 15 May 1912.

23. US, p. 1,147, affidavit of 15 May 1912.
24. US, p. 1,109, dated Monday 13 May 1912.
25. BBC television series *First Hand*, episode 2, 'The Sinking of the *Titanic*', broadcast 28 November 1956. Available to view on www.youtube.com/watch?v=FVLiZo6Pkak.

6 Officialdom

1. *Hampshire Advertiser* and *Southampton Pictorial*, various dates in March/April 1912.
2. Various dates, 1912, national press advertising – e.g. *Daily Telegraph*, *The Times*.
3. Although the strike was voted to an end on 6 April, it took ten days for the pits to reopen and the market to begin to recover. The *Daily News* on Tuesday 16 April printed a picture of the scene at Wood Green 'on the arrival of the first consignment of steam coal in London since the coal strike began'. The headline on p. 10 read 'Welcome! First Coal Arrives in London'. But the front page had a starker message: 'Giant Liner Wrecked. *Titanic* Collides With Iceberg'.
4. Steward George Beedem wrote to his wife on 5 April: 'I found a stowaway last trip.' Letter cited in Hyslop, Forsyth and Jemima (1994), p. 96.
5. High Court Law Report, 5 March 1912. See the author's long-form essay on the case at www.encyclopedia-titanica.org/william-weller.html.
6. Br. 97–8.
7. Friday 19 April 1912.
8. *Daily Telegraph*, 20 April 1912.
9. Belfast colloquialism, thought to have originated in the shipyard soon after the disaster. Black humour was common at Harland & Wolff, with a song parody about its chief that made use of the *Titanic*'s yard number: 'There's not a friend like the good Lord Pirrie, 401, 401; He bought a house in the heart of Surrey, 401, 401', cited in Hammond, David, *Steelchest, Nail in the Boot & The Barking Dog. The Belfast Shipyard: A Story of the People Told by the People* (Flying Fox, Belfast, 1986), p. 107. The tourist attraction Titanic Belfast now sells T-shirts emblazoned with the slogan 'She was all right when she left here.'
10. PRONI trans 2A/45/381A.
11. A 'jobsworth' is an official who upholds minor or even illogical rules, even at the expense of common sense.

12. *Faringdon Advertiser and Vale of the White Horse Gazette*, 30 November 1911, p. 2. Though this source puts his address as the New Forest, Kelly's Directory of Southampton for 1911/12 lists 'Smith, Commander Edward J., R.D. R.N.R.', with an address at 'Woodhead' on Winn Road, in the north of the city, near the common.

13. 'Morgan in auto races train', *Hartford City Telegram*, 11 September 1907, p. 5.

14. Lightoller (1939), p. 141.

15. Recalled in *The Washington Times*, 17 April 1912, p. 1.

16. *Ibid.*

7 Exodus

1. PRONI trans 2A/45/381A.

2. 'Derby Man as Steward,' *Derby Advertiser,* 26 April 1912, p. 3.

3. *Ibid.* 'He spoke of his journey up and across the Irish Sea in the *Donegal*, and said the *Titanic* seemed a great deal better than the *Olympic*, which he called an unlucky ship.'

4. *Ibid.*

5. Based on a comparison between the crew agreement for the Belfast to Southampton trip and that for the maiden voyage from Southampton to New York. See Appendix 1.

6. Similarly reported in the Dublin *Daily Express*, 26 April 1912, p. 9, under the headline 'From *Titanic* to Police Court'.

7. 'Survivors in Belfast. Fireman's Graphic Narrative', *The Belfast News-Letter*, 6 May 1912, p. 8.

8. Hyslop, Forsyth and Jemima (1994), p. 56.

9. The *Titanic* was regularly characterised in her brief career as a 'floating hotel'. The British Titanic Society regularly uses the same Southampton hotel as convention venue. Imagine if only 5 per cent of delegates re-booked their stay the following year, with fully 95 per cent choosing either elsewhere or to stay at home – could one deduce that some serious problem must have occurred?

10. 'Black Squad' was a term used to describe soot-smudged firemen and trimmers (wheelbarrow men), and occasionally greasers, but not the engineers who kept them all at it.

8 Men of Affairs

1. Body 245, recovered by the *MacKay-Bennett* search vessel, was clad in evening clothes.
2. *Peterborough Advertiser*, 6 April 1912, p. 2.
3. Walter Lord, whose book *A Night to Remember* (Henry Holt, New York, 1955) revived post-war interest in the *Titanic*, made reference in his acknowledgments to an interview with one Louis Mickelsen in the *Cedar Rapids Gazette* of 15 May 1955, prior to his book being published. Mickelsen – whose name does not appear on the crew list, and who must be treated as an impostor – claimed to be 'serving aboard a cattleboat when it put into Southampton, England, shortly before the scheduled sailing date of the *Titanic*'. He 'happened to hear that White Star Lines were advertising for firemen for the luxury liner … he signed on immediately'. Mickelsen's name appears on other crew agreements of the period, for instance, the *Cornishman* of the Leyland Line in 1915, with the correct age (he was born on 25 August 1889). Even if he was never aboard the *Titanic*, it is likely he did hear about her urgent need for firemen. Mickelsen gave accurate details of the disaster when no *Titanic* book of any kind had been published in fifteen years, the last being John B. Thayer Jr's privately printed 1940 account, of which only 500 copies were made. Mickelsen specified 711 survivors, a figure that has only come to be accepted as almost precisely accurate in the twenty-first century. He became a US citizen in 1920 and died in 1975.
4. William Hawkesworth, whose namesake father and uncle James, both stewards who died in the disaster, told the Southampton *Echo* in May 1970 that his mother began to cry while watching the *Titanic* leave. 'On asking her why, she replied: "That boat will never reach New York, dear."' Reprinted in Hyslop, Forsyth and Jemima (1994), p. 106.
5. 1972 Canadian Broadcasting Corporation radio documentary by Neil Copeland.
6. Hyslop, Forsyth and Jemima (1994), p. 77.
7. On 4 June 1914. Viewable at www.titanicinquiry.org/lol/depositions/ismay02.php.
8. US, p. 957.
9. Br. 18761.

9   Passing Muster

1. Oldham, Wilton J., *The Ismay Line: The White Star Line and the Ismay Family Story* (Journal of Commerce, Liverpool, 1961), p. 186.
2. Author's collection.
3. Don Lynch, Becker family account, *Titanic Commutator*, the Official Journal of the Titanic Historical Society, Vol. 14, No. 4, Winter 1990, quoting contemporary recollections, p. 47.
4. Article written for *The Belvederian*, 1912, school annual of Belvedere College S.J. Dublin, established by Francis Browne and still produced today.
5. US, p. 642.
6. Br. 19239.
7. Wilson, Rufus Rockwell, *The Sea Rovers* (B.W. Dodge and Company, New York, 1906), p. 32.
8. Br. 24112.
9. Br. 24174.
10. Br. 24129.
11. Br. 24193.
12. Br. 24211.
13. Br. 24120.
14. Br. 24121.

10 Drilling Down

1. Lightoller (1939), p. 148.
2. US, p. 54. 'I should say the marine superintendent was with him the whole time.'
3. In 1987 Maurice Weaver, industrial correspondent for the *Daily Telegraph*, interviewed Steel's son Edwin, who revealed his father had sworn him to secrecy about a near-accident to the *Olympic* in June 1912, seven weeks after the loss of the *Titanic*. The eighty-two-year-old retired chemist disclosed that a gross navigational error left her 'within an ace of running onto the jagged Cornish coastline', requiring emergency action. 'My father knew that if the information ever got out it would have done irreparable harm to the company, probably finished it off completely.' He added: 'He told me in confidence. I agreed never to say anything, but after three-quarters of a century, I believe I can be released from that promise.' *Daily Telegraph*,

15 April 1987, p. 17. Reprinted in the *Titanic Commutator*, Vol. 12, No. 1, 1988, pp. 40–1.

4. Br. 21966–8 and 21986.

5. Br. 21997.

6. It was the only time Moody would be in a *Titanic* lifeboat on the water, though Lowe urged him to take command of boat 16 at the height of the crisis. Moody instead stayed aboard to the end and died aged twenty-four.

7. Henry Aldridge & Son, November 2012, Lot 344.

8. Manning meaning the numbers of crew members assigned to different departments and tasks.

9. US, p. 377.

10. Br. 505. 'Number 13 boat I was in.'

11. Br. 502.

12. Br. 520.

13. Scarrott was a bigamist, having abandoned one wife and married another without the latter's knowledge of the original (who happened to be still alive and living but a few streets away in Southampton). A trial was told Scarrott would probably not have been discovered had he not 'as the result of depression, made a confession to his second wife' in 1913. Perhaps survivor guilt prompted the admission, but wife number two went to the police 'because she did not like another woman being in it'. The *Hampshire Advertiser* ironically reported the case on Valentine's Day. Survivor Scarrott, who had been stunned by his love's reaction, served one month's hard labour in 1914. His Lordship insisted when passing sentence that 'the law must be respected', a stricture previously lost on officials of both the Board of Trade and the White Star Line.

14. *Pier Review* (Southend Council), No. 8, March 1912. Also Nos 9 and 10, June and September 1932.

15. A discharge book is a crew member's personal passport to sea, containing dates and details of voyages and brief accounts of conduct, e.g. 'very good'.

11 Short on Fuel

1. Beesley (1912), p. 11.

2. Bullock, Shan F., *Thomas Andrews, Shipbuilder* (Maunsel & Co., Dublin, 1912), p. 58.

3. *Ibid.*, p. 60.
4. *Ibid.*, p. 58.
5. Maxtone-Graham, John, *Titanic Tragedy* (W. W. Norton & Co., New York, 2011), p. 88.
6. *Ibid.*, p. 86.
7. *Ibid.*, p. 87.
8. Reports by Board of Trade Officers, appendix to the British inquiry report p. 905, signed M. H. Clarke on Wednesday 10 April 1912. Cited in evidence Br. 19101, 5 June 1912.
9. Br. 23888.
10. Rostron, Sir Arthur, *Home from the Sea* (Macmillan, New York, 1931), pp. 247–8.
11. *Ibid.*, p. 248.
12. De Kerbrech, Richard P., *Down Amongst the Black Gang: The World and Workplace of RMS Titanic's Stokers* (History Press, Stroud, 2014), p. 42.
13. US, p. 966.
14. *Ibid.* The Plimsoll mark is a safe-loading measure on the hull, devised by the British visionary Samuel Plimsoll.
15. US, p. 966.
16. *Ibid.*, p. 967.
17. Eaton, John P., *Voyage* (official journal of the Titanic International Society), No. 42, Winter 2003, p. 73.
18. Letter sold at auction for £4,200 at Henry Aldridge & Son, October 2016, Lot 232.

12 Away at Last

1. The third sister ship was the *Britannic*, launched in 1914. She never entered service as, while serving as a hospital ship, she hit a mine in the Aegean in 1916 and sank. The *Olympic* survived the war, sinking a U-boat with her prow, and was finally scrapped in 1935.
2. The *New York Tribune* of Thursday 22 June 1911 reported: 'The ship's officers … preserved a sphinx-like silence on the subject of coal consumption. The *Olympic's* boilers took on 6,000 tons of coal at Southampton and she had not a great deal left on arrival. It was said aboard unofficially that she consumed between 775 and 825 tons of coal a day.'
3. Beesley (1912), p. 4.

4. *Ibid.*, p. 15.
5. *The Belvederian*, 1912 edition.
6. London *Globe*, 12 April 1912, p. 1.
7. Beesley (1912), p. 22.
8. *The Southampton Times*, 13 April 1912.
9. 'An hour late,' said the *Birmingham Gazette* of 11 April 1912, adding: 'It was a relief to everyone when the *Titanic* at last passed the bend and glided slowly away to sea. It was a thrilling start for the maiden voyage of the largest steamer in the world.'
10. US, p. 332.
11. Wilson (1906), p. 48.
12. *Ibid.*, p. 49.
13. *New York Tribune*, 20 April 1912, p. 6.
14. Br. 5242.
15. Br. 5243–4.
16. Br. 2296–7.
17. Br. 2339.
18. London *Daily News*, 9 May 1912, p. 7.
19. Br. 2338.
20. Br. 2340.
21. De Kerbrech (2014), p. 39. This work is important to a technical understanding.
22. *Ibid.*, p. 41.
23. Discussion in Harold Sanderson's testimony, subsequent to Br. 19634.
24. *Ibid.*
25. The man asked Harris, 'Do you love life?' (see Prologue). A similar incident with a woman aboard *Titanic* involved a conversation between Thomas Andrews, head of the guarantee group, and stewardess Annie Robinson. He told her to put on a lifebelt and to walk about and to let the passengers see her in it. She protested: 'It looks rather mean.' Andrews replied: 'No, put it on.' He followed up: 'Well, if you value your life, put your belt on.' Robinson recounted the meeting and quotes it in her evidence at Br. 13291.

13 The News Leaks Out

1. *The New York Times*, 25 April 1912, p. 4.
2. *Ibid.*

3. Wilkinson, Norman, *A Brush With Life* (Seeley, London, 1969) and quoted in Hyslop, Forsyth and Jemima (1994), p. 94.
4. *Irish Independent*, 17 April 1956, p. 10.
5. Hyslop, Forsyth and Jemima (1994), p. 111. The seaman is not named.
6. The *Seattle Post-Intelligencer*, 27 April 1912. Dorothy Kendle, the granddaughter of Mrs Brown, has a typewritten statement in her possession, prepared in 1912, in which her grandmother makes the same claim that an officer of the ship denied there was any fire aboard, which was an untruthful statement, whether knowingly or unwittingly made. Elizabeth's note says: 'They denied it, but I had it on good authority that there was [a fire], that this was true.' Dorothy wrote a 1995 book about her mother, Edith, with the author James Pellow, entitled *A Lifetime on the Titanic*.
7. Haisman, David, *Titanic: The Edith Brown Story* (Authorhouse, Milton Keynes, 2009).
8. *Ibid.*, p. 54. Elizabeth Brown told the *Seattle Post-Intelligencer* of frequently meeting William Harbeck, 45, who was lost.
9. *Ibid.*, p. 86. The *Seattle Post-Intelligencer* account of the fire is reprinted in Haisman's book, p. 83. It was also carried in the *Titanic Commutator*, Vol. 19, No. 2, August–October 1985, contributed by Don Lynch.
10. *Ilford Graphic*, 10 May 1912.
11. The others at their table who died were René Pernot, forty-year-old chauffeur to millionaire Benjamin Guggenheim (also lost), and fifty-seven-year-old Southampton woman Mary Mack, who intended to visit her daughter in Manhattan. Her body was recovered but reconsigned to the deep because of its condition.
12. *Irish Independent*, 17 April 1956, p. 10. Dorothy Kendle, daughter of Edith Brown, mentions that as her mother's lifeboat (No. 14) was lowered she saw four of the lift boys laughing together looking over the rail. All were lost.

14 Arrival in Ireland

1. This introduction is directly from Browne's account in *The Belvederian* (1912). The Lizard is a peninsula in southern Cornwall, the most southerly point of the UK. Two White Star liners, the *Suevic* and the *Bardic*, separately went aground on rocks at the Lizard (from 'Lios Ard', high fort) in 1907 and 1924 respectively.
2. Included with the piece was a photograph, 'supplied by the gentleman', but it was a view forward from the stern, rather than his picture of the S-bend wake.

3. Walter Lord writes in *The Night Lives On: The Untold Stories and Secrets Behind the Sinking of the "Unsinkable" Ship* (Penguin, London, 1986), p. 44: 'The *Titanic* began practising turns, leaving a wake of lazy S's, as Captain Smith continued to educate himself on the ways of his immense new command.' The ability to turn is, of course, of key importance in the saga.

4. Sennett, Richard and Oram, Henry, *The Marine Steam Engine* (Longmans, London, 1898, 1906 and 1910) declares: 'Considerable care is necessary to prevent accident from explosion of gas in bunkers … ventilating pipes are usually carried from the upper parts of the bunkers to the funnel casings to allow the impure air and gases, as they form, to pass away freely to the atmosphere' (pp. 448–9). Conduit tubing was used as 'gas was lighter than air, so surface ventilation was necessary to carry it away, and whenever possible bunker lids or hatches were removed in fine weather to facilitate this': de Kerbrech (2014), p. 39.

5. Beesley (1912), p. 26.

6. *Ibid.*, p. 24.

7. *Cork Free Press*, 12 April 1912, p. 6.

8. *Ibid.*, 18 April 1912, p. 5.

9. *Cork Free Press*, 12 April 1912, p. 6. 'Every part of the vessel from the lower gangway to the upper boat deck was shown to the visitors. Needless to say, both the Pressmen and the other visitors were much impressed with all they saw.' They were not shown the boiler rooms, only the passenger accommodations and public spaces.

10. *The Belvederian* (1912). In this article Browne mistakenly wrote 'Nicholson' for Williamson. There was no one named Nicholson aboard. McElroy and James Bertram Williamson were fellow Irishmen, the former with roots in Wexford, the latter a Dubliner. Both died. Williamson's mother received a letter from the Lord Lieutenant expressing deep sympathy on behalf of Lady Aberdeen and himself. 'Your son, after having, in conjunction with his brave colleagues, made every effort for the safety of the mails, devoted himself to the assistance of the women and children. And so his name is securely placed in the illustrious and imperishable roll of fame.' But Eleanor Williamson had to sue the Postmaster General in October 1912 to seek compensation for the loss of her sole support. She died in 1913.

11. *The Cork Examiner*, 18 April 1912, p. 11.

12. Also cited in Hyslop, Forsyth and Jemima (1994), p. 111.

13. *The Whitstable Times and Herne Bay Herald.* On the return voyage the *Mauretania's* passengers raised a princely £650 for the *Titanic* benefit fund.

14. Limitation of liability hearings, 30 April 1915. See www.titanicinquiry.org/lol/depositions/turner01.php.

15. *The Cork Examiner*, Monday 9 April 1912, p. 5.

16. The surviving card shows Katie was in Cabin 161 in Q section, starboard side, E deck, aft. (A four-berth room, she shared with Kate Mullen, Margaret Mannion and Ellen Mockler. All were saved.) Another Irish female to embark at Queenstown, Nora Keane, told roommate Edwina Troutt 'every day that the ship was doomed and would not reach New York': *Titanic Commutator*, Vol. 8, No. 1, Spring 1984. Keane, a Harrisburg hotelier, aged forty-six, did not explain the reason for her view.

17. Reprinted in the *Titanic Commutator*, Vol. 37, No. 197, 2012, p. 54.

15 Consultation at Queenstown

1. Testimony for limitation of liability hearings on 4 June 1914. Available at www.titanicinquiry.org/lol/depositions/ismay02.php.

2. The *Carpathia* docked at 9 p.m. on Thursday 18 April. Ismay was sworn into evidence at 10.30 a.m. on Friday 19 April.

3. US, p. 3.

4. In his first thirty seconds of evidence, Ismay agreed he was a 'voluntary passenger', not travelling as managing director to supervise the voyage (US, p. 2). Asked about any consultations with the captain, he replied 'absolutely none', adding 'it was absolutely out of my province. I am not a navigator. I was simply a passenger.' US, p. 7.

5. The British inquiry's index entries for *Titanic*'s speed are somehow serially misleading, referring to times other than the moment of impact. Wheelsman Hichens, however, devastatingly testified (Br. 965) that before 10 p.m. the ship had been travelling at 45 knots every two hours, i.e. 22.5 knots, and he had this information from the cherub log, meaning it was not opinion but solid fact. Lightoller eventually agreed to this figure, but firemen in New York claimed the speed had been 23 knots at 11.40 p.m., an hour and a half afterwards, and a few specified an ever higher rate of travel.

6. Br. 18392.

7. See Sanderson Marconigram revealing that Hill Dickinson solicitor John Furniss joined the *Adriatic*, with Ismay aboard, at Queenstown, accompanying the vessel to Liverpool.

8. Br. 18392.

9. Br. 18396.

10. Discussion during Ismay's evidence after Br. 18399.

11. US, p. 523. He reiterated his evidence at the British inquiry. Br. 17603: 'Did you look at the patent log?' 'I did, after the iceberg was cleared.' Br. 17613: 'How long after the ship struck do you think it was you looked at this patent log – ten minutes or a quarter of an hour?' Rowe: 'About half a minute.'

12. *The Cork Examiner*, 12 April 1912.

13. *Cork Constitution*, 13 April 1912, p. 4.

16 Undertaking the Atlantic

1. Marcus, Geoffrey, *The Maiden Voyage* (Viking, New York, 1969), attributed to 'private information', p. 58. Also cited in Hyslop, Forsyth and Jemima (1994), p. 118.

2. US, pp. 944–5.

3. *New York Tribune*, 4 March 1893, p. 3.

4. Lightoller (1939), p. 179. 'In Washington it was of little consequence, but in London it was very necessary to keep one's hand on the whitewash brush. Sharp questions that needed careful answers if one was to avoid a pitfall, carefully and subtly dug, leading to a pinning down of blame on to someone's luckless shoulders.' He added (p. 180): 'A washing of dirty linen would help no one.' What dirty linen he had in mind he did not specify.

5. Br. 24537.

6. Lightoller enjoyed 'swapping lies with kindred spirits' (p. 133), with shipboard japes 'kept jealous secret' from passengers (p. 140). But the lie-teller went too far in setting off a gun from a Sydney harbour fort one night in 1900, having first erected a fake Boer flag. Informed upon, he denied responsibility. White Star promptly transferred him to the North Atlantic. His 1935 memoir (from which the above quotes are taken) trumpeted Lightoller as the 'sole surviving officer' of the *Titanic*, even though ex-officers H. J. Pitman and J. G. Boxhall were both yet living.

7. Copies of the Bristow letters kindly supplied to the author by Maureen Landreth, New Zealand.

8. Audio recordings made by McGiffin's descendants, kindly supplied to the author by Maureen Landreth, New Zealand.

9. McGiffin had gone aboard the *Olympic* at Queenstown during her maiden voyage the previous year. *The Cork Examiner* of 16 June 1911, p. 6, said: 'Captain McGiffin, Marine Superintendent, White Star Line, exercised his charge with unfailing kindness and consideration.' An illuminated 1912 testimonial of farewell from Queenstown burghers declares: 'It soon became evident that you were an official whose worth and efficiency, tact and courtesy, stamped you as one possessing the qualities essential to the proper discharge of the onerous duties of the important office you held.' A copy of the address was pointedly sent to the White Star Line, even though it was losing his services. The *Cork Constitution* of Monday 28 October 1912, reporting on his leaving event, quoted Captain McGiffin: 'I endeavoured to discharge the duties of the position I held in your important port with fidelity to the companies I served.'

10. Rowe wrote the letter to Ed Kamuda, founder of the Titanic Enthusiasts of America as it was then, renamed the Titanic Historical Society in 1975. He repeated the story, with slight variation, in another letter to Kamuda dated 3 September 1963. It was reprinted in the *Titanic Commutator*, Vol. 25, No. 56, 2001, p. 270.

11. Beesley (1912), p. 30.

12. *The Times*, 22 April 1912, p. 12, quoting the newspaper's Boulogne correspondent. In terms of vulnerability, the *Titanic* was 'dangerously near' to the trawler, rather than the other way around. Collisions of liners and fishing boats were said to be not uncommon in the days of 'ram-you, damn-you' navigation, with speed sometimes undiminished in fog.

17 The Blue Concourse

1. Lightoller (1939), p. 62.

2. *Ibid.*, p. 63.

3. *Ibid.*, p. 67.

4. Richard O'Connor writes in *Down to Eternity* (Fawcett, New York, 1968), p. 61: 'Among the *Titanic*'s crew there also was said to be talk of bad luck and increasing whispers about the fire smouldering in Bunker Six [*sic*] ... but the passengers were not privileged to share in sailors' gossip.'

5. *Topeka State Journal* (Kansas), quoting its New York correspondent, Monday 22 April 1912, p. 2.

6. US, pp. 1,446–7, dated Wednesday 15 May 1912.

7. *Irish Independent*, 18 April 1956.
8. Rostron (1931), p. 53.
9. Beesley (1912), p. 33.
10. *Ibid.*, p. 32.
11. *Ibid.*, pp. 35–6.
12. *Ibid.*, p. 34.
13. *Ibid.*, pp. 34–5.
14. US, p. 1,042.

18 The Myth of 'Exceptional Strength'

1. The fire's seat was given in New York press reports on landfall, both by firemen and 'an officer'.
2. US, p. 985.
3. On one of his father's whaling ships, off Taiwan, in 1877, when he was aged twenty-two.
4. US, p. 985.
5. Solicitor General of the United Kingdom Sir John Simon explicitly told the British inquiry at Br. 2100: 'The side of the ship is one of the sides of the coal bunkers there.' He also said (Br. 2072): 'If you imagine this box is the bunker, and that [side] is the starboard skin of the ship.'
6. Bisset, James, *Tramps and Ladies: My Early Years in Steamers* (Angus and Robertson, London, 1959), p. 266. Bisset had vast experience, rising to become captain of the *Queen Mary* and commodore of the Cunard Line, having been captain of six other Cunarders. He first went to sea in 1898 and was aboard the *Carpathia* when she rescued the *Titanic* lifeboats.
7. The Line took out full-page diagrammatic advertising with these phrases and arguments outlined within. They ran in all major British and American illustrated magazines, and some newspapers, throughout March 1913 and sporadically thereafter.
8. *The Sphere*, 8 March 1913.
9. Davie, Michael, *The Titanic: The Full Story of a Tragedy* (Bodley Head, London, 1986), p. 19: 'Claimed at the time to be an effective safety feature, although it only came up seven feet above the keel.' It did not even reach the waterline, which could be twenty-five feet higher again, depending on loading.

10. Br. 20636–9. Testimony of Edward Wilding.

11. Davie (1986), p. 19. He interviewed a former Harland & Wolff shipyard worker named Dick Sweeney, quoting him: 'They called it steel plate, but it was not really high-class steel in those days; it was really raw hard iron. Most ships now are made of high tensile steel, which is much tougher.'

12. *Titanic: The New Evidence*, Channel 4, 1 January 2017.

13. Thursday 13 May 1915, 4 p.m.

14. Beesley (1912), p. 9.

15. *Weekly Irish Times*, 12 October 1912.

16. Belfast *Weekly Telegraph*, 14 October 1911.

19 Interference by Ismay

1. Fireman George Kemish, letter of 19 June 1955 to author Walter Lord: 'We had a full head of steam and were doing about 23 knots ... when there was a heavy thud and a grinding, tearing sound.' Nat. Mar. Mus. LMQ/7/1/49. (Quoted in Barratt, Nick, *Lost Voices from the Titanic: The Definitive Oral History* (Preface, London, 2009), pp. 155–60.)

2. Br. 18869–71.

3. Br. 18871.

4. Br. 18872.

5. Br. 18875.

6. Br. 18877.

7. Br. 18655.

8. The secretary's body was recovered and interred in Fairview Lawn cemetery in Halifax, Nova Scotia. His body (No. 110) was the first buried there. A large stone monument, paid for by Ismay, stands sentinel. After his evidence in London, Ismay 'sent for Mrs Harrison and notified her that he intended paying her £300 a year for the term of her widowhood', reported the *Yorkshire Post*. The legal documents executing the terms were signed in early June.

9. Br. 18651.

10. *Irish Independent*, 17 April 1956.

11. Testimony taken at the American Consulate-General in Paris on 22 November 1913.

12. Her deposition was made on 4 June 1913.

13. Letter to W. R. Cross, traffic manager of the Marconi company, New York, 27 April 1912. Nat. Mar. Mus. LMQ/7/1/12.

20 Gauging Speed, Time and Distance

1. Beesley (1912), p. 33.
2. *Washington Post*, 11 April 1912. Also reported on the front page of the evening newspaper *Richmond Palladium* (Virginia) on the day the maiden voyage started, 10 April 1912.
3. US, p. 135.
4. US, p. 633.
5. US, p. 618. In some lines, even the lifeboat masts were installed and sails erected, all while the boats still hung in the davits with the ship at sea.
6. 1972 Canadian Broadcasting Corporation radio documentary by Neil Copeland. Interview transcript.
7. Br. 2239–41.
8. 'Slogging our guts out and nearly roasted with the heat,' said fireman George Kemish, in his letter of 19 June 1955. Nat. Mar. Mus. LMQ/7/1/49.
9. New York *Evening World*, 22 April 1912, p. 6.
10. New York *Sun*, 23 April 1912, p. 3.
11. US, p. 3.
12. Limitation of liability hearings, 4 June 1914.

21 The Sinful Sabbath

1. Br. 2067–70.
2. Br. 1942.
3. Br. 5243, 2301 and 2341.
4. Br. 5246–8.
5. Br. 5249. A blaze would have to be of prolonged intensity to visibly warp a steel bulkhead.
6. Br. 2304. Corroboration of 'damage' to a bulkhead must mean it has lost some of its structural integrity, quite apart from metallurgical changes to the properties of the steel.
7. Br. 2305. This corrugation could be considered to be an S-warp in profile.

8. Br. 2302. 'The Chief Engineer, Mr Bell, gave me orders.'

9. Br. 2248.

10. Br. 2336.

11. US, p. 1,141; Br. 2337. One of the most circumspect replies in the entire transcript.

12. Br. 3940–1.

13. Br. 5252. Again the question is about 'any effect on the collision', rather than the sinking.

14. Br. 20882.

15. Br. 20883–5.

16. Br. 2305. Rein: see note 4, p. 272 above.

17. *Titanic: The New Evidence*, Channel 4, 1 January 2017.

18. 'as soon as possible' (Barrett, Br. 2296); Lightoller's 'potential volcano' is from Chapter 13 of his memoirs (1939, p. 63) about spontaneous combustion in the *Knight of St Michael's* coal when he was aboard in March 1893.

19. Geological Society of America, '*Titanic* Disaster: New Theory Fingers Coal Fire', *Science Daily*, 11 November 2004: www.sciencedaily.com/releases/2004/11/041108020906.htm.

20. New York *Sun*, 19 April 1912, p. 1.

21. Letter of 23 April 1912 by Sir Roger Casement, held by the National Library of Ireland. 'Enquiring into the loss of a British ship on the high seas, issuing subpoenas and having "flashlight" court sittings. A fine body to elicit truth! No one seems to realise the enormous impertinence of these proceedings.' Lightoller agreed, writing in his memoirs (1939, p. 178): 'It was a colossal piece of impertinence that served no useful purpose.' The *Saturday Review* said the United States was 'acting in defiance of all precedent and of international law and without regard to decency,' denying the committee's right to detain Englishmen as witnesses. Senator Smith was a 'blustering ignoramus' and 'ignorant bully'. The *Outlook* also questioned the legality of the tribunal, which it termed a 'burlesque by senatorial busybodies'.

22. The senator and his son had made a 1906 voyage with Captain Smith aboard the *Baltic*. Wade, Wyn Craig, *The Titanic: End of a Dream* (Penguin, New York, 1986), p. 100.

23. Passenger Archibald Gracie pondered the same riddle in his book, *The Truth About the Titanic* (Mitchell Kennerly, New York, 1913), p. 102: 'Who can satisfactorily explain this heedlessness of danger?' This book attempts to explain why the

considerable risk was knowingly run. Gracie remarks: 'The *Titanic*'s officers were no novices and were well trained in ... dangers of the sea' (p. 101).

24. Speech on presentation of his report to the US Senate on Tuesday 28 May 1912. 62nd Congress, second session, document No. 850, Government Printing Office, Washington DC.

22 Forewarnings of Fate

1. The British inquiry lists 'Ice Messages Received' on pages 26–8 of its official report. Lord Mersey concluded: 'The foregoing evidence establishes quite clearly that Captain Smith, the master, Mr Murdoch, the first officer, Mr Lightoller, the second officer, and Mr Moody, the sixth officer, all knew on Sunday evening that the vessel was entering a region where ice might be expected.'

2. British inquiry report, p. 26.

3. Thayer, John B., *The Sinking of the S.S. Titanic* (privately printed, 1940), p. 13.

4. US, p. 1,102.

5. Ismay statement issued to the press. Reported by *The New York Times* on its front page, 22 April 1912.

6. On 6 June 1913. Available at www.titanicinquiry.org/lol/depositions/ryerson1.php.

7. Deposition, 6 June 1913 (Ryerson and Bowen made sworn statements, one after the other, in Ms Bowen's house at Cooperstown, NY), www.titanicinquiry.org/lol/depositions/bowen1.php.

8. *New York Tribune*, 20 April 1912, p. 3.

9. Br. 18913–15.

10. Br. 18336.

11. Br. 18348.

12. Br. 18358.

13. Br. 18360.

14. Deposition 4 June 1914, www.titanicinquiry.org/lol/depositions/ismay02.php.

15. Br. 19028.

16. Br. 19031–2.

17. De Kerbrech (2014).

18. *Ibid.*

19. British inquiry report, p. 27. On page 29, Lord Mersey declared: 'The alteration of the course ... was so insignificant that it cannot be attributed to any intention to

avoid ice.' But while noting this significant anomaly, he did not supply any reason at all for the delayed turn. Nor, remarkably, did any of the officers giving evidence. There appeared to be a collective shrug of the shoulders.

23 Conversations and Contradictions

1. *Irish Independent*, 18 April 1956.
2. Evidence given on 31 October 1913, www.titanicinquiry.org/lol/depositions/Shiers01.php.
3. Turner's testimony to the liability hearings was given in New York just five days before he sailed for Liverpool as master of the *Lusitania* on her fatal crossing when she was torpedoed off the Old Head of Kinsale by U-20, with the loss of 1,198 lives. www.titanicinquiry.org/lol/depositions/turner01.php.
4. Thayer (1940), p. 14.
5. *Ibid.*, p. 13.
6. Original Bride report, dated 4 June 1912. Auctioned by Henry Aldridge & Son, 31 March 2012, Lot 314 fetched £7,500 and was sold to a prominent American collector.
7. British inquiry report, p. 28.
8. Br. 16925.
9. Br. 13629.
10. Br. 13615 and 13617.
11. Br. 13635.
12. Br. 13538. Lord Mersey: 'In your opinion when in point of fact would you have reached the vicinity of the ice?' Lightoller: 'I roughly figured out about half-past nine.'
13. Deposition, 14 November 1913, www.titanicinquiry.org/lol/depositions/rheims01.php.
14. US, p. 1,149.
15. Affidavit, 15 May 1912. US, p. 1,147.
16. Letter to Senator William Alden Smith, 11 May 1912. Appendix to US inquiry transcript, p. 1,110. She wrote to the chairman of the US inquiry: 'I have given you my observations and experiences after the disaster, but I want to tell you of what occurred on Sunday night, April 14.'

24 To the Edge of the Field

1. *Irish Independent*, 18 April 1956.
2. Mrs Clark went to fetch her husband after being shaken awake by the ship's shivering. She found him unconcerned in the smoking room, still playing cards. He later waved her off in lifeboat 4, sure the vessel would remain afloat. Mrs Clark was reportedly prostrate with grief for weeks after his loss, their overseas trip having been a postponed honeymoon. Nonetheless she was remarried before the end of September 1912.
3. Deposition, 14 November 1913, pp. 10–11. Hunt, Hill & Betts, 165 Broadway, New York City.
4. Lord (1955), pp. 177–8.
5. *Pier Review*, 1932.
6. The letter, printed in the *Westmeath Examiner* on Saturday 4 May 1912, continued: 'This was kept up even after we had struck, for the stewards came through and told us that we need not be afraid, that everything was all right. There was no danger, they said. Most of those assembled believed them until it was too late. That is why so many of the steerage were drowned.'
7. Letter home composed on the *Carpathia* three days after rescue, printed by *The Cork Examiner*, Monday 13 May 1912, p. 7.
8. Beesley (1912), p. 47. First-class passenger Archibald Gracie by contrast noted the singing of *O God Our Help in Ages Past* in his book (1913), reporting it was No. 418 of the White Star Line's hymnal (p. 8).
9. Beesley (1912), p. 45.
10. *Ibid.*, pp. 52–4.
11. *Titanic Commutator*, Vol. 37, No. 197, 2012, p. 55. She was roused by Eugene Daly: 'a young man who used to play the bagpipes at night, knocked on my door and said that something was wrong with the ship'.
12. Thursday 13 May 1915, www.titanicinquiry.org/lol/depositions/wilding06.php. Lightoller had typically lied, claiming to the 1912 inquiry that the speed on this leg had not exceeded 18.5 knots. Br. 13436.
13. Br. 1410.
14. The British inquiry left this warning out of its list of 'Ice Messages Received' in its final report.
15. Br. 8992–7. Testimony of Cyril F. Evans.

16. Reported in the *Cork Constitution*, 18 April 1912, p. 3.
17. *Ibid.* Also on the bridge for thirty-six hours was the captain of the *Franconia*, C. A. Smith.
18. *Irish Independent*, 18 April 1956.
19. Rowe letter to Walter Lord, June 1955. Nat. Mar. Mus. LMQ/7/2/21.

25 Was Impact Inevitable?

1. US, p. 456. 'I couldn't see nothing … I might as well [have been] locked in a cell. The only thing I could see was my compass' (in the wheelhouse).
2. Br 17383 and 17389.
3. Br. 17314.
4. US, p. 320.
5. Br. 17390.
6. US, p. 450. Hichens, on the same page, also put Chief Officer Henry Wilde on the bridge, even though it was not his watch. 'The chief officer rushed from the wing to the bridge, or I imagine so, sir.' Perhaps he was imagining, or it was a slip of the tongue, intending Murdoch, whom he named correctly as the first officer in his next response. Or perhaps it was no slip at all.
7. US, p. 220.
8. Boxhall said (US, p. 228) he did not see the iceberg at the time the warning bells were rung from the crow's nest. Nor did he describe it as it struck beside him, but said it did not interrupt his stride. He then confessed (US, p. 230): 'I was not very sure of seeing it.' Yet passenger George Rheims testified, during the US limitation of liability hearings, to spying it from amidships on A deck as he looked to a starboard window.
9. US, pp. 230–1.
10. Br. 15366.
11. Russell: *Irish Independent*, 18 April 1956; Boxhall: US, p. 230.
12. Rowe repeatedly made this comparison. He was rushed through evidence in London but said in America that he saw 'a mass of ice' (US, p. 519) and it looked 'like ordinary ice', ergo not black, '100ft high' (US, p. 521). The windjammer comparison features in many of Rowe's letters and was uttered by him on screen in a 1956 BBC South television recording of *Titanic* survivors: 'At twenty minutes to twelve, I was pacing up and down the deck, and I felt her give a jar. I thought that was peculiar,

and I looked along the side and I saw what I thought was a windjammer, but as it came astern I saw it was an iceberg.'

13. Br. 15321.

14. *New York Tribune*, 20 April 1912, p. 3.

15. US, p. 352. Lightoller was enquiring about the conduct of Quartermaster Hichens in Peuchen's lifeboat, he claimed. The Canadian passenger then took the opportunity to get a signed note stating Lightoller had ordered him into a boat because he was a yachtsman. Peuchen had anticipated a public backlash against male survivors.

26 Presentation of Ice

1. Br. 2441.

2. Br. 351. Abaft means behind, and towards or near the stern.

3. Br. 359.

4. Br. 361–2.

5. US, p. 974.

6. *Ilford Graphic*, 10 May 1912.

7. *The Washington Herald*, 20 April 1912, p. 1.

8. US, p. 347.

9. *The Times*, 20 April 1912.

10. *Philadelphia Inquirer*, 16 April 1912.

11. *New York Tribune*, 24 April 1912, p. 4.

12. US, p. 361.

13. Boxhall declared (US, p. 911): 'A sailing vessel does not show steaming lights or white lights.'

14. Geoffrey Marcus in his book (1969, pp. 81–2 and 303) relates a story told to him directly by Captain Edwin Jones of serving aboard the *Arabic* with *Titanic* First Officer William Murdoch one night in late 1903, westbound to New York. The lookout reported a dimly glimpsed vessel immediately ahead and urgent evasive action was required. Murdoch was told to prepare to 'port your helm' – i.e., to go to starboard in accordance with the rules of the road. That order was then given. The other, a sailing ship, had not seen the *Arabic* and was crossing to pass down her starboard side. Murdoch realised this, and aborted the starboard turn, collision being avoided. The story demonstrates the natural instinct to apply the Rules of the Road – by evading always to starboard. 'Chang' Jones separately told the same story

to Alan Villiers, who included it in his book, *Of Ships and Men: A Personal Antho-logy* (Newnes, London, 1962), p. 124. The incident was not entered in the *Arabic*'s official log.

15. Br. 2447.
16. A 'mystery ship' approached the stricken *Titanic* that night, displaying both running lights (red and green), Fourth Officer Boxhall testified. This vessel had 'probably gotten into the ice' because she next showed her red light only, lying stopped for some time before moving away. This is clear evidence of her making a turn to starboard when presented with an obstruction ahead. US, p. 934, 29 April 1912.

27 Horror on the High Seas

1. US, p. 427.
2. Deposition, 30 April 1915, www.titanicinquiry.org/lol/depositions/turner01.php.
3. Her captain, Stanley Lord, told the US inquiry (p. 732): 'on seeing the ice ... we turned the ship to starboard'. See also endnote 16, above. The mystery ship that directly approached the *Titanic* from the other side of the ice barrier soon turned to starboard when she saw the obstruction, presenting her red (port) light to observers on the maiden voyager.
4. US, p. 231.
5. Incidentally, Captain Lord of the *Californian* reached the rescue point and described the largest berg there as being 100–150 feet high and 700–800 feet long (US, pp. 723–4). 'It looked to me to be white' and would have been grey at night, 'not exactly black' (p. 725). He resisted a suggestion it could have been blue. 'I should imagine it would be grey' in darkness.
6. US, p. 320.
7. Patten, Louise, *Good as Gold* (Quercus, London, 2010), Afterword, p. 421: 'Bruce Ismay had told him (Lightoller) if the company was found to be negligent it would be bankrupted, and every job would be lost.'
8. *Ibid.*, p. 419: 'The fact that Robert Hitchins [*sic*] has turned the wrong way was a source of endless discussion, as was the switch from Tiller Orders to Rudder Orders which had caused him to make the error.'
9. US, p. 354.
10. US, p. 456.
11. US p. 450.

12. US, p. 949.
13. Br. 17296.
14. Lightoller (1939), p. 141.
15. Lord (1986), p. 44: 'The *Titanic* began practising turns, leaving a wake of lazy S's, as Captain Smith continued to educate himself on the ways of his immense new command.'
16. Browne account, *Irish Independent*, 18 April 1912.
17. Reprinted in *Voyage* (organ of the Titanic International Society), No. 96, summer 2016, 'An Unusual Voyage', contributed by Mike Poirier, p. 173.
18. Hayes, Sir Bertram, *Hull Down: Reminiscences of Windjammers, Troops and Travellers* (Macmillan, New York, 1925), p. 230.

28 Communication Issues

1. Br. 14376.
2. US, p. 318. He used the phrase 'anything we see' in response to three successive questions.
3. Br. 14293.
4. US, p. 423.
5. US, p. 319.
6. US, p. 320.
7. US, p. 584.
8. US, p. 320.
9. *Ibid.*
10. US, p. 353.
11. US, p. 359.
12. Br. 17285.
13. US, p. 1,145.
14. Br. 17285–6.
15. *The New York Times*, 21 April 1912.
16. *New York World*, 19 April 1912.
17. *The New York Times*, 26 April 1912.
18. New York *Sun*, 24 April 1912, p. 3. Hichens attended with Reg Lee, a lookout when the ship hit the iceberg. 'Both said they were through with the sea ... Hichens told the committee that he had a wife and two children in England and he was

afraid they were in trouble. They needed the money. Hichens couldn't talk about the disaster.'

19. *New York Tribune*, Monday 22 April 1912, p. 2.

29 The Long Lead-in to Loss

1. Br. 15564.
2. *The New York Times*, 19 April 1912.
3. US, p. 354.
4. *The New York Times*, 19 April 1912.
5. Br. 14298.
6. US, p. 526.
7. Br. 337.
8. Br. 468.
9. Br. 343.
10. US, p. 317.
11. US, p. 359.
12. US, p. 361.
13. Br. 17475.
14. Lightoller was asked this question at Br. 14884.
15. Br. 17475.
16. *Ibid.*
17. Br. 17478.
18. Br. 17479.
19. Quote from the *Derry Journal*, 27 May 1912.

30 Individual Effects

1. Br. 14995. Pitman also referenced Ismay saying 'no time to waste' at US, p. 276. First-class passenger Karl Behr, in a private manuscript, even alleged that 'Ismay then told this officer to take charge of the boat'. Pitman commanded No. 5 boat, in which Behr was saved. Nat. Mar. Mus. LMQ/7/1/5. Cited in Barratt (2009), p. 183.
2. Windmilling his arm, it appears: Br. 15979. What was he doing to help the work? Pitman: 'He was going like this, "Lower away, lower away" (*showing*).' US, p. 912.

Boxhall: 'He asked me why I was not getting the boat away. I told him I had no orders to get the boat away.'

3. US, p. 389. Lowe also snapped to Ismay: 'If you will get to hell out of that I shall be able to do something.' *Ibid.*

4. Br. 15001.

5. US, p. 429. 'I may also say, in regard to the testimony in regard to Mr Ismay, although I can not vouch for the source, yet it was given to me from a source such that I have every reason to believe its truth ... It is that Chief Officer Wilde was at the starboard collapsible boat in which Mr Ismay went away, and that he told Mr Ismay, "There are no more women on board the ship." Wilde was a pretty big, powerful chap, and he was a man that would not argue very long. Mr Ismay was right there. Naturally he was there close to the boat, because he was working at the boats and he had been working at the collapsible boat, and that is why he was there, and Mr Wilde, who was near him, simply bundled him into the boat ... I forget the source. I am sorry, I have forgotten it.'

6. US, p. 521. Two days after Lightoller's claim, Rowe answered Senator Theodore Burton's question 'Did you hear anyone ask them to get in?' with 'No, sir.' He was watching the chief officer and did not see him speak to Ismay or the other man who entered collapsible C, William Carter. 'If he had spoken to them, would you have known it?' Rowe: 'I think so.' He repeated the same story in his London evidence: 'Did anybody tell them to get in?' 'I never heard anybody.' – 'You did not hear anybody say, "Get into that boat"? 'No.' – 'No officer?' 'No.' Br. 17638–40.

7. *First Hand*: 'The Sinking of the *Titanic*', BBC, 28 November 1956.

8. Br. 383 and 393.

9. Beesley (1912), pp. 107–8.

10. *Ibid.*, pp. 108–9.

11. *Collier's Weekly*, 4 May 1912.

12. *Harper's Weekly*, 27 April 1912.

13. US, p. 335.

14. New York *Sun*, 23 April 1912, p. 3.

15. US, p. 550.

16. US, p. 552.

17. US, p. 555.

18. Br. 17805.

19. US, p. 561.

20. Gracie (1913), p. 249.
21. *Ibid.*, p. 288.
22. US, p. 1,020.
23. *Ibid.*
24. Br. 4712.
25. US, p. 1,039. It was later photographed bandaged up in St Vincent's Hospital, NY.
26. *San Francisco Call*'s magazine of May 1912.
27. Portaluppi was interviewed by the *New York Tribune* of Friday 19 April 1912, p. 3: 'Following his arrival on deck, which was in utter confusion, one of the boilers of the *Titanic* exploded.'
28. Br. 4201–2.
29. US, p. 343; Br. 662.
30. US, p. 947.
31. US, p. 813.
32. US, p. 1,029. Syrian passenger Celiney Yasbeck claimed in a letter: 'We went to the engine room and saw the crew trying to repair parts of the ship.' Nat. Mar. Mus. LMQ/7/1/24. Cited in Barratt (2009), pp. 174–5.
33. US, p. 1,001.
34. *The Oregonian*, 27 April 1912.
35. Originally published in the *Atlantic Daily Bulletin*. www.encyclopedia-titanica.org/copy-letter-sent-mr-knowless-daughter.html.
36. Lord (1955), p. 43.

31 Dilley and 'An Officer' Describe

1. US, p. 332.
2. *New York Tribune*, 20 April 1912, p. 6.
3. *The New York Times*, 21 April 1912, p. 1.
4. Plymouth *Daily News*, 29 April 1912.
5. London *Globe*, 20 July 1912, p. 11.
6. *Huddersfield Daily Examiner*, 10 September 1914, p. 3.
7. *New York Tribune*, 14 August 1922, p. 3.

32 What Happened Below?

1. *Western Daily Mercury*, 30 April 1912, p. 6.
2. British inquiry transcript of evidence, p. 131.
3. *Western Daily Mercury*, Monday 29 April 1912, p. 5. Hurst later wrote to Walter Lord to describe his experiences, adding a postscript: 'I went to London on the Inquiry, but was not called. I am sure it was because I spoke of the boats leaving half empty.' Nat. Mar. Mus. LMQ/7/1/44.
4. *Western Daily Mercury*, 30 April 1912, p. 6.
5. Br. 2026. Testimony of Frederick Barrett.
6. *Exeter & Plymouth Times*, Wednesday 1 May 1912, p. 3.
7. *Washington Herald*, 19 April 1912, p. 1.
8. Sloper, William Thompson, *The Life and Times of Andrew Jackson Sloper* (privately printed, 1949), p. 400.
9. *Oregonian*, 27 April 1912. The squash court was on G deck (with a viewing gallery on F deck) with first-class baggage rooms immediately further forward. G was the lowest accessible deck for passengers.
10. *Binghamton Press*, NY, Monday 29 April 1912.
11. *Belfast Weekly Telegraph*, 27 April 1912, p. 10.
12. US, p. 811.
13. US, pp. 811–12.
14. *New York Tribune*, 20 April 1912, p. 3.
15. Br. 5568. Scott and three others were killed by an explosion on *La Marguerite*, 28 September 1915.
16. Br. 5609.
17. US, pp. 531–2.
18. US, p. 599.
19. Br. 13757.
20. Beesley (1912), p. 63.
21. Letter now at the Nat. Mar. Mus. She also wrote to Walter Lord in 1972, declaring: 'I am hoping I may get a call from the CBS for their "I've got a Secret" TV programme as I had rather a good one about the *Titanic*.'
22. Patten (2010), 2nd paperback edition, p. 25 and original p. 419.
23. Lightoller (1939), p. 250.
24. US, p. 346.

25. Br. 3722.
26. Beesley (1912), p. 70.

33 Enabling the Flood

1. Br. 5585, 5587 and 5592–3.
2. Br. 5600–1.
3. After Br. 5606.
4. Br. 3738, 3745, 3777–88 and 3793.
5. Br. 3793.
6. After Br. 5606.
7. British inquiry report, p. 35.
8. *Ibid.*, p. 36.
9. Br. 5640 and 5689.
10. Br. 5889 and 5891.
11. Br. 5685–6.
12. Br. 5687–9 and 5693.
13. British inquiry report, p. 35.
14. Br. 5797.
15. Br. 3807.
16. Br. 3902.
17. Br. 3973 and 3976.
18. Br. 4262–3.
19. Br. 4283–91.
20. Br. 2357, 1868, 1898 and 1905.
21. Br. 1907–12 and 1945.
22. Br. 665–6 and 676.
23. US, p. 1,141.
24. Br. 2014.
25. Br. 1970 and 1984–5.
26. Br. 20883–5.
27. Br. 2038 and 2348.
28. Br. 2355 and 2044.
29. Br. 2349.
30. Br. 2255.

34 Götterdämmerung

1. Ship's clocks had to shed the five hours' time difference between Britain and the US east coast when travelling westbound. They did so in nightly instalments.

2. New York *Sun*, 20 April 1912, p. 3.

3. *New York Tribune*, 20 April 1912, p. 2.

4. A copy of the letter is in the Nat. Mar. Mus. LMQ/7/2/39.

5. *New York Tribune*, 20 April 1912, p. 4.

6. Br. 6040.

7. Br. 6224 and 6049.

8. Br. 6052.

9. *Hastings Observer*, 4 May 1912, p. 10.

10. *New York World*, 20 April 1912.

11. *Bureau County Republican*, 2 May 1912.

12. Account of Pierre Maréchal, Alfred Omont and Paul Chevré in a letter to *Le Matin*, reprinted in translation by the *Daily News*, 20 April 1912.

13. Bagot, Alec, 'Roaming Around, Memoirs of a Marconi Operator' (unpublished).

14. Private collection. Cited by Stephen Cameron in *Titanic: Belfast's Own* (Wolfhound, Dublin, 1998), pp. 126–7.

15. Letter to another relative, cited in Bullock (1912), p. 68.

16. Br. 3363.

17. Br. 3366.

18. Newport *Argus*, 19 January 1998.

19. *The Kerryman*, Saturday 11 May, 1935, p. 1.

20. *Chicago American*, 22 April 1912.

35 Crisis Management

1. US, p. 961.

2. US, p. 951.

3. Ione Wyatt, personal correspondence with author.

4. US, p. 1,138. Sent from *Carpathia* to *Olympic* at 3.10 p.m. on Monday 15 April 1912.

5. US, p. 426.

6. This and subsequent messages were taken from p. 952 of the US inquiry transcript of Ismay's evidence on Day 11.

7. US, p. 953.
8. US, p. 436.
9. US, pp. 425–6. Ironically, one of the men on the *Cedric* had previously been offered a berth on the *Titanic*. Mrs Mary Heslin of Dublin received a letter dated 17 April, headed 'On board SS *Cedric*, New York City'. Her brother Thomas Geoghegan wrote to his married sister: 'I have had somebody's good prayer. I was not on the *Titanic*, as I had a chance of going to Southampton. The shore captain in the White Star asked me would I like to go on the *Titanic*, and only I could not get a train in time I would be on it now – at the bottom of the Atlantic.' *Larne Times*, 27 March 1926, p. 7.
10. *Washington Herald*, 21 April 1912.
11. Patten (2010), p. 421.

36 Inquiry and Non-Enquiry

1. *Evening World*, Thursday 28 August 1913, p. 1.
2. *The New York Times* of 21 April 1912 carried this from an undercover reporter aboard the *Celtic*: 'Some held … "that the law was on the side of the company, and all pay stopped the minute the ship was lost." Others suggested that surely "Mr Ismay would make some grant," and [lookout Fred] Fleet announced that he had already had an intimation that wages would be paid up to the time of getting home again.' In the same article the lookout was reported as talking of 'sittin' tight and waitin' for the boss's word … he had been drilled, and so when Mr Ismay said not to talk, it meant as far as he was concerned that there was nothing to be said.' Major's wage slip is in the author's possession. Fireman George Kemish confirmed in a letter of 19 June 1955: 'All we got out of it was what would have been a normal trip's pay', i.e. for a voyage out and back. He also referred to a 'promise' from the White Star Line of a job for life, but ruefully reflected: 'I have never had anything from them. I have had long unemployment at times.' Nat. Mar. Mus. LMQ/7/1/49, cited in Barratt (2009), pp. 155–60.
3. *Washington Herald*, 21 April 1912, p. 1.
4. Reprinted in the *Irish Independent*, 30 April 1912, p. 6.
5. Application at the beginning of the fourth day of proceedings. British inquiry transcript, p. 58.
6. Discussion after Br. 19634, testimony of Harold Sanderson.

7. Discussion after Br. 24344, testimony of William D. Archer.
8. British inquiry transcript of evidence, p. 732. Holmes submission, 24 June 1912.
9. British inquiry report, p. 35. A 1914 bulkhead test caused bending and bulging of metal and signs of incipient fracture.
10. Discussion after Br. 23974.
11. Br. 23983 and 23985.

37 Thomas Whiteley

1. British inquiry report, p. 30.
2. *Ibid.*
3. *Ryan v. Oceanic Steam Navigation Co.* Read the author's detailed précis of the case at www.encyclopedia-titanica.org/ryan-v-osnc.html.
4. Reported, for example, in the *Washington Star*, 16 January 1914, p. 2.
5. *New York Herald*, 21 April 1912, p. 1.
6. US, p. 328.
7. Br. 2419.
8. *New York Herald*, 22 April 1912, p. 1.
9. Whiteley subsequently appeared on stage in Lowell, Massachusetts, giving his account of the wreck, as surviving crew and passengers did elsewhere. The local *Sun* newspaper declared on 28 May 1912: 'His story is first hand and contains many features not touched on by the press, either at the time of the terrible catastrophe or since.'
10. *The Times*, 17 January 1914, p. 3.
11. *Nottingham Evening Post*, 28 May 1914, p. 6.
12. *Daily Mirror*, Friday 19 April 1912, p. 8.

38 It Happened Before (and Again)

1. Cited in C. H. Milsom, *The Coal Was There for Burning* (Marine Media for the Institute of Marine Engineers, 1975), p. 54. The same account of the wreck quotes T. H. Ismay's statement to the court of inquiry: 'It is not the fact that the mixed coals were used for reasons of economy', p. 68.
2. Beesley (1912), p. 5.
3. *The New York Times*, 14 October 1913.

4. *The Times*, 29 November 1913, p. 12.

5. *The Washington Herald*, 15 October 1913, p. 7.

6. *John Bull*, 18 October 1913.

39 Summary Decisions

1. *Liverpool Daily Post and Mercury*, 7 May 1912, p. 8. '*Titanic*'s Successor – Work Suspended.'

2. PRONI, cat. D2805, October 1912.

3. G. A. Pratt, publisher, nautical bookseller, stationer, etc., Southampton. Author collection.

4. *Daily Express*, 3 March 1995.

5. Walter Lord papers, Nat. Mar. Mus.

6. Official finding: 'The damage extended over a length of about 300ft.' British inquiry report, p. 32. Lord Mersey also decided that floodwater had flowed over the top of bulkheads as compartments flooded, thereby ruling out any catastrophic failure of these obstructions.

7. British inquiry report, p. 50. Board of Trade principal surveyor William David Archer cited in evidence Rule 12, by which total boat accommodation might be reduced if a vessel were divided into efficient watertight compartments. 'Mr Archer's view was that shipowners should be encouraged to increase flotability of the ships they built, and that the way to encourage them was to relax the legal requirements as to boats … The great object was so to build the ship that in the event of the disaster she would be her own lifeboat.' Archer stated in the witness box that since the disaster of the *Titanic* he had modified his views and thought Rule 12 should be discontinued. Br. 24256.

8. Delivered in a lecture to the annual convention of the Geological Society of America in Denver, 2004.

9. Br. 4383–9.

10. Br. 4397.

11. Br. 4398.

12. Br. 661.

13. Br. 660.

14. New York *Sun*, 23 April 1912, p. 3. To the *Evening World* the previous day he said: 'From Queenstown out, all the firemen had been talking of the orders we had to

fire her up as hard as we possibly could ... we were carrying full pressure. From the time we left Queenstown until the moment of the shock we never ceased to make from 74 to 77 revolutions.'

15. *Maclean's* magazine, Vol. 91, No. 2, 23 January 1978, pp. 38–9.
16. Lightoller (1939), pp. 132 and 182.
17. US, p. 956.
18. US, p. 947.
19. US, p. 3.
20. *Ibid.* On 23 April, Ismay wrote to the chairman of the US inquiry (US, p. 962) seeking to be released. He said about the day of his Bell admission: 'I voluntarily appeared before the committee [on] Friday, April 19, and though not in the best of condition to give evidence, I testified at length.' He added that he had been under 'severe mental and physical strain'. He would undoubtedly have been legally advised on this letter, which anticipated his giving evidence in Britain: 'The committee is also aware that an inquiry into this disaster has been started by my own Government, which has jurisdiction to deal with matters of serious importance to the interests of the company, which I understand are outside the scope of the present inquiry, and which urgently require my personal attention in England.' A possible 'confusion' argument is thus pre-established.

40 Epilogue

1. Lightoller (1939), p. 13.
2. *Ibid.*, p. 36.
3. *Ibid.*, p. 136.
4. *Ibid.*
5. Fred Fleet actually used the phrase a 'narrow shave' to his crow's nest companion Reg Lee after the collision, not realising the damage that had been done. He cheerfully admitted the comment in both America (US, p. 321) and Britain (Br. 17323).
6. Lightoller (1939), p. 142.
7. *Ibid.*, p. 144.
8. *Ibid.*, p. 165: 'Murdoch couldn't find them when they were wanted.' p. 166: 'Into the first officer's cabin we went – the chief, Murdoch, the Captain and myself – where I hauled them out, still in all their pristine newness and grease.'

9. Patten (2010), 'Afterword: The *Titanic* cover-up', p. 3.

10. *Ibid.* Patten says that in addition to the conversation in Murdoch's cabin there had also been 'snatched briefings while the lifeboats were being loaded' about what led to the collision.

11. *Halifax Chronicle*, 29 April 1912, p. 8. The news clipping can be seen here: http://thechronicleherald.ca/titanic/archive/82879-the-death-ship-will-arrive-tomorrow.

12. *The New York Times*, 5 February 1904, p. 1. The *New York Tribune* of the same date (p. 6) reported that the *Oceanic* was two days late in arrival.

BIBLIOGRAPHY

Barratt, Nick, *Lost Voices from the Titanic: The Definitive Oral History* (Preface, London, 2009

Beaumont, J. C. H., *Ships – And People* (Frederick Stokes & Co., New York, 1926)

Beesley, Lawrence, *The Loss of the SS Titanic* (Houghton Mifflin, Boston, 1912)

Bisset, James, *Tramps and Ladies: My Early Years in Steamers* (Angus and Robertson, London, 1959)

Bullock, Shan F., *Thomas Andrews, Shipbuilder* (Maunsel & Co., Dublin, 1912)

Cameron, Stephen, *Titanic: Belfast's Own* (Wolfhound, Dublin, 1998)

Davie, Michael, *The Titanic: The Full Story of a Tragedy* (Bodley Head, London, 1986)

De Kerbrech, Richard P., *Down Amongst the Black Gang: The World and Workplace of RMS Titanic's Stokers* (History Press, Stroud, 2014)

Gracie, Archibald, *The Truth About the Titanic* (Mitchell Kennerly, New York, 1913)

Haisman, David, *Titanic: The Edith Brown Story* (Authorhouse, Milton Keynes, 2009)

Hammond, David (ed.), *Steelchest, Nail in the Boot & The Barking Dog. The Belfast Shipyard: A Story of the People Told by the People* (Flying Fox, Belfast, 1986)

Hayes, Sir Bertram, *Hull Down: Reminiscences of Windjammers, Troops and Travellers* (Macmillan, New York, 1925)

Hyslop, Donald, Forsyth, Alastair and Jemima, Sheila, *Titanic Voices: Memories from the Fateful Voyage* (Southampton City Council, Southampton, 1994)

Jessop, Violet (edited by John Maxtone-Graham), *Titanic Survivor: The Memoirs of Violet Jessop, Stewardess* (History Press, Stroud, 2007)

Lightoller, Charles, *Titanic and Other Ships* (Bay Tree, London, 1939)

Lord, Walter, *A Night to Remember* (Henry Holt, New York, 1955)

Lord, Walter, *The Night Lives On: The Untold Stories and Secrets Behind the Sinking of the "Unsinkable" Ship* (Penguin, London, 1986)

Marcus, Geoffrey, *The Maiden Voyage* (Viking, New York, 1969)

Matarasso, Pauline, *A Voyage Closed and Done* (Michael Russell, Norwich, 2005)

Maxtone-Graham, John, *Titanic Tragedy: A New Look at the Lost Liner* (W. W. Norton & Co., New York, 2011)

Milson, C. H., *The Coal Was There for Burning* (Marine Media for the Institute of Marine Engineers, 1975)

O'Connor, Richard, *Down to Eternity* (Fawcett, New York, 1968)

Oldham, Wilton J., *The Ismay Line: The White Star Line and the Ismay family Story* (Journal of Commerce, Liverpool, 1961)

Patten, Louise, *Good as Gold* (Quercus, London, 2010)

Pellow, James with Kendle, Dorothy, *A Lifetime on the Titanic: the Biography of Edith Haisman, Britain's Oldest Survivor of the Titanic Disaster* (Island Books, London, 1995)

Rostron, Sir Arthur, *Home from the Sea* (Macmillan, New York, 1931)

Sennett, Richard and Oram, Henry, *The Marine Steam Engine* (Longmans, London, 1898)

Sloper, William Thompson, *The Life and Times of Andrew Jackson Sloper* (privately printed, 1949)

Stenson, Patrick, *Titanic Voyager: the Odyssey of C. H. Lightoller* (Halsgrove, 1998)

Thayer, John B., *The Sinking of the S.S. Titanic, April 14–15, 1912* (privately printed, 1940)

Villiers, Alan, *Of Ships and Men: A Personal Anthology* (Newnes, London, 1962)

Wade, Wyn Craig, *The Titanic: End of a Dream* (Penguin, New York, 1986)

Wilkinson, Norman, *A Brush With Life* (Seeley, London, 1969)

Wilson, Rufus Rockwell, *The Sea Rovers* (B.W. Dodge & Co., New York, 1906)

INDEX

ABOUT THE AUTHOR

Senan Molony is Political Editor of the *Irish Daily Mail* and is a national award-winning journalist. Born in 1963, he has over thirty-five years experience in his profession, with wide exposure to tribunals, hearings and inquiries. He has led and featured in a number of TV documentaries and addressed conventions of the British, Belfast and Titanic International societies. Senan has discussed the *Titanic* in interviews on CNN, CBS, NBC, ABC, NPR, and other stations internationally, and lectured on memorial voyages to mark the centenaries of the sinking of the *Titanic, Lusitania* and *Britannic,* as well as working as a host for the Titanic Channel. He lives in Dublin with his wife Brigid, daughters Pippa and Millie, and son Mossy. His other books include: *The Irish Aboard Titanic; Lusitania: An Irish Tragedy; Titanic and the Mystery Ship; The Phoenix Park Murders; Titanic: Victims and Villains; Titanic Scandal: The Trial of the Mount Temple,* and *Titanic Unseen.*

CPSIA information can be obtained
at www.ICGtesting.com
Printed in the USA
BVHW092345270521
608252BV00003B/3